Releasing the Dove

RELEASING *the* DOVE

R. N. Miller

Copyright © 2021 R. N. Miller

All rights reserved. No part of this book may be reproduced or transmitted in any form or by any means electronic or mechanical including photocopying, recording, or by any information storage and retrieval system without permission in writing from the publisher.

Aurora Books, an imprint of Eco-Justice Press, L.L.C.

Aurora Books
P.O. Box 5409 Eugene, OR 97405
www.ecojusticepress.com

Releasing the Dove
Written by R. N. Miller

Cover design by Wendy L. Stasolla

Library of Congress Control Number: 2021946920
ISBN 978-1-945432-48-4

*For those whose hearts long, whose dreams sometimes die,
but who never stop resurrecting themselves despite the pain;
for the obsessed, the weary, and the resilient.
And for those whose healing can take decades,
and whose scars never really disappear.*

INTRODUCTION

When I wrote this book, even at the beginning, I always imagined a soundtrack. Songs are the background to so many of our memories and our dreams and imaginings. I love all kinds of music, and wanted to include, in some way, the compositions, the voices of the songs that rang through my head as I wrote.

For your extra dimensional pleasure, I have therefore created a playlist on Spotify of the songs I felt best helped frame the story as it progressed. You will see little headphone icons and notation of each song's composer as you move through the book. I encourage you to open up Spotify, search for the playlist titled, "Dove," put on some headphones, and listen to each track as you come to it in the story. Stop reading for a moment. Let the sounds and the emotions and the meaning of the words become another aspect of the storytelling. Then return to the story until the next song is indicated.

Many, many thanks to the singers and songwriters whose work I love and treasure and listen to, and have referenced in my book. Your art helped me express my art during the process of writing, and in the re-reading. Please continue to make your incredible music.

PROLOGUE

June 3, 2005

Victoria and Patrice moved in a subtle ellipse around the stadium as they approached a sign overhead that read "Sections 312–313." Patrice's son and his friend were up ahead a bit, keeping as much preteen distance as possible between themselves and the two women. Patrice called out to them, "Wait up! Our seats are in the next section!"

Their seats were just through the next entry ramp and to the left, down about three rows; the boys distanced themselves by sitting two rows in front of them in unoccupied seats. Their view of the field was cut off at the top by the overhang from the balcony above them. The smell of hot dogs and beer and sweat drifted on the evening air. The weathermen had predicted intermittent storms all evening, and the swollen, dark gray clouds rolled slowly, just above the stadium seats.

"Well, these are pretty good seats, considering," Patrice commented.

"They're great!" Victoria replied. "And if it starts to rain, hey, we're already under cover. Guess I didn't need this umbrella and poncho," she said, lifting the wrinkled blue plastic camping poncho she'd brought along.

The stadium wasn't crowded. The Nationals were a relatively new baseball team, the first team Washington, D.C., had had in umpteen years, Victoria had heard. She wasn't a particularly big sports fan, baseball or otherwise. Still, the tickets had been free, and Patrice was fun to be with, one of the few single friends she had who wasn't a barfly but still liked to have a good time.

They'd arrived a little late, so they'd missed the first three innings. Victoria browsed the section they were sitting in. There didn't appear to be any single men in their age range nearby. A couple men sitting several rows ahead of them looked potentially viewable, but then she caught sight of the telltale gold bands and immediately averted her eyes to three young men to the left. They looked like they maybe were 30, but most likely were still in their 20s. Victoria laughed a little to herself at her inability to refrain from checking out the scene. As a 42-year-old divorced mom, she held little hope of just happening to run into a sane, unattached, and not repulsive man who maybe was at least her height, if not taller, and within five years either direction of her age. Still, no point in putting blinders on...

The music bounced in muffled tones beneath the overhang roof, encouraging shouts of "Charge!" during the course of the next couple innings. The mascot, purportedly an eagle, looked like a big-headed chicken in a Nationals jersey that kept running by with signs that read "Nats!" while bobbing his (her?) head and punching his/her feathered fists into the air, eliciting cheers from the crowd. The Nationals even scored some runs, and Victoria stood and clapped and whooped with everyone else. Live games were definitely more fun than televised ones.

"Oh, watch out! Here comes the wave!" Patrice warned. She and Victoria stood up as the ripple moved through their section. They laughed as they sat back down.

"There's something about the wave that is just irresistible!" Victoria said. "Did you see the movie *When Harry Met Sally*? There's this great scene when Harry and his buddy are at a baseball game talking about Harry's wife having just left him, and they're so into the conversation, and the wave comes through, and they stand up, raise their arms, and sit back down, the whole time still talking, never missing a beat. It's hilarious. Have you seen it?"

"I think so," said Patrice.

"Great movie," Victoria said, replaying the scene in her mind and chuckling. They settled back into their seats, returning their attention somewhat to the game. Victoria's eyes drifted to an empty set of seats down and to the right.

And there he was. Without preamble, without forethought, without any conscious attempt to think of him, he appeared in the aisle seat, slouched down, left leg stretched out into the aisle. He leaned on one arm, and his head turned back over his left shoulder, towards her, smiling that smile she recalled so well. Playful, sexy, and addictive. If she really focused, she could see that he was wearing the white button-down shirt and black slacks. His tie was loosened at the neck and hanging askew, lying against his chest where the top of his white undershirt was peeking above the last buttoned button, just a few chest hairs escaping over the collar.

It could go like this: he could be there, watching the Nationals, maybe on assignment. Or maybe he was there with friends, down to check out the Nats, out for a night of b-ball and brewskies. Yes, it could go that way. He'd been drinking and was a little buzzed. And he turned around and there she was, and their eyes would meet. They'd see it right away, a magnetic draw that was out of their control.

He would have to somehow end up with her…yes, the story could go like this: Patrice would give him a ride. He could sit up front, squeezed up against the door, Victoria in the middle. Just an old friend she'd run into who was going to come back to her house for the night. In the morning, she could offer to drive him to wherever his friends were.

His thigh would be pressed up against hers, a heat emanating all along the length of their legs, every shift of movement creating invisible sparks. She would be able to smell him, a little bit of beer mixed in with his intoxicating scent. They'd have to make small talk the whole way back from

D.C. to her house, keeping it G-rated for the sake of Patrice and the boys.

Okay, yes, yes. Now she had it. He would come back to her place. She'd be a little coy. Where had he been, anyway? And why hadn't he ever written or called? She was going to be more cautious this time, not just diving in, not just getting swept away. But all the while, they'd both know where it was heading, how it would turn out, how it would have to turn out.

Maybe he'd be too drunk to even let anything happen that night. She'd tuck him into bed after removing his shoes, socks, pants, tie, and shirt. Yes, she'd pour him into her bed, with him clumsily reaching out for her and babbling about how they were gonna have them some fun. And then he'd pass out, and she'd watch him a while. She'd study his face and his rising chest and his fluttering eyelids. She'd gently rest her fingers against his cheek, the cheek that needed a shave and prickled as she moved her fingers lightly down to his chin. Her eyes would feel that hot, sharp sting, but she'd squeeze them shut and wipe them quickly, reminding herself to live in the moment, not relive the past, not try to foretell the future.

Then she'd climb in beside him, being careful not to make the mattress bounce or to jostle his covers, laying her head ever-so-carefully down on the pillow, inches from his face. His features would be barely visible from the light coming between the slats in the window blinds, where outside a few streetlamps burned into the night. She'd pull the sheet up to her chin, breathe him in, and fall asleep to the rhythm of his inhalations and exhalations.

In the morning, by the pale light, he'd awaken first, his eyes groggily taking in his surroundings, maybe wondering where he was for a moment before remembering the events of the night before, and he'd see her, still sleeping, her hair spread out on the pillow. He'd reach over, his hand hovering just above her shoulder, hesitating, momentarily rethinking the decision his body had just made for him as it had responded to her proximity. He'd smile at her peaceful face, so youthful in slumber. He'd touch her shoulder while moving his body up next to hers and begin kissing her before she'd fully opened her eyes. And then...

"Amazing!" the sportscaster cried. "Bases are loaded! UN-BE-LIEV-ABLE!"

Victoria refocused on the baseball diamond and the players. Sure enough, the Nationals held all three bases, with a player warming up at home plate. She glanced back down and to the right, to the empty seats.

"I thought you were gone," she said silently. "I thought I'd let you go."

INVITATION

June 2, 2001

The ivory envelope arrived, with a breast-cancer commemorative stamp coloring the upper right hand corner with shades of blue, green, orange, red, and yellow. A clear address label had been pressed, slightly askew, in the center of the envelope, addressed in computer-generated script to "Vick Woolsey."

She smiled at the use of the childhood nickname, reminiscent of the friendship that had stumbled and faltered over the years. No one really called her Vick anymore, except maybe her baby sister. Her last name was spelled incorrectly, a not uncommon occurrence. Woolfrey was an unusual name, and people often substituted letters that made more sense to their minds.

On the flap of the envelope, a second label indicated the invitation was from Deena Cashell and Todd van Durst. She pulled out a 4 x 5" card. On it was a simply sketched groom and bride with spliced-in photo heads of Deena and her groom-to-be, Todd. They wore jolly expressions and stood outdoors, a two-tiered fountain topped with an angel drawn behind them. On the back, the invitation listed the address for the wedding and reception, a place in the heart of NYC. Victoria knew that the city was likely to be still balmy and colorful in the middle of September when the wedding would take place.

A carefully folded 8-1/2 x 11" piece of waxy, opaque paper listed hotel information for out-of-town travelers, and an RSVP card and return envelope were also enclosed.

Victoria had known the invitation was coming, and was thrilled. The last year or so had seen a renewal in her friendship with Deena. Right after Max had left her, Victoria had tried to boost her morale by making a trip to the Big Apple. She had called Deena and been invited to come and stay at her apartment in the garment district. It had been a fun getaway. Fine dining, an off-Broadway show, intelligent conversation. It had also been a change in scenery from a home that demanded attention and housed the ghosts of a happily married couple who had invested their dreams along with the down payment when they bought the place two years earlier.

Since that trip to New York, Deena and Victoria had stayed in touch, primarily via email. The announcement that there was going to be a wedding had come as no surprise: Deena and Todd had been living together for several years, and were ready to start a family.

Wife and mother. That was the job description Victoria had taken on almost eight years earlier, when she began staying home full-time with their daughter Chloe. All these years and a second child later, she still called herself a stay-at-home mom. The "wife" part, however, was now in name only. Max had left in January 2000, less than a month after the 40th birthday party she'd thrown for him.

Still, the divorce had not made her bitter about marriage, at least not theoretically. Her own had fallen apart slowly, turning tragic corners with the births of two children and the changes that come with family life after being double-income, free spirits for so long. She didn't think she could ever stomach marriage again. It had been, and still was, too hard dissolving this one, and too painful. But there was always hope for other people. She wished nothing but the best for Deena and Todd.

Besides, who didn't love a good wedding? She was sure it would be a good one, too. Deena and Todd had money, they lived in arguably the most exciting city in the world, and there would be many people there from the old days, people who would remember Victoria and maybe be impressed with her now.

One thing the separation had done for Victoria was to motivate her to exercise religiously and eat more sparingly. She'd hired a personal trainer and was taking better care of herself than she had in years, possibly ever. She'd bought contacts to replace her 80s-style, double-wide, pink framed glasses, and had let her hair grow out a little, coloring the gray and recapturing the chestnut brown she'd had naturally. Thirty-nine was around the corner, and she meant not to look it.

The kids were gone now every other weekend, Friday night through Sunday night, and though the wedding was on a Sunday afternoon, she felt sure she would be able to arrange to go.

LIGHTS OUT

September 11, 2001

The turning of the calendar to September had brought the excitement of new beginnings. An Indian summer had leisurely taken hold in Virginia, with the promise of a warm autumn. A new school year was starting. Connor and Chloe were entering kindergarten and 2nd grade. This would be the first time in Victoria's parenting career that she would have free time during the week. With Connor gone every afternoon, she wasn't sure what she would do with herself. She was watching two other children to make a little extra cash, but they slept in the afternoons and there might actually be time to watch a soap opera or exercise with a tape. Pay bills? Make phone calls? All without interruption!

It was great walking weather. The few times she found herself home alone, she would take walks around the neighborhood. Other times, she'd pull the kids in the Radio Flyer wagon she'd inherited from her older brother. She'd don her headphones, listening to Smashmouth or Nelly Furtado, and set out briskly, sending endorphins to her brain. Since she'd started working out more, she'd discovered how much better she felt when she worked up a sweat and got her heart pumping. Better than therapy, and a lot cheaper. The walks were healing.

This morning looked like another good walking day. Crisp blue skies, sunny, not too hot. She was guessing the temperature was somewhere in the 70s, though she hadn't read the paper or listened to the news lately. At 8:30, Victoria and Connor walked Chloe to the bus stop down at the corner. Their house was the second from the corner, and an easy skip from the front door to the stop sign. Connor and Chloe ran ahead, down the grassy slope in front of their house and onto the sidewalk.

It hadn't been that long ago that Chloe had gotten on the bus for the first time. Victoria remembered feeling a mixture of emotions: relief that someone else would be taking her daughter for part of the day, pride that her little girl seemed so ready to go on this adventure, fear that the bus would be in an accident, inexplicable sadness at her baby growing up. She had kept from crying until after the bus pulled away.

Now the bus made its familiar lurching squawk, the folding doors closed, the small stop sign extending from the side of the bus pulled back in, the brakes released, and the gears ground in succession as the bus moved up the hill. Connor and Victoria waved goodbye to Chloe, her face framed by the bus window. She gave a quick wave back, then turned her face away. Victoria took Connor's hand as they walked back together, down the sidewalk, up the driveway. Connor asked if he could play on the computer, a not-unexpected request. Victoria agreed, knowing it would grant her a few moments' peace.

Connor hopped down the stairs of the split-level foyer to the basement. Victoria looked up at the foyer's high ceiling. Cobwebs hung in strands from the light fixture. She ground her jaw and squeezed her eyes shut, thinking for the hundredth time that she would need to paint the foyer before the house went on the market.

Max's guilt had slowly run out after he'd left. At first, he'd been content to have Victoria and the kids stay in the house while he paid the mortgage and she remained home with the kids. But he had grown anxious as his bank account shrank. He had told her it was time to go back to work, time to sell the house.

She'd fought it at first. That wasn't what they'd agreed on, and she felt robbed of any ability to make a decision affecting her own life. He kept making them for her, against her will. But, after two lawyers, she'd come to see that the Hollywood version, where the asshole husband gets taken to the cleaners and the wronged wife gets to have it all, was just that: a Hollywood version.

The truth was, she had a master's degree in education and marketable skills, and both kids were in school. A court of law would not find alimony was in order. There was no way she could afford to stay in the house unemployed, even with child support, and she wasn't sure what kind of job she'd be getting, but it wasn't likely to be full-time, and it wasn't likely to pay the bills this huge house demanded.

Victoria plodded up the stairs towards the kitchen. Though she still had almost three hours before the afternoon kindergarten bus came, Victoria knew that it would soon be time to make Connor lunch and get him ready for school. Brandy would be arriving any minute now, and then things would start to get more chaotic. Brandy was dropped off each morning around 9:30. Since turning two, she had become quite a handful, pulling out toys, demanding to be read books, and wanting to be pushed on the swing in the back yard.

At a few minutes before 9:00, the telephone rang. It was Brandy's grandmother, Barb.

"Did you hear about the plane crash?" Barb asked. Her voice came fast and breathless.

"No, I haven't had the TV or radio on," Victoria answered.

"Well, apparently a plane just crashed into the World Trade Center," she went on. "It's all over the news."

Barb went on to say that she would be keeping Brandy home for the day. Victoria tiptoed downstairs and made sure Connor was still immersed in his computer game, then came back upstairs. He wasn't likely to come up for air for some time unless she insisted.

She was reluctant to turn on the television. So many times, the media covered stories—especially tragedies—ad nauseam. Special music and special graphics and even special fonts for special titles; disasters became prime time viewing. It was all a little much, and she didn't usually watch the news because of it. Still, it was pretty amazing that a plane had crashed into a building. Why was it flying so low? In New York, of all places? She decided to turn on the television and see if she could find anything out.

The L-shaped couch hugged half the perimeter of the living room, a large square cherry coffee table in its center, and an immense cherry entertainment center at its focal point. Max had called it their altar to technology, and she had always hated it. Hated how the only thing one could really do when sitting on the couch was look at the TV. Now she sat on the edge of the coffee table, volume down low, watching in shock as the story became clear.

The footage of smoke billowing out of the side of the tower was shown constantly as the correspondents tried to decipher its meaning. And then, another plane burst into the second tower. Victoria covered her mouth as smoke came pouring from the buildings and people ran, screaming, real-time, from the wreckage. Her hand remained on her throat as she watched, stunned.

As the story unfolded, the realization that it was likely not an accident revealed itself. The towers collapsed. There was a crash into the Pentagon, so close by, and another in Pennsylvania. For hours, she watched as the news began to reveal the unfathomable. All sense of safety fell away.

❧

The day was a nightmare. She sent Connor to school and continued watching the coverage, glued to the television she so skillfully avoided most of the time. When the bus brought the children home at 3:35, she met it shakily. She wondered if they knew anything about what had happened. Surely, the teachers and administrators had heard what was going on. Had they discussed it in front of the children? As she walked them back from the bus stop to the door, she hadn't been able to decide whether or not to ask them.

Chloe initiated the conversation matter-of-factly, stating, "Some bad men crashed a plane."

"Yes," Victoria answered. "That's right. Some bad men caused some accidents by making planes crash. Lots of people died because of it. But we're safe," she added.

She wasn't sure if that was true or not, but she'd needed to reassure the children, reassure herself that they didn't need to be scared. But her fear was all-consuming.

She waited to see if there were more details Chloe or Connor would provide, or questions they might have. They didn't seem to want to talk about it anymore, retreating to the security of their toys and books and crayons. Victoria wished she could do the same.

Tucking Chloe in bed later that night, she felt the tears begin to burn her eyes. All day, she'd maintained a front of stability and normalcy, not wanting to alarm the children or give in to the crushing sensation she was feeling. She climbed onto Chloe's bed and tried to squeeze in among the stuffed animals and Beanie Babies.

"I just want to hold you a little while," she said. She breathed in Chloe's scent, a mixture of little girl sweat and minty toothpaste and something more primal, more basic: the smell of a child that only a mother can recognize.

She held Chloe tightly, but Chloe pushed her away and looked confused. It was all Victoria could do not to completely fall apart. All she wanted was for her babies to be safe. She wanted comfort, and there was none. Human contact was what she craved, and all that was available was a 7-year-old girl who wasn't much of a snuggler and who couldn't understand why Mommy was crying and shaking. How could it have come to this? It felt as though a light had gone out and could not be relit.

VOWS

Over the next week, flurries of emails passed between Victoria and Deena. She and Todd were fine. They had not been anywhere near the Towers, nor had anyone in their immediate circle. Just days after the attack, Deena and Todd emailed their friends and families, encouraging them not to let fear dictate their lives. They still planned to hold the wedding, come together in joy and celebration, and overcome the shadow of fear that darkened the city.

Victoria was wavering. After all that had happened, she didn't think it was a good idea to travel, especially to New York City. The plan had been to drive up, and that certainly seemed the safest travel option. Still, anxiety was infecting her decisions. Should she leave her children behind? What if she didn't make it back? What if something horrible happened and she was away from her kids?

She ran the scenario through her head multiple times. She really wanted to go to this wedding, and the idea of letting the terrorists win by changing her decision was a thorn in her side.

After a day or so, Victoria talked herself into making the trip. She reasoned herself into believing that a car, as a moving target, would be safe. A church was safe, out of hundreds that must exist in the city. Security was higher than ever. Her kids were in good hands. Her mind was set in stubborn resolution. She adopted an attitude she only partially felt. She would not let the terrorists scare her into staying in her house with the shades drawn.

❧

Just weeks after the Twin Towers fell, Victoria drove into Lawrenceville, NJ, around lunch time. Sandy was a friend from her teenage years who had two children the same ages as Chloe and Connor. Since Sandy's move to New Jersey from Virginia, the two friends had spent many a weekend visiting one another, taking turns making the drive.

Victoria planned to go to the wedding, taking the train into the city and back. After spending the night at Sandy's, she'd drive back to Virginia in the morning. Victoria had dropped the kids off at a friend's house early, around 8:30. The friend would take the kids to church, then pass them off to Max, who would keep them overnight, then drop them at another friend's who would put Chloe on the bus Monday morning, watch Connor, and put him on the bus in the afternoon. Victoria would be back in time to meet the bus after school had ended for the day.

The drive had been easy, technically. She'd made it in about three and a half hours. There had been little traffic on a Sunday morning, but every bridge over 95 and the Delaware Memorial Parkway, and every overpass, was decorated with flags, flowers, and messages of patriotism and hope. In chain-link fences, plastic cups of red, white, and blue had been placed in the likeness of American flags, or used to spell out "USA" or "America the Free." Every overpass she traveled under brought the sober realization that she was heading into the very center of the world. Right now, all eyes were on New York and keeping tabs on its recovery.

After eating a quick sandwich at Sandy's, Victoria showered, giving her armpits and legs a fresh shave. She brushed her teeth and fixed her hair and makeup. The new dress she'd ordered from the Victoria's Secret catalog was a black, cotton-knit sheath, sleeveless, with a simple V-neck.

It came to mid-calf on her long legs. There was a short-waisted, three-quarter sleeve cardigan that matched and could be worn if it got chilly. It seemed appropriate both for an evening wedding, and to pay respects to the many lost lives.

She also had on a new black bra, lightly padded and of a silky material that made her small breasts seem rounder and of more equal size. Her new thong was of the same material, though in muted plum. She smiled at the memory of the conversation she'd had with Sandy about thongs before Victoria had ever worn one. Victoria had thought they must feel like a perpetual wedgie riding up one's ass, causing the constant urge to yank them out. Sandy claimed that not only did they not feel like a wedgie, but that the thong actually felt good, and if one moved in just the right way, one could get the extra benefit of a stimulating sensation that provided private pleasure.

So far, Victoria didn't think thongs felt either uncomfortable or stimulating. However, the thong alleviated the problem of panty lines. Control-top hose for extra esteem flattened her somewhat rounded belly. Despite hours of weight training, hundreds of sit-ups, and a diet low in carbs and high in protein, her post child-bearing paunch remained.

She finished off the outfit with chunky-heeled black sandals she'd bought last July for her 20th high school reunion. It was always a tough decision about wearing heels; Victoria's 5'11" frame felt so tall already. But dresses just didn't look that great with flats, and she had taken the attitude that she should be proud, not ashamed, of her stature. Besides, she was already taller than most people she knew. Would a couple more inches matter? She checked herself in the mirror and approved. Not bad for an old gal; not too frumpy for a stay-at-home mom.

It was amazing what the right clothes and careful makeup application could achieve. She moved her face closer to the mirror. Her eyes looked good. She had learned how to apply eye shadow, liner, and mascara back in high school, and achieved a look that made her slightly puffy eyes look more deep-set, less fleshy on the lids. She regularly tweezed her dark thick brows, and waxed her upper lip to remove the dark hair that grew there.

As it was September, she still retained a hint of a tan, so her normally pale skin had more of a glow. Though she still got pimples at this stage in life--a major disappointment of hers--she had expertly covered them with the right mix of concealer, foundation, and powder. She looked at her features, assessing herself for what must have been the millionth time.

She had a rather large nose, but straight, and not too big for her face. Her chin could have stood to be a little more prominent, but as long as she didn't pull it in, she didn't totally lose it in her neck. A mole below her right ear had always been touted as a "beauty mark," and, except for the two or three small pimples on her chin, her skin was smooth and even-toned.

She had bedecked herself with simple jewelry that had belonged to her grandmother: paisley-shaped gold clip-on earrings, with two small diamond chips embedded in each center; a gold chain with a dark blue, almost black stone set in a gold pendant made by her grandmother; a simple gold bracelet, about a half-inch wide; and her Nana's gold-and-silver watch.

She had also taken the time to paint her nails a sandy gold color the night before. Her long slender fingers with their tapered nails had always been one of her best features, along with her equally long and slender legs. She applied berry-colored lipstick, then lined her lips and used a brush to blend it all. This was a more recent addition to her beauty routine.

In earlier years, she had never quite gotten the hang of lipstick, always thinking it made her look like a clown. It wasn't until someone had shown her how to use lip liner and blend that she had figured out how to actually make her lips appear shapely and full. She smiled at herself, noting that braces had been a good decision on her parents' part.

She came out of the bathroom, switching off the light. Sandy was sitting in the family room.

"Well, what do you think?" she asked, doing a 360-degree turn.

"You look great!" said Sandy.

"Thanks," Victoria said. "I guess we should head out soon, huh?" It was approaching 2:00.

There was a 2:21 train out of the Hamilton station, just one exit away on 295. It would get her into the city just after 3:30. She could catch a cab from Penn Station and make it to the church in plenty of time for the 4:30 ceremony. For the return trip, there were trains at 6:32, 7:32, 8:33, 9:33, and 10:46, leaving lots of choices if the reception went late.

※

As New York's skyline slid into view, the mindless chatter on the train ceased and the faces turned toward the view in stunned silence. If she hadn't known better, Victoria would not have known what city she now approached, so foreign was its appearance. The telltale towers no longer protruded skyward. Sadness and respect filled her as she half-closed her eyes and made a feeble attempt at prayer. The wounds felt fresh, the pain still raw.

As the train pulled in to Penn Station, Victoria checked her lipstick in a small mirror sewn into the flap of her purse. All she had with her was her camera and the purse. In it were her driver's license and a credit card, the folded paper with the train times, some cash for cabs, her lipstick, and her cell phone.

She held onto her purse as she stepped off the train with the crowd. She moved along with the herd, pushing her way up a flight of stairs into the main lobby of the station. People milled around, looking up at the suspended departure board with its constantly changing train times.

Victoria followed the signs to the exit, walked out of the station and into the city bustle. She somehow expected a pall to have fallen over the city, for recent events to have taken the spring out of people's steps, for faces to be drawn and lifeless. By all appearances, however, nothing had slowed down a bit. Cabs lined the sidewalk, cars and buses honked and pulled out into traffic, people cascaded in every direction, and the city felt completely alive.

She walked to the holding area and waited for the next available taxi. As it pulled up to the curb and she climbed in, she told the driver the address she had memorized.

The driver was no more cautious than any taxi driver she'd been driven by in the past. Nothing was moving any more slowly or carefully than before 9/11. The cabbie swerved in and out of traffic, honking at people in his path, cursing and looking wildly around for an opening. There wasn't any newfound respect for human life or new politeness paid to the brotherhood of man. New York looked the way it had always looked, at least at first.

The cab smelled faintly spicy, and more strongly of male sweat. The cab driver's name was Luis Santiago, according to the cabbie license hanging from the dashboard. He didn't say much, only listened to a Latin radio station as he maniacally drove the city streets. Sometimes cabbies talked nonstop, trying to engage you in mindless conversation or tell you about their lives. Not Luis. He was perfectly happy to ignore his fare. He suddenly stopped in the middle of the street, pulling up next to a curb on the right that bordered Central Park.

"I only go this far. You have to walk down there," he said, and he waved his hand indiscriminately down a street to the left.

"Is this the right address?" she asked, not seeing any churches nearby.

"Yes, but you have to walk the rest of the way, okay?"

"Okay," she said haltingly. The fare came to $8.75. She handed him a ten and stepped out of the car.

She crossed the busy intersection as the cab pulled away and began walking down the street he'd pointed to. New Yorkers walk, she thought, and I'm in New York, so I'll walk. She put on an air of acceptance and looked up at the life pulsating around her.

The side street she now navigated was quieter, less traveled than the road onto which she'd gotten out of the taxi. It was lined with what seemed to be homes and small businesses. Here and there grew trees, coming up through squares of soil enclosed in short, iron-wrought edging that interrupted the sidewalk. Parked cars lined the curbs, so close together it seemed they'd pulled in one after the other in a long line. She wondered how they would ever pull away from the curb again. Would everyone wait for the first car in line to leave, and then follow, one by one?

She walked a couple of blocks but still saw nothing resembling a church. It was just after 4:00. She pulled out her cell phone and dialed Sandy. Sandy's husband Bob answered.

"Hey Bob, guess what I forgot? My wedding invitation! I don't know the name of the church, and I'm not sure where I'm going. Could you read me the name again, and maybe look it up on Mapquest?"

She walked while she talked, feeling that this was how New Yorkers behaved, always a cell phone to their ear as they hurried to the next appointment or meeting. Bob came back on the line and gave her the name of the church. It should be coming up any moment. For false security, Victoria kept Bob on the phone as she walked, somehow feeling like as long as she was connected to a voice, she was okay.

She soon approached some parked cars with passengers who were dressed up, some carrying gifts. Victoria had sent the Williams Sonoma® wooden mixing spoon set on ahead of her, not wanting to have to carry it with her as she traveled. She got off the phone with Bob, thanking him for keeping her company, and crossed the street to enter what she now realized was the church.

From the outside, it was a low, flat building built of bricks of a nondescript color with windows that showed nothing on the other side. There was a long covered walkway that snaked down from the entrance to the sidewalk and street.

She now noticed it was crowded with people. As she approached the building and moved through the mélange of faces, she recognized some, but rather than stopping to say hello, she hurried past, wanting desperately to find a bathroom.

Inside, she found the small, hidden restroom with one toilet and a dim bulb overhead. After relieving herself, she checked her lipstick. She moved a few stray hairs into place and turned sideways, checking her profile while sucking her stomach in. Maybe Todd had some tall brothers or cousins she could hook up with for the evening, at least to dance and flirt with.

When she reemerged, more people had come inside the church. She walked into the entry foyer and saw Deena's brother J.R.

"Hey J.R.," she said, tapping him on the shoulder.

He looked surprised and gave her a hug. "Victoria? Is that you?"

J.R. had been the cute boy in the neighborhood that all the girls had crushes on. Victoria had always just seen him as an annoying older brother. He used to walk in on her in the bathroom after they'd all told her that the rule in their house was no locked doors. She'd fallen for it, and then paid in embarrassment.

J.R. looked the same, if older and a little heavier. Still the same big blue eyes he'd inherited from his dad, and robust cheeks and mischievous smile. On his arm was a younger woman who turned out to be his wife Bonnie. She held onto him possessively but smiled at Victoria as they were introduced. Then more of the old gang began to arrive. There were the DeWitts, a couple who had been friends with Victoria's and Deena's parents. Mrs. DeWitt was from England originally, and had the accent to prove it. They enthusiastically greeted her and asked after the whole family.

There was Mr. Cashell, Deena and J.R.'s dad. More hellos, more family updates. And there was Joseph Lindner. He'd been Victoria's next-door neighbor growing up. His family had lived just down a short hill from them. Victoria remembered the large plate-glass windows that looked into each other's stairways and upstairs hallways.

When Victoria and her little sister used to take baths, they would run around the upstairs hallway naked before they realized that the Lindner children could look towards their house through the plate-glass windows and see them. Mr. and Mrs. Lindner still lived in the same house, though the kids were all out now. Victoria invited Joseph to sit with her. They found a pew and caught up on family events.

Joseph shared some scoop, explaining that a lot of people hadn't come due to recent events and fear of airplane travel. Joseph and Victoria sat on the groom's side to help even out the balance of guests. Todd's family was from New Zealand, and the pews were thinner on his side. Joseph and Victoria stood along with the rest of the guests as the bride glided down the aisle on her father's arm.

The ceremony was the usual parade of family doing readings and priests doing prayers. At the close of the ceremony, the guests were asked to wait outside until a bagpiper arrived and started playing. Everyone would then follow the piper back down the street to Central Park, walk through the park, and arrive at the reception at the Boathouse restaurant. While she waited, Victoria took the opportunity to take some photos with some old friends.

After about fifteen minutes, the piper arrived. His pipes began their wail, calling the guests to follow. The park was beautiful. It was after 5:30 now and people were out enjoying the warm evening, playing Frisbee with their dogs or picnicking on the grass. Groups of young men were tossing footballs or kicking soccer balls. The air had a fall crispness to it that smelled fresh and earthy. As the wedding party marched past, people stopped, pointed, or took photos. It was very exhilarating being a part of it all. Victoria was glad her shoes were almost comfortable. Higher, less stable heels would have been difficult to navigate for this distance.

At the center of the park they came to an open area paved with herringbone bricks, surrounded by intricately carved sandstone walls. Squared columns, about ten feet high, stood at each corner of the wall. Atop each column was a rounded, pagoda-like stone cap. The party approached the open area, called the Bethesda Terrace, by one of two wide stone stairways that bordered the bridge overlooking the area. Seven arches opened beneath the bridge, leading to other pathways through the park.

A central fountain stood at the center of the large circular terrace. Its pool was about 100 feet across. At its center was a stone two-tiered fountain, an angel with open wings balancing atop it. Victoria realized this was the fountain pictured in the wedding invitation. Several ice cream and hot dog vendors were set up beneath green-and-white striped umbrellas. Visitors from all over the world and New York City milled around, taking photos, tossing coins into the fountain, and watching the spectacle now emerging on the terrace.

The wedding party and guests stopped here for a group photo, as well as several other shots of the family and wedding party. The photographer commanded the guests from atop the bridge, They stood in a huddled mass with the bride and groom up front, the fountain behind them. Victoria stood just to Deena's right, and on the count of three, everyone raised their hands or fists and gave a loud whoop. The air was full of joy and excitement, ripe for beauty and laughter.

HAKA

The Boathouse was a rather swanky restaurant on a lake. To get there, the party exited the terrace via a path on the right. A black awning over the entrance bore the gold-lettered words, "Central Park Boathouse." A black metal fence surrounded the outdoor seating area and private gardens. To the left, green rowboats were stacked like books on a shelf. The lake lay just beyond, and rowers and gondoliers (in full gondolier regalia) could be seen navigating the water in the mild autumn weather.

The Boathouse was iconic and had been used in various movies. It was most famous for its scene with Meg Ryan and Carrie Fisher from *When Harry Met Sally*. Victoria recalled the scene in which Sally, played by Meg Ryan, had just told her two best friends that she had broken up with her long time beau, Joe. Immediately, Carrie Fisher's character pulled a Rolodex from her purse to start searching for available men. Another scene in the movie showed Billy Crystal and Bruno Kirby jogging through Central Park, right through the Bethesda Terrace where the wedding photos had been taken.

Just inside the entrance to the banquet room, displays on two round tables held photos of Deena and Todd as children. Victoria spent a few minutes perusing them, recognizing some of the photos of Deena from their old neighborhood. Round tables with seating cards were arranged throughout the main room, with a dance floor and more tables in a separate space two steps down from the dining room. Just past the dance floor, a balcony overlooked the lake.

The DJ was set up in a corner of the dance floor, just next to the balcony. The bar was on the other side. Pseudo Tuscan chandeliers, approximately five feet in diameter, pointed downward like full breasts. The wall to the right of the tables was made of glass and segmented into large rectangles, some of which were doors to the outside.

Victoria found her name on a small ivory card. Her name was spelled correctly this time, Vick Woolfrey. She was seated next to Joseph on the left, and Mary Thompson on her right, another friend from the neighborhood.

Mary and her husband Dan were both very nice, and enthusiastically greeted her and spent some time catching up. Also at the table were the DeWitts, Deena's Aunt Amelia and Uncle Tom, and next to them, a young man Victoria didn't know, but who turned out to be Deena's cousin Michael. Introductions were made all around as wine was served.

Conversations bounced around the table as they waited for dinner. Aunt Amelia knew Victoria's mother, it turned out. Michael worked for Kennels America, producing footage of dog shows and competitions. Since the movie *Best in Show* had come out recently, several jokes about his profession were tossed back and forth.

Maybe at first, she didn't pay that much attention. Maybe at first, she was getting used to the environment and settling down after the excitement of the ceremony and the walk through the park. But as she listened to Michael's voice, she became very aware of his smile and his laugh. As the night wore on, she noticed he spent a lot of time with his aunt and uncle, sitting with them in a relaxed way that didn't speak of any immediate desire to be elsewhere talking with, perhaps, single women or guys his age.

He was definitely attractive. His clean-shaven face reminded her somewhat of Hugh Grant's, only not as thin. He had a boyish smile and dimples. He had dark wavy hair and his smile was big and friendly. As he spoke, his voice—

the way he spoke—seemed somewhat self-deprecating and self-aware.

He knew how to hold a conversation, asking questions and looking directly into the eyes of the person with whom he was speaking. He wore a white dress shirt and tie, loosened at the neck. His suit jacket lay over the back of his chair, and his arm rested casually on the back of the chair as he turned his body slightly toward the person he was talking to. Victoria found herself desperately wishing she were sitting next to him, receiving his attention, close enough to smell him.

Dinner took a long time getting served. It was a choice between filet mignon and coq au vin, both accompanied by steamed vegetables, wild rice, and bread. Victoria chose the chicken, holding conversations through bites of food. The mood at their table was jovial and high-spirited. There was lots of laughter and constant chatter.

Then came dancing. The DJ did an adequate job playing popular tunes and fielding requests. Victoria danced with J.R., Joseph, Mr. Cashell, and even Todd's father, Mr. van Durst, who was three sheets to the wind. She wanted to ask Michael to dance, but every time she looked for him, he wasn't around.

There was an outdoor area she hadn't explored, but where some of the guests had congregated. The door frequently opened and shut, admitting people back into the main bar and dance area or releasing them into the courtyard. Through the periodic opening of the door, she could see that he was out there, drinking beers. She wondered if he'd found a young woman with whom to fraternize.

Back at the table, promises of staying in touch were made, and friendships refortified. Victoria had a long talk with Amelia and Tom about the family who couldn't be there. It turned out Michael's father was receiving treatment for cancer and not feeling well. Speaking of Michael gave Victoria the nerve to finally boldly ask about him.

"So, what's Michael's story?" she asked. By this time, Deena's stepsister Lindy and her partner Trish had joined the table.

Amelia said, "He's very single. You should go for it!"

Victoria blushed, not thinking her interest was that obvious, and said, "Yeah, but how old is he?"

After bantering back and forth, it was determined he was 32.

"That's a little young," Victoria said. When asked how old she was, she had to admit she was 38.

"That's not so much difference," said Amelia, clearly encouraging her to be open, at least, to the possibilities. "You should talk to him."

An announcement asked all guests to assemble on the dance floor. The men from New Zealand, young and old alike, gathered on the two steps above the dance floor and commanded the attention of the rest of the guests. From childhood, they had learned and practiced a Maori war dance and chant, the haka, which they wished to or had been requested to perform. Victoria, standing at the bottom of the stairs with the other guests, got out her camera. Michael was just next to her, video taping the whole thing. Her arm brushed against his as she raised her camera to take a shot. She felt the warmth from his body.

"Isn't this great?" she said.

"It's really something," he answered, camera to his eye.

The haka was intensely emotional. The men became Maori warriors, transforming before their audience. They stomped their feet, pounded their chests with their fists, and shouted, twisting their faces into grimaces, tongues lolling, eyes bulging, a challenge to their foes, a show of strength and fearlessness. The rhythmic movements echoed on the wooden floor and a silence surrounded their shouts. They ended with one rousing yell, intense facial expressions on each and every one of them.

With enthusiastic applause and cheering from the assembled wedding party, they performed again, this time without shirts. They stripped down, the slender, the hairy, the pudgy, the white-haired, the bare-chested, and again loudly chanted their war calls and stamped out the steps of the dance. Victoria's skin tingled and pulse quickened. The crowd cheered and applauded and laughed and the men reverted back from Maori warriors to drunken dinner guests.

It was a fun, rowdy group. The music was playing, the wine was flowing, the evening was lovely. And it was getting late. Victoria checked her watch. Almost 9:30. She checked the crumpled paper with the train times in her purse. The last train left at 10:46, which meant she'd need to get out of there soon and find a cab to take her to Penn Station. She spoke to Lindy about how to get out.

"Oh, you don't want to leave now. It's not safe in the park at night. We're all taking a trolley out together when the reception is over."

"But I've got to catch a train soon! How will I get back?" Victoria asked.

"Why don't you just stay over tonight? I'm sure we can find you a place to stay." Lindy seemed to think it perfectly okay to change the plan.

"I don't know...I don't want to leave, but then I've got to figure out how I'm getting home tomorrow."

"Let me see what I can do. Call your friends and let them know you might not be coming back tonight," suggested Lindy.

"Well, let's see what you find out first. Just let me know soon, okay?"

Victoria was running over the possibilities in her mind. How would she get back to Hamilton Station? What time did the trains begin in the morning? Would Sandy or Bob be able to come get her then? And would she make it back to Virginia in time to meet the bus?

Honestly, she didn't want to leave. She was having a good time, and she still hadn't danced with Michael. Within 15 minutes, Lindy came back with Deena's sister, Sabrina.

"Bri says you can stay with her and Mark," Lindy said. Mark was Sabrina's husband.

"We're staying at a bed and breakfast. There's only one bed, but there's a loft," Bri recounted. "Our cousin Michael slept there last night."

The words hit her like an aphrodisiac. She imagined sleeping in the same bed he'd slept in. It was rather erotic to think about smelling the sheets where he'd lain and imagining his body there. She thought about it for a minute.

"Come on, you don't want to leave now! The party's just starting!" said Bri, smiling.

Victoria thought about how short life was. How few opportunities there were. How fleeting the good times could be and how quickly all joy can be sucked out of you in an instant. Carpe diem.

"Okay, I'll stay!" she said. The girls clapped her on the back.

Victoria took her cell phone outside and called Sandy and Bob.

"Hey, I've decided to stay the night. They've found me a place to stay, and I have no way to leave anyway. I'll catch a train first thing in the morning. Is that okay?"

They confirmed that she could catch the 7:34 train in the morning and that Sandy could come pick her up. Once the plans were settled, Victoria turned off her phone, put it back in her purse, and returned to the party.

ప

"Everything all settled?" Bri asked Victoria when she came back in.

"Yes, all set. Thanks again for letting me stay with you guys. I really didn't want to leave just yet."

"No problem," said Bri. "We talked to Michael, and he didn't have a problem with sharing the loft with you."

One giant thud sounded within Victoria's chest cavity as all the sounds around her became momentarily muffled. Did Bri just indicate that not only would Victoria be sleeping in the loft where Michael had slept the night before, but that he was staying there again tonight? In other words, were they going to be sleeping in the loft together? She realized she wasn't breathing, and took a breath. She forced her mind to focus, she felt her body, alive and kicking, and her mind racing, and she found that, despite her surprise, she was not upset or freaked out.

"Oh! Well, okay then..." Victoria shakily responded. She was tipsy and the whole experience was so exciting and fun, she had adopted the attitude that she would just go with the flow; when in Rome, etcetera.

She struck up a conversation with another of Deena's cousins, though clearly with different parents than Michael. He was dark-haired and barrel-chested. He was not as tall as Michael, and a little rounder through the middle. While exchanging information on how each of them knew either the bride or groom, a young woman with short dark hair, his wife it turned out, promptly appeared at his side.

Victoria was so tired of married women feeling uncomfortable about her existing. It was as though her mere presence was a threat. Frankly, she wasn't at all attracted to this cousin, but was enjoying making conversation and working on not following her urge to remain a wallflower. Then Michael appeared, Heineken in hand, jacket casually slung over his shoulder. The two cousins bantered about the old days, recalling various family get-togethers. Then the first cousin, whose name had completely vanished from Victoria's mind, walked off with his wife.

"Nice meeting you," Victoria called as they moved away. She was alone with Michael for the first time. This was the man she'd been eyeing all night. This was the man she'd be sleeping next to tonight.

"So," Victoria jumped right in before the alcohol could wear off and she lost her nerve, "I hear we're sleeping together tonight!" They had a laugh at that, and his eyes didn't leave hers.

"My aunt said you were asking about me," he said, smiling mischievously.

Victoria felt her face go scarlet. He raised his beer to his lips, tipping the bottle up, taking a long drag. His eyes remained focused on her.

"I thought you were with that guy you were sitting with," he continued, referring to Joseph.

"Oh, no. Joseph's just an old friend. We were neighbors growing up," Victoria said, a little too quickly.

"Good," he said. They smiled at each other.

The reception began to wind down, and there was talk of another party at Deena and Todd's apartment.

"Do you want to go to it?" Michael asked. He hadn't left her side since they'd parted ways with the other cousins. His interest in her had been switched on all of a sudden, and now there seemed to be a shift in Victoria's reality. He wasn't there, and then, he was.

Victoria shrugged.

"I'll do whatever everyone else is doing, I guess. It's fine with me," she said. She felt she was at a disadvantage because she was at the mercy of Bri and Mark, who had the room she was to sleep in with Michael. She was tired, but she was along for the ride, which seemed to be getting ready to roll somewhere else.

The guests meandered out to the front of the Boathouse, waiting for the trolley to take them out of the park. The park was dark and empty at this hour on a Sunday night. Victoria shivered in the cooler night air. She was glad she hadn't tried to leave alone. She pulled her cardigan on and hugged herself.

"I should tell you," Michael said, standing close, "that there may be some--how do I put this?—recreational drugs being used there. I don't know if that bothers you or not, but I thought you should know."

"Oh," Victoria said. She didn't think of herself as a prude; on the other hand, she hadn't smoked pot since she was a teenager, and she'd never tried anything harder. Sitting around watching other people get high would probably feel uncomfortable.

"Actually, thanks for telling me," she said to Michael. "Now that you mention it, I probably don't want to go. Do you think there's some way I can get a key or something to the room, and just go on ahead of everyone else?" she asked.

"I don't know. We could check," said Michael.

He went off to find Sabrina and Mark. He came back a few minutes later and said, "I have the key."

"Great," she said. "Someone just needs to tell me the address I'm going to, and I'll be good to go." She held her hand out for the key. Michael held onto it. She laughed a little, looking quizzically at him.

"I'm not going to go to the party either," he said. "I'll just go back with you."

Victoria's heart skipped a beat. When it resumed, she was sure everyone could hear it pounding.

"I'm sure I can find it okay…you really don't have to," she said weakly.

"No…I want to," he replied. "Is that okay?"

Victoria swallowed the lump that had suddenly grown in her throat. Blood was pounding in her ears, but she was fairly certain she said, "Sure…that's fine."

Then the trolley pulled up.

LIGHTS ON

The trolley rolled bumpily through the park. Inside its brightly lit interior, the guests still laughed and conversed. Michael and Victoria shared one vinyl-covered seat, directly behind Mr. van Durst, whose head was lolling precariously on the metal rim at the back of his seat. Every now and then he'd sit up and say something incomprehensible in slurred speech, bringing gales of laughter from those sitting nearby. Michael and Victoria exchanged knowing looks, as if to agree that he was definitely going to be paying for his fun the next morning.

Once outside the park, the guests clamored off the trolley and began to part ways, but Deena, Todd, Bri, Mark, and a handful of others stayed on a corner trying to decide who needed what cabs and where to head next. Michael stayed close to Victoria.

"I guess we'll just get our own cab," he said. Her palms were sweating.

When a cab finally pulled over, the rest of the group was still trying to decide what to do. What an odd bunch they must seem, a bride in a long white gown and veil and a bunch of drunken people in dressy garb on a street corner under a single street lamp on a Sunday night. Actually, being that it was New York City, it probably went unnoticed.

"Come on, let's get in this one," said Michael, and he held the door open for her.

She slid over to the left side and he climbed in after her. Some of the guests looked at them as they got in.

Deena called out, "Aren't you coming with us?" She looked confused, though she was smiling.

"No, but thanks! Have fun!" Michael yelled as the cab pulled away from the curb.

Victoria's blood was pumping furiously through her veins. What was going to happen here? It seemed too obvious, too easy. She was just going to go back to some room in some B&B, the location of which she didn't even know, where until an hour or so ago, she hadn't even known she would be staying, with a stranger she had just met whom she just happened to find attractive, and they were going to be alone together, spending the night in the same bed? And he had chosen to come with her?

She dug her fingernails into her palms, trying to see if she was asleep. Michael told the cab driver where to take them. He was in total control. He had the address, he had the key, and he had the upper hand. She was a little nervous; however, it surprised her to note that she was curious as to what would happen next on this adventure.

Her thoughts were derailed, however, by what she saw out the cab windows. Rows of candles lined the sidewalks, with bunches of flowers interspersed between them. On the walls were posted sketches and photographs of those still missing from the Twin Towers. Time slowed down as she stared at each image. It went on for blocks.

"This is the saddest thing I have ever experienced," she said, her tone becoming serious and melancholy and humbled.

Michael touched her shoulder with his left hand. "Look over there," Michael said, pointing down the street they were just passing. "See those lights?"

"Yes," she answered. She placed her fingertips against the cool smooth glass of the window.

"Those are the searchlights at Ground Zero," he said. "They are on 24 hours a day. They're still digging through the rubble."

This sobering thought made Victoria want to cry and take refuge in his arms. The sorrow, pain, and horror hung in the air, leaving her feeling cold and sober.

"Here we are," Michael said as the cab came to a stop.

They were in front of some darkened buildings on a street that wasn't exactly bustling with activity. Victoria thought she remembered someone saying that the B&B was somewhere in Greenwich Village. Michael paid the cabbie and they got out.

"Let's see if I can remember which door it is," he said, looking up and down the street and at the different stairways and doors. "I was here last night; I'm just not sure exactly which one of these it is."

Victoria took a moment to assess the situation. She recalled a time she'd been in Denver visiting an old friend. They had gone out to a bar, Studebaker's, that boasted big cars from the 50s one could sit in, and waiters and waitresses who danced and sang on the bar. They had gone there in hopes of lots of free drinks since the friend knew one of the bartenders. They met a lot of cute guys, even taken pictures with them.

As the night came to a close, they'd met a couple of guys who wanted to take them to breakfast. They were drunk and the guys were cute, so they said yes and went to a Denny's for eggs and hash browns and bacon. When they'd finished eating, Victoria was propositioned by one of the guys, a blonde with a moustache (what was his name? John? Jack? Something simple like that...).

She agreed to go back to his apartment, with the agreement that he would drive her back to where they were staying later on. Her friend seemed a little concerned, but didn't try to talk her out of it. She went home with this guy, who had performed some of the best oral sex she'd ever experienced, and then he puked his guts out, which sobered them both immediately, erasing all feelings of erotica or romance.

He drove her home on a dark back road. By then, she was completely sober and realized she was with a complete stranger in his truck on a dark road in the middle of the night with no clue where she was or how to get back to her friend. She inched closer and closer to her side of the truck, hand near the door handle. The guy knew she was freaked out and kept reassuring her, in a somewhat irritated tone, that he wasn't a murderer or rapist and that he was definitely taking her home. Even though she arrived safely, the knowledge of the danger she'd put herself in at the time had been a real dose of reality.

Now Victoria found herself in a somewhat similar situation. But now she didn't feel scared. Cautious, maybe, but not scared.

Out of the corner of her eye, Victoria noticed a young man swaggering towards them. He was giggling and pointing, and clearly drunk.

"Look!" he cried out, "Look in that window! Do you see it? Look."

He was pointing and waving in the general direction of where Michael and Victoria now stood. She inched closer to Michael, not sure what the drunk was going to do.

"What is it?" Michael asked.

"It's a cat. He's just lying there!" Michael looked where the man was pointing.

Victoria followed his gaze. Sure enough, a mostly black cat lay on the table in a storefront window, now dark. His head, with two streaks of white just on the inner side of where his ears came out, lay peacefully on his front paws.

"How about that?" Michael said to the young man. His friendly tone seemed to disarm any concern or threat.

"Well, have a good night!" he called to the young man as he escorted Victoria up some stairs.

"I think this is it," he said, pulling out the key and inserting it into the lock.

"Well, that's a relief," Victoria said. Michael sensed her hesitation.

"I'm sure we're there. But this doesn't look too familiar...I don't recognize the doors."

They had entered a foyer, and a narrow staircase led up to another level.

"Well, your key worked, so it's got to be the place, right?" she asked.

"Yes, I'm sure it is, but it isn't looking familiar."

"Maybe it will look familiar when we go upstairs. Shall we try it?" she asked, trying not to sound nervous or concerned.

They walked up a flight of stairs. A small sitting room led off to the left.

"This sure looks like a bed and breakfast to me," she commented, wondering how he could not remember what room it was.

"I think maybe we're in the wrong place," he said.

He walked up another stairway. What if he entered someone's private room?

"No, this doesn't look right. I know it sounds crazy, but I think we have to go back outside. Trust me. Don't worry, I know it's near here."

Victoria wasn't so sure about this anymore. Had they come to the wrong place? But then how would the key have worked? She laughed nervously, and followed him back down the stairs and outside. He looked around at the different doorways.

"I think it's that one," he said, pointing to another doorway next to the first one. "Let's try it, shall we?"

He sounded a little nervous too. He inserted the key into the second door. It opened.

"There we go," he said, relieved. "It's just another part of the same place."

"Does it look familiar now?" she asked.

"Yes, this definitely looks more familiar. I think it's up these stairs."

She followed him up another flight of stairs, and he opened a door at the top.

"Yeah, this is it. Now I recognize it," he said, entering the dark doorway.

He flipped on the light switch to reveal a small, crowded room. To the left, an unmade double bed was squashed right up in the corner with a floor-to-ceiling window to its left. At the foot of the bed stood a dresser with a digital clock and a small television. Toiletries, clothing, and suitcases lay scattered about the room. To the right of the doorway, there was a small table and two chairs in an alcove beneath an overhang. Also in the alcove were a small sink and refrigerator. A shallow shelf above the sink held some wine glasses and two gallon jugs of water.

Behind the alcove a doorway led to the bathroom. The overhang turned out to be the loft. A steep ladder led from the left of the alcove to the loft, where a small space contained a mattress under a low ceiling. It smelled mildly damp, though clean.

"I'm so thirsty. Do you want some water?" Victoria asked.

Michael had closed the door and was sitting in the chair closest to the door. The back of the chair was to the wall. He half-slumped in the chair, head resting against the wall, hands clasped and hanging between his knees. She poured some water for them both out of one of the jugs into two wine glasses, placing one before him and sitting in the other chair so that she faced Michael at a right angle.

The table was littered with dishes and trash and more belongings, ostensibly Bri's and Mark's. Michael took his wallet out and placed it on the table, along with his keys. He had set his video camera down next to the chair, and he'd hung his jacket over the back. He loosened his tie some more, then removed it, laying it atop the jacket on the chair. His shirt was unbuttoned at the top and she could see a white t-shirt beneath, with a hint of chest hair peeking over the top. Victoria drank her entire glass of water.

"I didn't realize how thirsty I was!" she said. He was looking shy and nervous, and she felt a shift in power.

"So, tell me about your life," she said.

They talked for some time. He told her about his job, his family, his connections to Deena and her family. He was the youngest of five children, the only one not married. He had always been close to the Cashells, particularly Bri.

She told him about growing up in the same neighborhood as Deena, about how her brother and his family now lived in the same house Deena had grown up in; she talked about her separation and her kids, her upcoming 39th birthday party. He talked about his breakup with his long time girlfriend of eight years.

"Why did you break up with her?" Victoria asked.

"She just wasn't 'the one,'" he answered.

"The one?" she asked. "What do you mean?"

"I don't know. I just realized I wasn't going to be able to spend the rest of my life with this person."

"Wow," Victoria said. She wondered how someone knew who "the one" was, and what, after eight years, could make it suddenly become clear that the person you were with was not the one. They did have in common, it seemed, the fact that they had both recently come out of long-term relationships and were currently floating freely.

She stretched her legs out before her as she sat. She had taken her shoes off almost as soon as they'd arrived. Her feet hurt from all the walking and dancing. As she stretched her legs towards him, her feet nearly touched his thighs. He reached out to her feet, as if to take them in his hands. She nervously put them back down on the floor.

The conversation stalled. The room felt small and close. Victoria felt a trickle of sweat slide down her temple. Her heart pumped volumes of blood through her body; she could feel it moving through her veins. Michael sat forward and looked down at his feet, elbows resting on his knees, hands together. He laughed a small laugh.

"What?" she asked.

"I want to kiss you," he said, glancing up from under his brow.

"What's stopping you?" she asked, standing and walking towards him.

She felt as though she wasn't even in control of her own voice and actions. It was just happening and she was going with it. As she reached him, he stood up. He was about three inches taller, and built solidly. He put his hands on her shoulders and drew her closer. It had been so, so long since she'd been kissed. His mouth was right there, on hers. She tasted his salty lips. Their tongues began to explore each other's mouths. His chin was just a little scratchy with stubble. It rubbed against her chin as his ardent kisses pulled her closer. His hands were on her back now, moving downward. She was shaking. He kissed her neck, and she groaned. They embraced for a moment.

"I'm really nervous," she said.

"Me too," he agreed, though she found it hard to believe.

"It's been a REALLY long time," she said. And it had been. At least two years had passed since she'd even been with Max. Even longer since she'd been kissed or touched by a man.

He took both her hands in his, then drew her toward the chair he'd been sitting in, and he sat back down. She stood straddling one of his legs. He inched her dress up past her thighs, past her hips, up over her stomach. She reached down, grabbing the hem, and pulled it off over her head.

"Wow, you have a beautiful body," he said. He looked at her completely, from top to bottom.

His words were a drug, a numbing and enhancing sensation. She felt a little self-conscious that he was seeing her this way, but was grateful she'd worn the nice bra and underwear. He pulled her close again so that her right leg, between his legs, brushed gently against his trousers at the crotch. He reached up and moved her bra up over her left breast. His hands moved to the bottom of her shoulder blades as he put his whole mouth over her breast and began to pull hard. She closed her eyes and lifted her chin, letting her head fall back.

She had her hands at the back of his head. His hair was thick and wavy and full. She opened her eyes and turned her head to the right, noticing, as if in a dream, that the curtain was open and it was raining outside.

He returned to kissing her. Her chin began to feel raw from his sandpapery whiskers. She didn't care. It was as if a dam had broken inside her. All her longing, all her desire had been locked inside for years of loveless marriage, and then alone and cold she had sat, dormant. Now it was as if he had taken that key to the door and it fit her lock, too. She was opened up, inviting, ready. He stopped kissing her for a moment and looked into her eyes.

"Shall we go up there?" he asked, indicating the loft.

"Okay," she said, somewhat breathlessly.

"Umm, should we worry about birth control?" he asked. She couldn't even remember the last time she'd had need of it.

"Well, I don't have anything with me, that's for sure," she said. Oh please, she thought, don't let this stop.

"I could run out and try and get something..." he offered.

"Don't you dare leave," she said throatily as she grabbed him possessively and kissed him again.

It was a good twelve feet up to the loft. She went first, feeling silly wearing only a thong as she carefully climbed up the rungs. Down below, he was taking off the rest of his clothes. She nearly fainted from the sight. He had removed his shoes. He took off his pants, laying them over the back of the chair, then removed his socks. He was still wearing a pair of boxers. She bit her lower lip. As he started to take them off she lay down, staring up at the ceiling, listening to the heavy rain pounding on the roof.

 *"Skin," ©1998, by Madonna & Patrick Leonard*

Everything he did, everything he said, was electricity passing through her body, jolting her and giving her renewed energy to keep going.

"How are you going for so long?" she asked in amazement.

"Tantra, baby," he said.

The lovemaking went on for what seemed like hours. Her chin was rubbed raw. Later, as they lay exhausted and sweaty beneath the low ceiling of the loft, sheets tangled around their ankles, she recalled the reference he'd made.

"Have you seen the movie *Go*?" she asked

"Yes!" he said in disbelief. "I can't believe you knew that!"

He stroked her cheek and whispered, "Did you...?"

It touched her, his concern for her satisfaction. Truthfully, it had been the best sexual experience she'd ever had. But despite all the unbelievable serendipity of the night and the incredible way her body felt, she was just really tired. It had to be past 3:00 in the morning by now.

She could tell he was disappointed that she hadn't had more of a climax.

"Are you okay?" he asked. His eyes sought hers and his hand touched her cheek.

"I'm fantastic," she said.

And she was. Her body felt completely spent, used up, exorcised of its demons. She lay like that for a few minutes, feeling exhaustion start to cover her like a thick blanket. Still, she felt drenched in sweat and other fluids and wanted very much to wash it off.

"Do you want to take a shower?" she asked.

"Sure," he said.

Bri and Mark had still not come back. They both climbed carefully back down the ladder and walked into the small bathroom. Their legs were shaking. Used towels lay strewn on the floor and hung on a hook on the door, along with travel packs for toiletries. It looked as if the last occupants had showered and gotten ready in a hurry.

Victoria turned on the water, waiting for it to get to the right temperature. Michael stood behind her, pressed against her with his nakedness, so warm. He kissed her shoulders. They stepped in together. She took the soap and lathered his back and chest. She couldn't believe she was with this man, naked in a shower.

"This is amazing," she said. "How did this happen? I still can't believe it did."

"Yeah," he agreed. "It was quite a surprise. A nice surprise."

"Very serendipitous," she commented. "I mean, I thought you were really cute, but I had no idea we'd end up together, like this..."

"Well, my Aunt Amelia said you'd been asking about me," he said.

"Really? How embarrassing! I was sure you wouldn't be interested," she said. "Then, when you came up to talk to me, well, I guess I could tell you had become more interested..."

He kissed her again, long and slow, as the water cascaded over their shoulders.

They finished washing and rinsing. She tried to keep her hair dry, realizing she wouldn't get to style it again, and hoping it had retained some semblance of a hairdo after all the sweaty thrashing. They got out of the shower and grabbed the two towels that seemed the least soggy.

She tried not to look at her reflection as she got out of the shower. Her makeup was rubbed off and her chin was red. She quickly removed her contacts, setting them in two shot glasses and borrowing Bri or Mark's contact solution. Perhaps not thoroughly sanitary, but a respite for her exhausted, dry eyes and a relief that her vision was too blurry to get a good look at herself in the mirror. She borrowed some of Bri and Mark's toothpaste to brush her teeth with her finger.

Once outside the bathroom again, she said, "I guess I'll put my dress back on in case they come home soon."

She found it in a heap on the floor, turned it right-side-out, and slipped it over her head. He put on his undershirt and boxers. She rubbed her forehead.

"I think I bumped my head."

"Let me see," he said, concerned. He moved her hair off her forehead and looked for a bump or red mark. "I'm sorry," he said.

"That's okay," she smiled. His tenderness melted her. "You remind me of a movie star, but I can't think of his name," she said, looking at his face closely.

"Hugh Grant?" he asked.

"Well, now that you mention it, you do kind of look like him, but there's someone else I'm thinking of."

"Jay Mohr?" he asked. He had obviously been compared to these celebrities before.

"Who's Jay Mohr?" she said.

"He was one of the two cops in *Go*, Scott Wolf's partner," he said.

She looked at him closely. Yes, something in the set of his mouth, the high forehead, did remind her of Jay Mohr.

"Oh yeah...you do kind of look like him. But that's still not who I'm thinking of. It's the guy in *Ghost*, not Patrick Swayze, but the mean guy. What's his name? Tony Goldwyn, that's who I'm thinking of!" She was pleased she had remembered.

"I'll have to watch that again and see what you mean," he said.

"The only star I've ever been told I resemble is Pee Wee Herman," she said, giggling. "It was the roommates I had after college...I think they were teasing me. I hope they were!"

They returned to their chairs, had more water, and talked some more. This time when he reached for her foot, she let him take it. He began massaging the sole of her foot. Such an intimate act. She was glad she'd gotten a pedicure. It felt so good. His thumbs pressed firmly into the arch of her foot, making small circles as he moved his hands slowly from the middle of her foot towards her toes. He then took each toe, one by one, pressing them between his thumb and forefinger and rotating them on the knuckle. Victoria felt her body become more and more relaxed. Combined with her pure exhaustion, she realized she couldn't stay awake much longer.

After he'd released her first foot, she told him, "I'm wiped out."

"Should we set the clock?" he asked. "I know you have to catch a train in the morning."

"Thanks. Yeah, I guess we should," she said.

She followed him over to the dresser where he fumbled with the clock a few minutes until he figured out how to set it. He set it for 7 a.m., only a few hours away. She turned to go back to the loft. He came up behind her and put one arm around her belly, the other hand moving her hair off her neck where he gently kissed the space between her shoulder and her neck. Now both his arms were around her. He was just holding her and resting his chin on her shoulder.

She leaned back into him, feeling his strong warmth. If this was a one-night stand, it was the most intimate, loving one-night stand she had ever experienced. They both climbed back up into the loft. They lay next to one another, suddenly spent and exhausted. They tried out a few different sleeping positions. Finally, he cuddled her spoon-style, holding her hands in his, kissing her neck goodnight.

WAKE, NOW

As tired as she was, Victoria didn't sleep well. The mattress was uncomfortable, she was unaccustomed to sleeping with anyone, and she was worried she'd oversleep and miss her train. She had to be back to Virginia in time to meet the school bus. She even had a session with her personal trainer that she was hoping not to miss. At one point during the night, she heard Bri and Mark return. They were noisy and bumping into things and shushing each other. At another point, she sat straight up in bed, suddenly realizing she had to pee. She bumped her head on the ceiling again. He sat up with her, placing his hands on her arms as if to steady her.

"It's okay," he murmured, consoling what he thought was a sudden bad dream or stark realization of where she was, what she had done.

"I just need to go pee really bad," she whispered.

She gently released herself from his hold and carefully climbed back down the steep ladder and found the bathroom. She peed, but didn't flush, not wanting to wake Bri and Mark. She climbed back up and repositioned herself with him. He was so beautiful. His face, his smile, his chest, his hands. He was such a tender, giving lover, but so ardent and passionate, with lots of energy and control. He was good at balancing the need to be in charge with the desire to be taken. He seemed to know exactly what to do to please her and please himself with no one feeling cheated. She smiled as she drifted back into a twilight sleep.

In what felt like minutes, she woke again with a start. The faintest lessening of night time's darkness had crept in past the closed curtains, and she knew it was morning. She didn't want to leave. But she had to leave. The alarm clock hadn't gone off yet, but she knew it was almost time to go.

She whispered to him, "Michael? Michael, oh my god, I don't want to get up, but I think it's time for me to go."

He groaned. "Already?" They commiserated a little more about not wanting to move, how tired they were. Finally he sat up, rubbing his eyes.

"You don't have to get up," she whispered. "Just tell me how to get out of here."

"No, no. I'll come with you. It's going to be hard to find a cab," he said. "I really wish you didn't have to go…"

"I know." She looked at his sleepy face in the dim light. She wanted to be held by him again, maybe sleep a little longer, maybe even resume the night's activities.

They climbed down the ladder for the last time. While he went to turn off the clock before its alarm went off, she tried to fix her face in the bathroom mirror. She looked hung over and tired and puffy. Her face looked red, and the blemishes so expertly covered last night were out in the open. She brushed her teeth again, and attempted some lipstick on her somewhat swollen lips. She put her contacts back in, wiping away the smudged mascara and eyeliner beneath her eyes, It yielded little in the way of positive results. She flicked off the bathroom light, quietly inched open the door, and found him moving things around on the small table.

"Have you seen my wallet?" he asked, a note of panic in his voice.

"I thought you put it on the table," she said.

He moved some more things around, lifted his jacket and felt the pockets. He was looking concerned. Then he spotted it on the floor. He gathered his things and they tiptoed toward the door. Mark rolled over as they reached the door, opening his eyes to mere slits.

"Hey," he mumbled.

"Bye," Victoria said quietly. "Thanks!"

They closed the door carefully, and she and Michael descended the stairway. It all seemed so surreal. She was going home. They walked down a very quiet street; she was still not sure where they were. She'd never seen New York at this hour. It was quite peaceful. She slipped her arm through his.

"I really like that dress on you," he said, admiring her. She felt self-conscious.

"Thanks. I got it from Victoria's Secret."

He moved her arm from his and took her hand instead. She felt like she was slowly waking from a dream. They walked several blocks, and finally were able to flag down a cab.

"Penn Station," he told the driver. They both slumped into their seats, too tired for talk.

When the cab pulled up, all too soon, she asked Michael where he was headed.

"I think I'll head over to Deena and Todd's. I hear there's a brunch there later today." He got out of the cab and helped her out, holding her hand as she stepped onto the curb. They stood facing each other for a moment.

"Well, goodbye," she said awkwardly.

He pulled her toward him and kissed her deeply once more. It surprised her in the dawn, with her true age showing and the alcohol all worn off.

"Goodbye," he said. He looked at her once more, and then climbed back into the cab.

He watched her out the window as the cab drove away, and she stood outside Penn Station, making the transition: back to the train, back to Sandy and Bob's, back to Virginia, back to her kids, back to being alone.

On the train to Hamilton Station, Victoria laid her head back on the vinyl covered seat. There were not many riders out of the city that morning. She closed her eyes and the images returned, one after the other, as if a movie of the previous night were playing in her head. Every touch, every breath she'd taken, she felt again, replaying every word and action, as if watching from a distance, yet physically reacting again and again. She was almost afraid to move or open her eyes in case it had really been just a dream.

"Here With Me," ©1999, by D. Armstrong, P. Statham & P. Gabriel

BURNING FUSE

Journal Entry:

9/24/01
I think I just had the best lay of my life. All the stars were aligned, and it all came together (no pun intended)...the wedding, the reception, ending up staying overnight in the city, and ending up with him...and I was able to go through with it because (a) I wanted to so badly, and (b) Deena's cousin Michael was so good to me and so careful and so perfectly capable and responsive and attentive. We made love for hours! We were drenched in slippery sweat, and he wanted me to have an orgasm so badly that he just kept going and going and going...he was so affectionate too, and polite and cute and funny. I asked him how he could keep going for so long, and he said, "Tantra, baby"—a quote from the movie Go, which not that many people have seen, but we both had. And he just kept complimenting me about what an incredible body I had, and what a good kisser I was, and so on and so on. And even afterwards, we took a shower, then had a great conversation while he rubbed my feet and then we slept together for the rest of the night (what was left of it), snuggling, touching, gently kissing and caressing. It was really quite lovely. I don't think I've ever been so satisfied, tired, cherished, cared about during sex—and after. This morning he held me in his arms and we both groaned about having to get up. We walked a few blocks together holding hands, then got a taxi and rode to Penn Station together, where he kissed me goodbye. Outta sight. I couldn't have imagined a better experience. I couldn't have asked for a better-suited lover with my situation of feeling nervous and rusty and somewhat fragile, though that quickly disappeared. Anyway, this wasn't

your typical one-night-stand. I'm feeling grateful, happy, tired, satisfied, horny, and relieved.

From: Vicki Woolfrey [vickwool@aol.com]
Sent: Tuesday, September 25, 2001 11:47 AM
To: MB@ka.org
Subject: Smiling

Hey Michael...I made it back in time for my training session, and somehow stayed awake till the kids were in bed. I slept like a log. How bout you?

I just wanted to say again that I can't stop smiling, and I have you to thank. What a lovely person you are, and what a wonderful time we had! You can get tantric with me any time!

Take care. I hope it was okay to email you...got your address from Bri.

Victoria

Victoria pressed the SEND button, blowing out a pent-up breath as she did so. She didn't know how he would respond to being contacted. They had said goodbye, no promises, no expectations. Somehow, though, she had not been able to shake the urge to reach out to him. It had been entirely too easy to get his email address from Bri, after a friendly email about how great it had been to see everyone, and so on. She'd used the excuse that she had enjoyed talking to Michael, they had hit it off, and it would be great to get in touch with him.

But would he answer? Would he take one look at her email and wonder how to get rid of her? Would he be excited to hear from her, or at least flattered? And even if he were, would he think twice before typing out a reply and hitting his own SEND button?

It took less than an hour of constantly checking her email to get her answer.

From: Michael Bellamy [MB@ka.org]
Sent: Tuesday, September 25, 2001 12:35 PM
To: vickwool@aol.com

Subject: RE: Smiling

Hey there!

Of course it's OK to e-mail me! But, how coy did you have to be with Bri in getting my address?

How you pulled off your training session is baffling! I was all proud to get to work on time and look the part of an energetic worker, fresh as a daisy...then by 9:30 I was doing the head-bob. Sounds like you stayed awake for your stop, but you must have dozed just a little. I still need another night to recover; even THIS morning has been tough!

I'm happy to report that the crazy New "Zeal"anders appear mortal after all...I headed down to Deena's for their brunch yesterday and all the "down under-ers" were quiet as church mice, sprawled out everywhere in the apt., just dozing. Of course, by the time I left, the Bloody Marys were starting up and another rally was beginning.

Bri thanked me for letting you stay in my bed... "Oh, no trouble really, I was happy to help out," I casually replied. I had a great time with you as well! That you're smiling makes me happy too. We had a few hours to spend together and get along rather nicely (putting it mildly!). It was, as we already agreed, rather serendipitous. If the situation presents itself again, i.e. I'm in your neck of the woods, or vice versa, I don't think I would mind very much finding out if lightning can strike twice. We'd have to be more careful in the future though...I hope everything is ok this time around, considering we kinda threw caution to the wind. And thank you for a very nice compliment. I think you're a lovely person too and it was a pleasure to be with you, if for just a night.

I still smile thinking about how you knew what I was referring to about the Tantric thing...don't know about you, but I think there's always room for improvement! Didn't Taye Digges say in Go they lasted 14 hours? Phew! But of course, it is Hollywood...

Well, back to the salt mines as they say.

Thanks for e-mailing me... I'm glad you felt comfortable doing so and I was wondering how you fared yesterday.

Take care as well and we'll chat again soon.

—Michael

From: Vicki Woolfrey [vickwool@aol.com]
Sent: Tuesday, September 25, 2001 1:08 PM
To: Michael Bellamy
Subject: RE: Smiling

There were a lot of people instrumental in making that night happen the way it did, and I want to thank them all!

Anyway, glad you're recovering, and to hear that New Zealanders need sleep too. I told my mom in great detail about the wedding and reception (uh...left out my sleeping arrangements), and she loved hearing about the Maori war dance. I hope my pictures turn out. Don't think I got one of you. Doesn't matter...you'll be imprinted on my brain.

Just so you know, I don't care WHAT Taye Digges said...you're amazing. I don't think I could have survived 14 hours anyway. Why did I think I needed to go to the gym after that?

I'll talk to you again soon. Thanks for getting back with me.

Victoria

From: Michael Bellamy [MB@ka.org]
Sent: Tuesday, September 25, 2001 1:53 PM
To: vickwool@aol.com
Subject: RE: Smiling

OK, fess up! Not necessarily in order but, on my end, I told you what my Aunt Amelia mentioned to me Sunday night, heard you needed a place to stay in lieu of leaving early, found out you have 2 children, (honestly can't be sure from whom – might have been Mark), and then I looked for you and decided to say "hello" again. Followed by several hours of more hellos!

So, the key players on my end were my aunt, Sabrina and Mark. And yours?

And now that you're making me blush, I'd say your many talents were on display as well. You mentioned it had been a while; could have fooled me. Maybe that goes to show that once you've got the talent, it's always there when you need it. Yeah, I'd say things went pretty well! Can tinker with a few things, though...

All right, now let's take a moment to thank the supporting cast behind the scenes of Sunday night: we all have Deena and Todd for starters...and then?

—Michael

From: Vicki Woolfrey [vickwool@aol.com]
Sent: Tuesday, September 25, 2001 4:17 PM
To: Michael Bellamy
Subject: RE: Smiling

You're so funny. I really am laughing at this very moment! I had an acceptance speech prepared...I wanted to thank everyone who was instrumental in my getting laid...first, Deena and Todd, of course; then the three different people who watched my kids so that I could come to the wedding; then there was your aunt who encouraged me quite openly to go after you (I don't usually go after anyone and wouldn't have thrown myself at you), and Lindy who intuitively knew I didn't want to leave the wedding so early and arranged the whole thing, and of course Sabrina and Mark who shared their space, if only for an hour or two (did you hear them come in? I thought I did). Oh, and there is one other person I'd like to thank. If it hadn't been for Michael Bellamy, well, none of this would have been possible. He is an extremely talented, caring individual without whose efforts I would still be suffering from what some would call a LONG DRY SPELL. On behalf of all those who were there for me in my hour of need, I accept this honor. Thank you, thank you, thank you.

What did my having 2 kids to do with it? Usually that makes men run the other way!

From: Michael Bellamy [MB@ka.org]
Sent: Tuesday, September 25, 2001 5:04 PM
To: vickwool@aol.com
Subject: RE: Smiling

Nice speech! And they didn't even have to cut you off and go to commercial! Ahh, to give it up for those that make it happen behind the scenes! So Lindy had something to do with our meeting? She might deserve an honorary award if she knew anything yesterday. Your having children doesn't faze me – obviously – and after I heard you had inquired, I sought you out for a little conversation. Apparently you were OK talking with me (being a little younger was a concern), since you opted for the green-lighted cab ride for relief for the both of us! Thanks to you and everyone!

Time to close up shop and catch the train back for more recovery sleep (thank you very much again, Victoria!) Have a good night!

—Michael

9/25/01
Feeling good today after solid night's sleep. Also got to gym again. Have been emailing with Michael. He is really funny, but more importantly, he doesn't mind staying in touch—in fact, he seems to like it. I wish I had that kind of relationship with someone all the time. I suspect this may fade after we don't see each other for months. I am happy for today, though. Aack, too much to do, though, planning this bday party. What was I thinking?

From: Vicki Woolfrey [vickwool@aol.com]
Sent: Thursday, September 27, 2001 8:56 AM
To: Michael Bellamy
Subject: Hey You

Good morning Michael. How are you today? I was thinking of you as the news showed live shots from Manhattan. I don't know what time you go in to work, but I was imagining you somewhere in that vast city. There are so many people there! It makes me realize how limited my own world is here in Manassas.

I am slowly going nuts trying to plan for this party. I am spending lots of money and figuring on cleaning the house Friday night after my kids go to their dad's. Why bother before that? I have out-of-town guests arriving Friday night and Saturday, and I stupidly planned this thing to start at 5. Why would I do that? Anyway, be here with me in spirit Saturday night, okay? I'll privately toast you at some point.

Victoria, Party Hostess Extraordinaire

P.S. Just got a recipe that makes 5-½ gallons of margaritas at one time. Mind boggling.

From: Michael Bellamy [MB@ka.org]
Sent: Thursday, September 27, 2001 11:27 AM
To: vickwool@aol.com
Subject: RE: Hey You

Good Morning, Victoria—

Things are OK so far today, but my spirits are lifted by the autumn that is rapidly arriving. I love the cold morning air and the bright blue skies we'll have for the next few months. Undoubtedly, my favorite season. I sure feel like an ant in this crazy place, but when you see shots from the air, the city kind of looks peaceful. As you know, street level is another story.

Manassas, huh? Please describe it as it is today; I know of it only in its significance in the Civil War. There must be all kinds of touristy things around your area.

My job is usually pretty fun, esp. when you get to work on location with the pups. I'll miss it when it's all said and done this December, did I tell you all this? But yeah, it is a pretty unusual job. It is part of a surprisingly large business — the pet world, that is. And occasionally, I'll see my stuff on National Geographic and Animal Planet, even at the airports on the CNN Airport Channel!

Please try not to go nuts planning YOUR own party! I know, I know, easier said than done, but of course I'll be with you in spirit on Saturday. I wish I could be there in more than spirit, though. I would love to help you ring in your birthday, as it was so fun last weekend. I could have spent all day in bed with you last Monday. I think that would have been OK with you, yes? Well, maybe someday we can rendezvous where there is no one imminently coming back to their room, we have a few more hours, and there's a tad more head room!

Well, no rest for the weary this weekend. Just when I thought it was safe to go out again, a friend is having a bachelor party that will undoubtedly rival the New Zealanders'. At some point in the evening, however, I'll return the private toast to my friend in VA!

Five and a half gallons!? How many people are you having? Sounds like you're in for it as well!

Talk to you later if you have time amidst the preparation!

—Michael

From: Vicki Woolfrey [vickwool@aol.com]
Sent: Thursday, September 27, 2001 1:25 PM
To: Michael Bellamy
Subject: RE: Hey You

You make my day. You are so nice (I mean that in a GOOD way!) and interesting and funny. Fall is my favorite time of year also. I just took my two young charges (I watch some friends' kids a couple days a week) out for a walk, pulling them in a wagon. My kids are at school, but lucky me, I get to play! The leaves are turning, and falling (the only part I don't like...I have a big back yard, and raking is a bear). Everything smells good and looks good. As for Manassas, it looks like two different places depending on where you are. The main interstate (Rte. 66) that comes out here from DC takes you into the part that looks like strip mall, fast food, car sales heaven. People that only see this part of it think, YUCK. But then you keep going, and you come to the old town part where there's antique shops, cool little restaurants and cafes, shops, churches, a train station. It's quite quaint, actually. I live in one of the many residential areas. It's a quiet street with mostly retired people on it. All single family homes. When I buy a place in the spring, it will most likely be a townhouse. Still in Manassas, though. You should come check it out some time. I'd love to show you around.

Now, why will you be done with your job in December? Was it a contract of some kind? What will you do next? WOW! Animal Planet, really? How would I know if it was work of yours? That's so cool!

And the party...well, I just made a double batch of my homemade salsa, so that's one thing to check off my list. A couple of friends just loaned me coolers, and another friend is bringing a giant thermos for the large margarita batch. I have friends coming in from out of town to help set up and cook, etc. So actually, it'll be okay. I just can't believe I'm doing this. The last big party I threw was for my husband's 40th, two months before he told me he was leaving. Well, I figured I deserve a party now! Especially since I probably won't have the room to throw one after I move! Lots of parties to still throw before spring, right? I have a nice deck with a tree coming up through it and a hot tub sunken into it. I plan to spend a good portion of the evening there.

Don't worry, I won't go crazy, at least not in a bad way! I might get a little wild, though. So far I have 52 confirmed yes's. Once, in New Orleans, I took my bra off in the middle of the street and started swinging it around. I always look to that memory as one of the times liquor and the atmosphere really had their way with me.

As for you, I can't think of anything that would be more fun, satisfying, and exciting than spending a much more leisurely time with you. The last thing I wanted to do Monday morning was leave the warmth of your arms. Would you ever have any reason to come down this way? I don't know when I'll next be up your way, but it COULD be arranged if we both wanted to...is that hoping for too much? I must be dreaming.

Arrgghh! Time to go wake up and be a mommy and upstanding woman of the community. Thanks for making me feel so good. You really are a treasure.

Victoria

From: Michael Bellamy [MB@ka.org]
Sent: Thursday, September 27, 2001 4:18 PM
To: vickwool@aol.com
Subject: RE: Hey You

Hey Victoria—

Just a short note before I shut up shop for today...thanks for the kind words. I'm happy to put you in a good mood every now and again. You can show me around some time (wink, wink)... I'd like to think we can rendezvous again; of course it will probably be a while before that can happen, at least looking at my schedule.

I'll elaborate more tomorrow on all things...

Here's hoping you ably balance family life and party preparations in an efficient manner tonight!

Until tomorrow, take care!

—Michael

From: Vicki Woolfrey [vickwool@aol.com]
Sent: Friday, September 28, 2001 4:40 PM
To: Michael Bellamy
Subject: have a great weekend!

Your day must have been as busy as mine! Hope you have fun at the bachelor's party. Talk to you next week.

Victoria

From: Michael Bellamy [MB@ka.org]
Sent: Friday, September 28, 2001 4:45 PM
To: vickwool@aol.com
Subject: Re: have a great weekend!

Yes, it has been a nutso Friday, trying to wrap up ASAP. Is it possible to dive into that tub of margaritas you made?

Have a fantastic day tomorrow. I'll hoist one aloft for you, provided I'm still standing that is!

All the best on your birthday and every day thereafter in your new year as well.

If I awake before dawn Sunday (for some reason), and see the Southern hemisphere aglow, I'll know the party in Manassas is still raging!

Enjoy your weekend and happy birthday again!

—Michael

From: Vicki Woolfrey [vickwool@aol.com]
Sent: Sunday, September 30, 2001 4:36 PM
To: Michael Bellamy
Subject: FW: Thanks again

Thought you'd get a kick out of this email from Sabrina! My reply was minimal.

-----Original Message-----
From: MarkBri Kirby [mailto:BriMark@earthlink.net]
Sent: Saturday, September 29, 2001 11:51 AM
To: Vicki Woolfrey
Subject: Re: Thanks again

Hey Vic, It was great to see you if even for a short while. Weddings always seem to spread people a bit too thin. I never got to ask ... what is everyone doing? I know that your mom is not feeling too well; I know your brother is living in the old house, but beyond that, I'm clueless, even about you. We got in at about 5 a.m. after the wedding and I'm surprised that we didn't wake you because Mark, who is a notorious klutz without the sauce and in broad daylight, ran into everything in the room, which made me laugh. I hope that you did not feel that we stuck you with our cousin Michael ... we quite like him. He is the only cousin from Mom's side who will have anything to do with the freaky Cashells and he has seen a lot, I can tell you. He is a very nice person and had I thought for a minute that he would have made himself a nuisance to you, I would have insisted that he find a different place to sleep. I hope that it all turned out ok. We came back to work dead to the world and are just now catching up on our sleep and work. I'm going to have to get to the latter now. Much much love to you and your family. Hope to stay in touch, Sabrina.

From: Vicki Woolfrey [vickwool@aol.com]
Sent: Sunday, September 30, 2001 4:43 PM
To: Michael Bellamy
Subject: Party On, Garth!

Hi Michael!

Well, I survived the party, and it was so much fun! I felt really loved and special. Had about 60 people here, but the main thing was my friends that helped out so much. My brother and his wife came early and did so much work setting up, and my friend from Boston did all the food...I mean all night long, she kept it coming! My friends from New Jersey took care of ice and errands and got me a cake and tons of people brought wine and food and gifts (oh my god...I really felt overwhelmed!). Some of the party was video taped, and we watched it this morning. I'd say two of the highlights were my "fuck you" dance, which frankly, I can't remember what instigated it, and then there was the disco ball. I don't have a disco ball, but someone gave me a crystal, and someone else figured out that if you put it on a flashlight and shone the light at the ceiling, you got this really cool effect. Whatever. We danced a lot, drank margaritas (of course), and I never made it into the hot tub till this morning. I was actually in bed before 3, which surprised me, but seeing as the party started at 5 pm, that was actually a long haul.

Well, I have MUCH to clean up, though my girlfriend did most of the dishes and swept the floors (I'm really lucky). I'm going to go start the cleanup process and eat some more cookies (I make these cookies I like to call "O" cookies because they are SO good, it's almost better than sex...almost).

Anyway, hope you had a fun weekend! Victoria

P.S. You turned up in exactly one picture from the wedding...but it was from a great distance as we walked through Central Park, and it was blurry. Oh well... weren't you carrying a video camera? Did you ever take any video?

9/30/01
Just about a week ago, I was at Deena and Todd's reception, unaware of what the night would hold for me. In only a few hours, I would blissfully be in the arms of a good lover, and a nice person, too. Wow. All this past week, we emailed one another. It was nice that he was okay with that, but I feel weird about it now. I mean, is there a point to continuing communicating? Will I ever see this person again? Is it worth investing time and energy into a long distance relationship that might never even rekindle? I don't know. I just know how he made me feel that night: beautiful, sexy, desirable...all the things I was sure I no longer was.

Releasing the Dove

From: Michael Bellamy [MB@ka.org]
Sent: Monday, October 01, 2001 11:30 AM
To: vickwool@aol.com
Subject: RE: Party On, Garth!

Hey Victoria—

Trying to type this thru the fog left over from the weekend – hope I'm coherent. We had quite the shindig ourselves, starting at about 1:45 on Saturday. We played paintball and I have to admit it was pretty fun. Took the groom to Yankee Stadium to see Cal Ripken's final game in NY and we froze our asses off and got rained on – ugh. I imagine you were still lounging around, dozing on the couch. If not, then you should have been!

Happy to hear your party was a success! Sounds like you have a good core of friends who pitched in substantially. And you needed it with 60 people – quite the gathering. Was it a little raucous, or a lot? Any upset tummies? Bed by 3? Tsk, tsk. Actually, I ran out of steam around 12:30 and dozed for a bit in the back of someone's car, tried to rally but everyone else was toast too, thank God. Any left over booze, i.e., the margaritas? Where were your little guys during all this? Hopefully far enough away when Mom started doing the f-u dance. To whom/what was that directed?

Yes, I had my video camera for Deena's wedding so that must have been me in the fuzzy background. Haven't looked at my footage much yet, but I do know I recorded that kid making the racket with his new whistle as the service wound up!

Gonna try to rally at work now, fight thru this haze and see if I can accomplish something!

How is 40 thus far?

—Michael

From: Vicki Woolfrey [vickwool@aol.com]
Sent: Monday, October 01, 2001 12:21 PM
To: Michael Bellamy
Subject: RE: Party On, Garth!

Hey! Let's not push it! I didn't turn 40 yet! This was 39! Please, don't send me out to pasture yet!

Glad you had fun with the bachelor party. That must have been cool seeing Cal's final farewell. I was supposed to go to a Redskins game with my dad on Sunday, but I cancelled since I knew I'd be wanting to sleep in and take it easy. My brother got to go instead.

There were no margaritas left...at least, not any that I mixed up ahead of time. I still have a large bottle of tequila that I'll just have to find a use for eventually. And a ton of lime wedges. Don't know what caused the f.u. dance...think someone made a rude comment. The party didn't get too crazy, at least not compared to the ones I used to throw. We did some coffee table dancing, and my sister in law tried to give me a wedgie, but when you're wearing a thong, it doesn't really work. She also started to undress at one point, and I threatened to lift my shirt a couple times. Other than that, I didn't personally witness any puking, stripping, or particularly loud or obscene behavior. My music was up pretty loud though...hope the neighbors dealt with it. We were listening to everything from disco to Van Halen to the Doobie Brothers to some weird stuff by a group called Soul Coughing. My kids were with their dad. He wasn't invited. I didn't even have a hangover the next day! What's up with that? Good for me, though. Sorry you're still suffering.

BTW, you were going to tell me about why your job is up in December and what you're going to do after. Also, I wanted to tell you two more things about you that I like: I liked how you spent a lot of time with your aunt and uncle at the wedding. I just thought that was cool. I also liked that you actually seemed concerned when I said I thought I had a bump on my head. Thanks. That was sweet.

Well, I ramble a lot. I'm going to run some errands and go to the gym now. Gotta work off all those chips and queso. Hope to hear from you again soon. What did you think of Sabrina's email?

Victoria, the Party Animal

10/01/01

I am not sure there's any future with Michael. We're still emailing, but I don't sense any energy coming from him—I guess it really was a one-night thing. I am sad, but a little relieved. I don't need another obsession. Not now.

10/2/01

Happy Bday to me. I felt pretty sucky today, but rallied enough to go to training session. I'm so sore. Took kids to Japanese steak house and frozen custard place—we had a really good time. My biggest bummer of the day was not hearing from Michael. I fear he's over the novelty, if he ever was into it. And, no, I can't tell if this is fear and insecurity and PMS talking, or what. I guess I wasn't as emotionally ready to be with someone as I thought. He was a sensitive and caring lover, but he isn't my soul mate—I became too attached because he's the first man who's cared in any way for years. How could I help it? But I don't believe he's as enamored of me as I am (was?) of him. I wrote a poem today about my reflections on Derek and Michael.

CAVITY

Derek—now there was another story.

After about a year of feeling numb after Max's departure, Victoria started working out at the gym at every opportunity. She had lost some weight, and was starting to feel a little more attractive, but had remained oblivious to the scene around her. Her workouts were focused on the sweat and the burn, not on the people.

She remembered the exact moment her switch was pulled back on. She looked up from the elliptical trainer where she had been sweating profusely, headphones blaring Madonna, when she saw him. A beautiful, perfect statue of a man. He was young and black and unbelievably built. She felt an electric current rev up inside her that had not been there for some time. She hadn't even noticed any men for the last year. After she saw him, she couldn't not look at him. And every time she saw him after that, she felt the same.

She finally got the nerve up to say hello, using the excuse of asking him how to use one of the pieces of equipment. After that, they talked now and then. She found out his name was Derek and he worked as a mortician at a local funeral home. She craved him in the most physical way. She knew he was a lot younger, she guessed mid-twenties. Still, she couldn't resist the temptation to look, and fantasize. Sometimes she even fantasized about sex in the funeral home laid out amongst the corpses. That was when she knew it had been too long.

Finally she decided to ask him over. She found out he was moving and thought she'd give it one last hurrah. He agreed to stop by, but at the last minute, she lost her nerve. She called and cancelled, suddenly unsure that she wanted anything to do with a man, especially in a physical sense. She had freaked out, woken from the fantasy. And then, he was gone.

Just Desserts

One year of craving
Chocolate dreams and fantasies
Hunk of solid chocolate, edges and corners
Hot chocolate sauce dripping over cold vanilla ice
Melting a cold heart, an icy core of suspended life
Swirling together in a dance of temperatures and colors and flavors
Coming together, a mocha soup
I tried to take a bite
But the chocolate was hollow and waxy and left a bad taste in my mouth
In the end, it only gave me a stomachache
I turned my head and found a man.
He wasn't holding any candy
Unpretentious and kind and smiling
He held my hands and kissed my bruises and touched me
He looked into my eyes when I spoke
His arms were solid and warm and real
Those hours, more delicious and lasting than any dessert
Erasing years empty of love or comfort

10-2-01

From: Michael Bellamy [MB@ka.org]
Sent: Wednesday, October 03, 2001 9:19 AM
To: vickwool@aol.com
Subject: RE: Party On, Garth!

Good Morning, Victoria —

Oops! Sorry bout that — I thought that was why the b-day party was on the grander scale. You certainly look younger than 39 and your physical prowess is quite impressive...let's just say you know how to handle yourself in certain "close-quarter" situations. I could go for a replay of that evening right now, as a matter of fact. For some reason, mornings are often when I'm feeling most "randy." (I tried to come up with a synonym for horny — that's the best I could do) The bachelor we toasted last weekend gets married this Sunday, yes another Sunday wedding. Only good memories bout the last one!

Went to a Yankees game last night, yes another, as a spontaneous decision and my friend and I threw a few more back than is allowed on a school night. A little groggy so far...

OK, job stuff — my department (me) has been deemed too expensive to maintain (even though our revenues far exceed expenses), so in effect, I'm being laid off. The co. has already laid off close to 20 people out of 70 over the past several months, so there were ominous signs. My boss, who fought with me to keep the dept. open, worked it out so I had the choice to work thru the calendar year. So, can you hook me up come Jan. 1? I could be your "extra-personal" trainer, hot tub repairman, or your personal slave (you decide what goes after...). But don't worry bout me, I'll land on my feet somewhere, just not sure where. I've wanted to get back to New England for a few years, so maybe I'll head up to Maine and be "nay-buhs" with J.R.

Sabrina's e-mail was fun to read — so did they know or not? They're cool enough that if they did, they wouldn't razz you about it.

If it looks like I'll be heading your way some time, we'll need to rendezvous without any cousins in the same room!

Work calls, what remains of it, that is...

Hope your day is a good one!

—Michael

Releasing the Dove

From: Vicki Woolfrey [vickwool@aol.com]
Sent: Wednesday, October 03, 2001 9:47 AM
To: Michael Bellamy
Subject: RE: Party On, Garth!

Michael, may I say that I agree with your replay wish? I think about you and that …uh, morning…way too often. You can't move to Maine! How will we EVER hook up again? Yes, I'll pay you to be my love slave!

I'm sorry to hear about your job ending. That is a bummer. Why don't you look for work down this way? (See above) Thanks for the compliments on my youthful look. I want to send you a picture from the party. Would you give me your address? I should get the pics back tonight, and hopefully there's one that isn't too embarrassing and maybe even a little flattering. Do you have any recent photos of your bad self? I wouldn't mind having one to stare at when I'm all alone…

Okay, 'nuff o' that. Listen, one serious thing, then I'll let ya go…just wanted you to know we're "safe." Thought that might ease your mind.

I wrote a poem about you yesterday. One day I'll show it to you.

Okay, little ones beckon me. Did you see the movie Almost Famous? I just bought it. It's so good.

Victoria

From: Michael Bellamy [MB@ka.org]
Sent: Wednesday, October 03, 2001 10:24 AM
To: vickwool@aol.com
Subject: RE: Party On, Garth!

OK, I'm really worked up right now; just have to bottle it up for a road trip down south. Do you have anything against shacking up at a cheap hotel down your way to work out this pent up energy? Any moral qualms with just a crazy, decadent night or two? Any objections to getting so sweaty and making so much racket that we get a call from the front desk? Good, me neither. At least you get to work out today at the gym and vent a little energy…

So, who have you told about our little tryst? I've mentioned you to a couple of friends…seems hooking up with an older woman is something guys get turned on by. And your friends? I'll look for a respectable photo to send you, could take a while though.

I've had the notion of Maine for some time, (sorry!) and I might want to see if I have the guts to make a bold move like that. The mountains, lakes and oceans are undoubtedly a big reason why I like it so much up there. Manassas, huh? I just thought of an obvious job solution – Victoria's personal masseuse! I've got to keep working on those feet you know! And then let my hands start to wander up your legs, start working your thighs, etc...oh boy.

How do I get to read this poem and when? Can you drop any hints? And yay! for being "safe"! That's good to know and thanks for telling me. And Almost Famous? I do not know it – who is in it?

—Michael

From: Vicki Woolfrey [vickwool@aol.com]
Sent: Wednesday, October 03, 2001 11:14 AM
To: Michael Bellamy
Subject: RE: Party On, Garth!

Wow. Who is working WHO up, here? No objections, whatsoever! I like sweaty. I can do loud. Let's meet halfway! Hey, I'm serious! My next weekend free is the 27thish...are you serious? Who have I told? Wow, well let's see...my best friends who all care so much about me and were thrilled that I broke my record of celibacy! Guys are turned on by older women? Where are all these guys? You crack me up. Younger men are a turn-on too! In any case, since I currently am (turned on, that is), you are making it really difficult to color pictures with 2— and 3-year-olds.

A respectable photo? Oh, okay. But it can be unrespectable too. Personal masseuse. I like that one too. I have several openings you can fill...

The poem makes you look like a saint, and honey, right now, you seem pretty far from sainthood! It is a contrast of my experiences with men, and you came out on top...

Enough of these double entendres! Get down here! Now! I'm about to explode! 10..9..8..7..6..5..4..3..2..1 KAPOW!

We are sorry to have to report this, but the woman you knew as Victoria has exploded. Pieces of her are scattered all over the room. We did find her mouth intact, though, and it was smiling.

Okay, GROSS. What am I on? Anyway. Almost Famous was directed by Cameron

Crowe, and it has Kate Hudson in it (Goldie Hawn's daughter). It is so cool. It's about groupies that follow rock stars...pretty appropriate after meeting up with a bunch of Matchbox 20 fans in NYC last March who were not too far off from the characters in the movie.

How can you get any work done if you keep emailing me sexy messages? BYE!

From: Michael Bellamy [MB@ka.org]
Sent: Wednesday, October 03, 2001 11:48 AM
To: vickwool@aol.com
Subject: Back to work, everyone!

Yup, my mind is wandering all over the place this morning. Work? Oh yeah, I almost forgot...so a short note as I re-direct my attention back to the video world.

Let me see what's upcoming. A road trip could be fun. But maybe I should go out on top? (kidding – I'm referring to the poem) I'm very much flattered by what you write and fear that I can only slip in stature. What if it's just a weekend romp now and again? Is that going to be all right? I certainly don't want you to think less of me if we just get together now and again. But if you want to re-visit our bedside maneuvers, I'll check the calendar. And I'll bring along my bomb-defusing kit, but maybe we don't need that, it can be fun to explode/implode under the right circumstances...

Several openings I can fill? Whew...ok, deep breath, time for lunch!

Talk later!
—Michael

From: Vicki Woolfrey [vickwool@aol.com]
Sent: Wednesday, October 03, 2001 3:35 PM
To: Michael Bellamy
Subject: RE: Back to work, everyone!

Michael, I hope you don't think I'm expecting you to drop your life and become mine. I am really happy for the time we had together, and I would LOVE to get together again. Whenever and whatever works out, that would be great. Would I love it if you DID live around here...uh, yeah. Would I love it if we met regularly for great sex? Uh, yeah. But I'm not a teenager anymore (as we both know), so I think I can deal with the circumstances we have. My life is crazy and busy and full, as is yours, and logistically, there are some obstacles. As far as measuring up to some standard, there's no way you could fail. It wasn't just your "talents" I liked...you were wonderful in every way, and that's what made it so special to me...special enough to write about. I was afraid I'd scare you off eventually... rats. I hope I haven't done that. I am just being honest about how I feel. I am not good at reading other people, especially via email, so you'll have to be honest with me too. Am I freaking you out with talking about seeing you again? I'll leave it up to you. If you were just joking around, then say so and I can go with that. But remembering everything that we shared makes me shiver and I wouldn't want to miss an opportunity for that again if it were presented. Life is too damn short!

Still smiling, Victoria

From: Michael Bellamy [MB@ka.org]
Sent: Wednesday, October 03, 2001 4:08 PM
To: vickwool@aol.com
Subject: RE: Back to work, everyone!

Hello Ms. Victoria –

Thanks for being honest. You're not freaking me out – but I wanted to make sure both of us are on the same page with all of this. With things somewhat up in the air with me, your response was what I was hoping for. We'll talk about this more, but the opportunity to have a fun weekend together is basically the essence for both of us. We had a great time together (in all regards) and didn't want to tarnish it, ya know? But as they say, I'm good if you're good, so I think it's time to check the calendars. I can't wait to pick up where we left off! With that...

In response: I have 3 words for you:

Havre de Grace!

I looked at a map and saw that the midway point between you and me is roughly around the Philly area, then I zoomed in on the northern tip of Maryland and recalled seeing signs on I-95 for Havre de Grace. So, I did some more searching and the town looks like just the ticket – quiet and ideally situated for both of us. There's a 4-Points/Sheraton Hotel, actually located in Aberdeen, one town over, that looks good. What do you think? Anything better?

I think you can tell by this point that I'm quite worked up and looking forward to getting together with you.

I agree, life is short – let's give it a ride then!

—MB

From: Vicki Woolfrey [vickwool@aol.com]
Sent: Wednesday, October 03, 2001 5:30 PM
To: Michael Bellamy
Subject: RE: Back to work, everyone!

Well aren't we the little busy bee? My heavens you work fast! Okay, then, you let me know what your calendar looks like. I basically have every other weekend starting the 27th without my kids. I feel like I'm in a movie. Should I be thinking of interesting clothing articles? I'm glad you are into this. I'm really going to have a hard time waiting. Oh well, hunger is the best sauce, right? I'm licking my lips...

So, this is a "tryst"? Ooo la la.

From: Michael Bellamy [MB@ka.org]
Sent: Wednesday, October 03, 2001 5:33 PM
To: vickwool@aol.com
Subject: RE: Back to work, everyone!

Hello, hello –

OK then!

Tomorrow I work out of the office, so probably won't get a chance to converse until Friday. Have a chance to look at the calendar too. Until then...

Pretty crazy, huh? I'm looking forward to it!

Take care.

—MB

10/3/01

What a weird day. I emailed back and forth with Michael a lot today, and I guess what it boils down to is sex. I guess I wish it was more, but it's not. I'm trying to accept that. Believe it or not, I acted all progressive and realistic and told him I knew our lives weren't going in the same direction. "I'm not a teenager" I said, convincing him I was cool with a rendezvous which he immediately began planning. It's all very surreal. I think I want it, but I feel a little removed from it. It's like I'll be watching from a distance, and I'd really rather be present in the moment. I'm so full of talk and then carrying through with the action freaks me out, just like with Derek. But that was not the same at all, was it? I don't have to feel cheap or used, because I am in control of this. It was my idea—at least 50%—to get together with Michael again. What good reason do I have to NOT go through with it? He is a really good lover, and I really need some good love. REALLY. Yet, how empty will I feel when the next "event" comes to an end? Without any promise of future meetings, and with only sex as the focus? We did spend a lot of time talking and cuddling that night, and that made it more of a connection. I wonder if he'll think less of me after this next time—a woman willing to meet in a hotel for a weekend of sex. Very odd. I guess I get to choose how to respond to the whole situation. I can choose to go or not; I can choose to enjoy it for what it is, or feel bad because it isn't something more. I have time to think. It won't be for a few weeks, at least.

From: Vicki Woolfrey [vickwool@aol.com]
Sent: Thursday, October 04, 2001 8:48 AM
To: Michael Bellamy
Subject: No reply necessary

Hey Michael, I know you're busy, so don't bother with a reply. Just wanted to say you're all I could think of yesterday. Have a good day! (You've never taken viagra, have you?...just keep wondering about that staying power...)

From: Michael Bellamy [MB@ka.org]
Sent: Thursday, October 04, 2001 9:39 AM
To: vickwool@aol.com
Subject: Re: No reply necessary

Viagra? God, I hope it never comes to that! The other thing that's kinda scary, we didn't get back to the B&B until 2 AM after a weekend of whooping it up, we easily could have just zonked out! Hmmm...maybe that's the secret.

Off to edit a video, will talk tomorrow!

Have a great day!

—Michael

PS – Hope no one is monitoring these e-mails!

From: Vicki Woolfrey [vickwool@aol.com]
Sent: Thursday, October 04, 2001 1:45 PM
To: Michael Bellamy
Subject: RE: No reply necessary

It's kind of like my trainer has been telling me about working different muscle groups to exhaustion. Must have something to do with that. Your guess is as good as mine. But you're right, where'd we get all that energy? Some kind of electrical storm. And if someone IS monitoring these emails, well maybe they'll get a cheap thrill. They sure are giving ME lots of cheap thrills! Later, dude.

From: Vicki Woolfrey [vickwool@aol.com]
Sent: Thursday, October 04, 2001 8:42 PM
To: Michael Bellamy
Subject: Waterfowl!

Well, Michael, Hot Diggity Damn! You didn't tell me Havre de Grace was the decoy capitol of the WORLD! They have a museum there solely dedicated to "documenting and interpreting waterfowl"! Yes I looked it up on the internet. It looks like you would have farther to travel than me, but if you like it, that's cool with me. But be honest, did you choose it because of the duck decoys? Come on now, tell the truth. What you DON'T know is that I once kept a collection of duck items, and even inherited the nickname of "Duck" from co-workers, so I will feel completely at home in this quack haven. I'm sorry, I'm not dissing your choice...anywhere will be great as long as it's with you. Uh, you don't want me to dress up as a duck, do you? I used to have a rubber duck beak. I guess that could make for an interesting evening, if you're into that kind of stuff. But if you want me to talk like Daffy, that's where I draw the line! Absolutely not! That is just TOO kinky! In fact, it's DESPICABLE!

Okay, now that I've spelled out the ground rules, I think we know where we stand. I'm glad we had this talk.

P.S. Hi!

10/4/01

I feel better about it today. I guess I long for a closer, more honest connection. On the other hand, this is honest after all. We are both agreeing to get together without strings to enjoy each other in every way. I got on a website about the suggested meeting spot, Havre de Grace, MD. I don't know what Michael has in mind, but there is stuff to do and see there. Whatever. I don't even know how realistic this all is. Geez. He could meet the love of his life before we're able to pick a date that works for both of us. It's fun imagining the possibilities, but realistically, I don't see that the plan has that much of a chance. My day-to-day existence doesn't leave much room for any of this. What am I thinking, anyway?

From: Michael Bellamy [MB@ka.org]
Sent: Friday, October 05, 2001 12:29 PM
To: vickwool@aol.com
Subject: Re: Waterfowl!

Hey there —

Not into waterfowl (as far as I know), sorry to disappoint...but that begs the question — what are you into? This could get really interesting for anyone snooping!

Time for lunch!

P.S. Hi back

From: Vicki Woolfrey [vickwool@aol.com]
Sent: Friday, October 05, 2001 2:00 PM
To: Michael Bellamy
Subject: RE: Waterfowl!

I'm not sure I'm into anything specific...got any ideas? I just ordered some stuff from Victoria's Secret...want me to dress up for you? Sorry, don't have any French maid costumes or anything, but hey, I'm open to suggestions! Or we could take a cue from Sharon Stone and drip some hot candle wax. Are you laughing as hard as I am? This is such a trip. Have you heard about the warm tea treatment?

Hope you had a good lunch. I just got taken to lunch for a belated bday present. I am stuffed. I'm going to go vedge out on the sofa for a while and think about what it would feel like if your hand were right there...then there...sigh

From: Michael Bellamy [MB@ka.org]
Sent: Friday, October 05, 2001 2:04 PM
To: vickwool@aol.com
Subject: RE: Waterfowl!

Whatever you'll be wearing, it's probably not going to be staying on long. Wax can be fun – warm tea? What's that? Do you need plastic liners on the mattress or something? Toys can be fun, too. Are you a wine, beer or liquor drinker?

From: Vicki Woolfrey [vickwool@aol.com]
Sent: Friday, October 05, 2001 3:40 PM
To: Michael Bellamy
Subject: Re: Waterfowl!

Hmmmm. Why the drinking question? Are you going to ply me with liquor, cuz I'll just tell you now, that won't be necessary. But, beer or tequila are my favorites. Wine gives me a headache anymore. The tea goes like this: Apparently, you swirl warm tea around in your mouth a few minutes, then I guess either swallow it or spit it out, then your mouth and tongue are nice and warm and have some properties of the tea that do something stimulating or numbing or something... use your imagination. I think it's called the velvet tongue. I've actually never tried this, but I've heard about it...as far as I know, no plastic sheets necessary. What toys were you referring to? This is intriguing. I'm thinking you are more worldly than you have let on thus far...I'm not going to have to spank you or anything, am I? Hey, maybe we could play a game! (I'm having entirely too much fun thinking about this). Maybe I could test you to see how long (we'll use a timer or something) you can go without ripping off my clothes, or vice versa?

Keep me posted Baby!

From: Michael Bellamy [MB@ka.org]
Sent: Friday, October 05, 2001 4:36 PM
To: vickwool@aol.com
Subject: RE: Waterfowl!

The whole teasing thing? Can't rip off clothes right away? That's S&M to me! The tea thing sounds fun, but no, I'm not as worldly as you might think. Just the basics with a twist here and there.

Didn't mean to imply we'd be relying on booze to get it on, not at all. Probably help with nerves though, as I'm sure there will be for a few seconds. But basically, you're in trouble.

With that, I'm shutting down for the weekend and trying to catch up on some sleep. Friend's wedding on Sunday and I've already taken Monday off as a recovery day. It could get rough.

I hope you have a great weekend! Hope the weather is good and you can go outside with your guys!

Talk on Tuesday.

—Michael

10/5/01

Another day of hot emails. Seems our internet sex is just as good as the real thing. He still sounds serious, but no date has been set. I would love for this to happen, but like so many other things I've imagined, I half expect it to fall through. I am not feeling pessimistic. I'm enjoying just talking about it with him. He is funny and sexy and doesn't need to be subtle—he comes right out and says shit like, "Whatever you wear, it won't be on very long" and things like that. I ordered a bunch of clothes from Victoria's Secret today—way too much—but in the order, I included a sexy nightie. That's when I asked him if he wanted me to wear anything special, which prompted the above response. He also said something about, "You're in trouble"—implying that I was in for a long, hot night. We shall see. As I sit here with mild gas, my period, and a broken out face with tons of church shit to do and kid stuff too, I feel anything but sexy. But he makes me feel so attractive and hot—like I am the reason he is behaving the way he is—it just feels really good, even if we never actually follow through with it. That, of course, remains to be seen.

10/6/01

I spent a lot of time today thinking about Michael and the whole ridiculousness of the situation. What am I hoping to accomplish? Is this really going to happen? So many things could get in the way, I find it hard to believe any of it is going anywhere. Heck, he's going to another wedding tomorrow and he could meet the chick of his dreams or at least get a good lay. I shouldn't think about that. I shouldn't think about any of it. What am I thinking? It's not going to change my lonely existence. Even if we actually were to somehow plan and execute this rendezvous, what then? Just another wild weekend for the books? Is that what I want? Can I even ever hope to get what I want?

10/7/01
I had a good sleep, but my mind is in turmoil. Part of me can't wait to resume contact with him—he's not going to be back online till Tuesday—2 more days to go! I love how he teases me with promises of completely defiling me...then I feel ridiculous that I'm having these conversations with someone who it's likely I'll never see again, or if I do, it will be a once or twice kind of thing before he's out of my life completely. How bad will that hurt? How much will I let it hurt? It's all in fun, I remind myself, and aren't I trying to have more fun? But at what expense? It's a constant battle in my mind. And yet I don't seem to want to consider the alternative—never seeing or talking to him again. He's too amazing—I can't not want to connect with him. I must be insane.

10/8/01
Tomorrow I hope to hear from Michael again, but I'm so hot and cold with this whole thing, it's really hard to judge how I'll be feeling tomorrow. I've drafted two emails to him this weekend, and neither of them is likely to convey how I'll feel tomorrow. Every day I am different. What a fricking psycho.

I'm so unbelievably attracted to the memory of what he was like. I don't know how that will translate when (if) we see each other again. Will he still find me as attractive? I keep imagining what I'm going to wear, and what I'll change into for him later. Yikes.

From: Vicki Woolfrey [vickwool@aol.com]
Sent: Monday, October 08, 2001 7:58 PM
To: Michael Bellamy
Subject: Wish you were here, or even there...

Hey Michael! Talk about your S&M...this long weekend of yours is killing me! I haven't had any dirty or suggestive emails since Friday! Good grief. I have had a crazy weekend...did a Fall Jubilee in old town Manassas Saturday morning with my kids...crafts, food, moon bounce, etc. Then I cooked all afternoon for a dinner party the next day, then we went to an Oktoberfest in my old 'hood (oompah band, German food, scarecrow stuffing); Sunday I taught Sunday school with an active bunch of 2nd and 3rd graders, then had 18 people to dinner Sunday night. It turned into quite the drink fest, with many glasses of wine and margaritas consumed. I hot tubbed with a friend till late, and realized it was all a big mistake since no matter what I do the night before, my kids will always wake me at 7. How was your weekend? The wedding a hellraiser? Hope you're all recovered.

So, I'm in trouble, huh? I like your kind of trouble. I can't wait to get into some more. When is this lovefest marathon taking place? Have you had a chance to check your calendar? I wish it were going to be today. Waiting is so difficult. I think I will choreograph a special dance for you wearing only a skimpy, sexy piece of clothing.

Write back!

Me

10/9/01

Today I've prayed to hear from Michael, but so far, nothing. I'm sure he's busy after taking yesterday off, but I am so insecure I keep thinking he's tired of this game or met someone his own age or who lives nearby that it would make more sense to be with. What are my expectations, anyway? He is clearly not looking for a serious relationship, and for crying out loud, he lives so far away and plans to move even farther. I must prepare myself for not seeing him anymore. I keep asking myself what it is I want. I guess I want a man that is as good a lover—in every way—as he is, with some interest in remaining in my life. I don't want to marry or live with another man—not now while I'm raising my kids—but someone IN my life on some sort of regular basis who actually CARES about me would be nice. Having tasted it—i.e., being cherished, if only for a few hours—I feel as though I'll die without it. I won't—I know that. I can exist on my friends and family to love and support me, and rely on myself to take care of me. But there really is no substitute for that connection you feel when you look directly into someone's eyes and KNOW—I don't know, you know you've achieved something special and unique—not just good sex, I'm talking about understanding each other's needs and communicating them and responding to them. It's such an awesome feeling, and I don't think I ever had that with Max. We never really connected. We loved each other, but I never felt him touch me that deeply. I guess I know what I'm looking for now. It's just finding it that's an issue.

From: Michael Bellamy [MB@ka.org]
Sent: Wednesday, October 10, 2001 8:31 AM
To: vickwool@aol.com
Subject: Re: Wish you were here, or even there...

Hi Victoria—

A short note as I prepare to head out of the office for a second day for work stuff. Hopefully I'll be able to write at greater length later this afternoon if/when I get back to my desk. Still looking at the calendar, please be patient!

Hope you have a great day!

—Michael

From: Vicki Woolfrey [vickwool@aol.com]
Sent: Wednesday, October 10, 2001 8:38 AM
To: Michael Bellamy
Subject: RE: Wish you were here, or even there...

You have a great day too. Patience isn't one of my virtues, but I'll do my best. Talk to you later.

Victoria

From: Michael Bellamy [MB@ka.org]
Sent: Wednesday, October 10, 2001 7:04 PM
To: vickwool@aol.com
Subject: RE: Wish you were here, or even there...

Hola Victoria—

Ugh, one of those (consecutive) days...

Don't worry, I'm not 'dissing you, simply haven't been at my desk too much the last few days. Thursday looks like I'll be around for the most part and so will try to conjure up some devious thoughts to whet the appetite. I did survive the wedding for the most part, wasn't as fun as the last one though. Now, I have to survive tonight – a Rangers-Capitols hockey game for which I have to now literally run to meet my friend.

Hope you are having an above average day and will write more tomorrow.

Ciao, mamacita!

Cavity

From: Michael Bellamy [MB@ka.org]
Sent: Thursday, October 11, 2001 10:39 AM
To: vickwool@aol.com
Subject: Do I make you...

???? Cue the Austin Powers line.

Hiya Victoria or Vicki (which do you prefer?) –

As promised, a meatier e-mail today for you. Let me start off by telling you how horny I am – very. At this point, I would pretty much pull off your pants and...be very vigorous. How's that? I could be more graphic but will refrain slightly. I want you on top, on the bottom, from behind, standing up, on the edge of the bed (one of my favorites), sideways and? Whew! Now, I feel better! Slightly...did I mention that mornings are a time when I'm especially prone to being very aroused?

Now on a less fun tip –

It will happen, our little rendezvous, but as much as you alluded to not being the patient type, it might be a little while, because of very serious reasons. My dad isn't doing too well health-wise. My parents moved to South Carolina a few years ago (from CT) and my pop's been battling cancer and suffering thru the side effects of its treatment. It's this that has him in the hospital the past few days and my brother and I discussed flying down to see him and be with our mom at home. So, that's the gist right now. It sucks when your parents get old.

A weekend getaway with you promises to be very fun and a bit of an escape. I hope and think you and I can put aside our shit for a few hours and have fun like we did a couple of weeks ago. And maybe we can even hold a conversation if we come up for air every few hours. Like I said, you are in big trouble, because all signs point to an even longer session than before.

So, some serious stuff to deal with first and then the fun will happen. Of course, I'll keep you posted.

Here's hoping you get outside today for some fresh air and autumn sunshine!

Talk later.

—Michael

From: Vicki Woolfrey [vickwool@aol.com]
Sent: Thursday, October 11, 2001 10:58 AM
To: Michael Bellamy
Subject: RE: Do I make you...

Michael, I'm so sorry about your dad. Your aunt had mentioned he wasn't well. I can understand what you're going through, as my mom has been ill for some time now. You're right, it does suck getting old. Of course I understand your need to be with your parents right now. Keep me posted on how it's going. I can be a friend too, you know.

As for the rest, well, you just got me all jellied inside with your rather straightforward remarks! WOW. I will be ready and willing whenever you say! (I like the edge too...that would have been tricky in the loft...) Maybe Veteran's Day weekend? That's even a long weekend for some folks, but I won't push. (I'll leave the pushing to you...) Let me know when you know, and that will be fine. Meanwhile, I guess I'll have to get off on your emails. Wow, electronic sex. Who'd-a-thunk it?

Vicki or Victoria is fine

PS Sending you a photo

From: Michael Bellamy [MB@ka.org]
Sent: Thursday, October 11, 2001 11:12 AM
To: vickwool@aol.com
Subject: RE: Do I make you...

Hi Victoria –

Thanks for your message and the offer. Yeah, you would have met him at Deena's wedding if he had been feeling well enough. My mom, though, is ably holding the fort and sounds OK thru all this. What is going on with your mom? If you care to share...

Perhaps over the weekend, things will improve and a better idea of travel plans will emerge.

So I got you going, huh? Good. I can't wait to pick up where we left off. A few things that loft just would not accommodate, the edge certainly being one of them...we're not that tall! Leave the pushing to me? Not all of it I hope. Your skills in that area are part of what I'm looking forward to. You can ride me all night. I think we had better bring lots of energy bars and Gatorade along. And tell the Personal Trainer you'll be recouping on Monday, can't make it in. That is, if I have anything to do with it.

OK, will look at Nov. 10/11 – don't have any extra days off, but can take an extra day for spending with you —that is, if you think you can make it worth my while...

—MB

From: Vicki Woolfrey [vickwool@aol.com]
Sent: Thursday, October 11, 2001 2:05 PM
To: Michael Bellamy
Subject: RE: Do I make you...

As for my mom, it's been years of kidney disease, arthritis, emphysema and now heart trouble that have aged her too quickly and make her miserable most of the time and virtually unable to care for herself. My dad makes all the meals, does the chores and errands, and hooks her up to a machine twice a day that does the work of her kidneys. Smoking and poor health habits contributed a lot. I keep expecting her to die. It's been so long since the first shock of thinking she might that I'm almost used to the idea...anyway, I worry more about my dad as he'll be the one left behind. Thanks for asking.

As for you and me, oh, I think I can make it worth your while. I have been inventing all sorts of enticing things in my mind to keep you busy...and yes, you make me...you had better stop with all this talk, or I will have to change my panties. Giddy up, Cowboy. Maybe I should invest in some boots. I just want to turn you on, that's all I can think of...I want to know what does it for you, and then I want to do it. Whew! I need to go get some air!

Your Sex Kitten (purrrrrrrrrrrrr)

10/11/01 (palindrome!)
Well, I did finally hear from Michael, and it was quite the splash. He was— uh, well, horny. I couldn't help it—my body was going nuts. I don't know what his story is, but he sure turns me on. I went ahead and sent him this card I had picked out, but was considering not sending, along with a picture of me. We talked about his dad being sick, and Mom too. Seems our rendezvous is on

hold, but that's okay. I'd rather not make a whole lot of changes to my schedule, and my weekends are booked! Looking at Veteran's Day, mid November. Geez—only 4 weeks away. Guess it's better than the alternative. He still seems interested, but who knows. I'm going to focus on my training, and kicking ass at church in my role as membership chair. I think that will keep me busy enough to not be completely obsessive. I'm going to back off on the emails, but I can't help the fantasies. My latest involves videotaping myself being very sexy; modeling lingerie and dancing to music, then mailing it to him with the title "Preview of What's to Come"—get it? Hahahaha. Well, I'm going.

From: Vicki Woolfrey [vickwool@aol.com]
Sent: Friday, October 12, 2001 11:29 AM
To: Michael Bellamy
Subject: Still in town?

Just wondering if you left for SC today or are going this weekend. Hope all is well.

Vicki

10/12/01

Didn't hear from Michael today. I'm thinking he went to be with his parents. I dreamt of him last night, fueled by my fantasy of being with him at his father's funeral. I know that's morbid, but I guess part of me wants to believe he'll let me be a comfort to him as he deals with his father's illness, and possibly his death. I want to be important to him, but I know I can't force that. I just wish I knew how to be more in his life. And yet, that hardly seems like a reasonable wish, seeing as he plans to go up north at the beginning of the new year, and I don't plan on going anywhere soon. In some fantasies, I think about the possibility of moving away from this area, but it isn't an idea that holds much weight between family and church. I feel pretty rooted here. What are the chances I'll ever meet anyone in this little redneck Baptist town? Besides, how could I leave and separate the kids from Max? I couldn't!

I suppose it's crazy to be thinking any of these things, but when I look at the likelihood of meeting anyone, it seems like I met Michael for a reason. But he may not see it that way, and the reason may be different than what I'm thinking. It may just be that I met him because I deserved to be made love to correctly, or to show me that there is that possibility and to never settle for less. The reason may not make itself clear to me now or in a month or in a year. It's so hard to know why we experience what we do. I guess I have to remember it's the journey, not the destination. It's just that my soul aches to be with someone I can finally trust it with, and he seems like such a good candidate.

But life is complex, not simple; situations in our lives present obstacles, and I guess we have to balance our obligations and our desires and the needs of others with our own needs. I don't always know what it is I need. I think I need to be more independent, and rely on myself for inner joy and peace; I also want to learn from my past to see how better to make choices in the future. With all that in mind, I desperately still have some Cinderella fantasy about meeting "the one" and knowing it and not letting it slip away. I can't really base all my hopes on one chance meeting where sex was the primary focus, yet I feel so drawn to him. Is it just because there is no one else? Is it because it was a positive experience, so I'm grasping onto it for dear life because there have been SO FEW positive experiences with men? Am I actually capable of living with things the way they are (as opposed to the way I think I want them to be)? And do I really have a choice? It's really quite the puzzle. In any case, I guess I just have to see how this situation plays out.

10/14/01
I'm hoping I'll hear from Michael tomorrow, but not counting on it. I am assuming he went to visit his parents, but have no idea if he's back. Daydreaming, and I'm thinkin' of you...

10/15/01
Still 4 more weeks till the potential rendezvous. Will it happen? Will it be so awesome I'll never want to come home? Will he ever want to go home? I want to see him so badly, but I just have to wait. No choice.

EXPRESSIONS

Victoria thought over the possibilities. What had this chance encounter meant? Why was it having such an impact on her? It seemed that every time she thought it was silly, that it had played out, something more sprung up inside of her, needing to be nurtured, expressed, delved into. Every time she thought she should back away, she would be overcome with renewed faith that something should be done, contact should be maintained, and her desire would begin all over again. Victoria lay down her pen, feeling a sudden urge to write a poem. At times, the feelings she just had to express would pop into her head and need—no, demand—to be written down. She moved to the computer and began typing.

> The plant lay dormant.
> The dirt was dry and dusty.
> The leaves were withered and dull.
> The flower was colorless and closed.
> An early autumn rain fell unexpectedly from the sky.
> It blessed the blossom with its sweet serendipity.
> The soil became moist and rich.
> The leaves drank in the drops of life juice.
> The flower opened to the rain and basked in its supple shower
> And its petals burst into color.
>
> 10-15-01

Releasing the Dove

From: Vicki Woolfrey [vickwool@aol.com]
Sent: Tuesday, October 16, 2001 8:37 AM
To: Michael Bellamy
Subject: You okay?

Hi Michael. Assuming you're back. I was going to wait till I heard from you, but I am worried about you. Did you go to see your parents? Are you doing okay? I've been thinking of you since Friday, wondering how things were going. I lit a candle for your family at church on Sunday. Let me know how you're doing and if I can be there for you. Hope to hear from you soon.

Vicki

From: Michael Bellamy [MB@ka.org]
Sent: Tuesday, October 16, 2001 10:08 AM
To: vickwool@aol.com
Subject: Doing all right, thanks. And you?

Hey Victoria—

Thanks for your kind thoughts and wishes — they're greatly appreciated. I stayed home this past weekend, primarily at my mom's urging and because I'm under the weather. (My Aunt Amelia and Uncle Tom made it down for a visit though.) My dad is hanging in, getting better slowly and could be home in a day or two.

Worked away from my desk yesterday (again) so here I am replying. And what a good day to reply — I got a letter from this chick in Virginia, with a picture of her and her buds. Thanks for the card/photo! It's a very good shot of you (and your friends) and I really like the earrings. And a very flattering card to boot, which is what we'll be knocking in a short while. Work some energy out and de-stress. Are you ready?

Lots of little things to do today so bear with me in terms of response time, okay?

—Michael

From: Vicki Woolfrey [vickwool@aol.com]
Sent: Tuesday, October 16, 2001 11:09 AM
To: Michael Bellamy
Subject: RE: Doing all right, thanks. And you?

Michael, I'll bear with you no matter what. Deal? Sorry you're not feeling too good. Ever tried taking echinacea?...it seems to ward off stuff. Glad your dad is doing better.

Am I ready? Is there such a thing as being TOO ready? I am ready now, so how ready will I be when I finally fly into you and knock you to the ground? Who is making the arrangements, anyway? Do you need me to do anything? I have a slight advantage being in a job where there's no boss and no time frame and no deadlines that can't be pushed off by saying "There was just too much laundry to get to that today..."

Anyway, don't worry about immediate responses...besides, I like the way you hold off until I go crazy...wrote another poem about you, actually our "encounter." Don't ask to see it! These are my innermost feelings, and this one was way more...uh...suggestive (?) than the last one. Think I'm in my "ready" phase. Are you getting it that I'm READY?!

Okay, talk to you later. Glad you liked the picture.

Vicki

10/16/01

I heard from Michael, who hadn't gone out of town at all. I am projecting this, but I sense him losing enthusiasm for us continuing to correspond. I keep thinking I'm being too eager or pushy. I'm going to back way off, and just wait to hear from him, and only check the damn email 2 or 3 times a day! I'm obsessing and I know it. Anyway, he didn't have much to say except he's under the weather, and he got the card and photo I sent. Whoop-dee-doo.

10/17/01

Trying not to be bummed that, once again, no word from Michael. I keep thinking his interest has waned, with time passing and other opportunities presenting themselves perhaps. Hopefully it isn't anything I said or did that's stopped his already-getting-infrequent communiqués. I was intensely monitoring the emails, and I have to stop that. It's just that I desperately want to connect with someone, someone I can feel good with. I guess "desperate" is a word that should always raise a red flag for me. I really can't be acting out of desperation. What good will that do? Meanwhile, I feel myself withdrawing just a little as I take my little bruised ego back into its protective shell for safekeeping. If he does really have an interest, my pushing it won't make matters any better. Why must I always carry these false hopes around like a charm, believing something will happen if I just wish hard enough? If I just try and be happy and charming and funny and smart and pretty, the man I want will come to his senses and love me. But it doesn't work that way. It's so easy to fall into patterns and habits of behavior where men are concerned. I'm not going to let someone in just because no one else is knocking right now. And BTW, Michael may not email every day, but his emails have always been at least somewhat encouraging, so why must I put a negative spin on it and expect the worst? I'd be better served to let it happen the way it's going to happen. I wasn't looking for it when I met him, and I can't force it now. BUT GOD I WANT HIM AGAIN!

10/18/01
I started feeling cheap and easy this morning about Michael. I mean geez, I'm throwing myself at him for what? A romp in the hay? It sounds so good sometimes, but especially now when he thinks it's fine to treat me without courtesy or anything else, it occurs to me that this too has been my pattern, let a man have what he wants, always say yes and not to worry. FUCK THAT. I'm not doing it anymore. I don't feel very respected right now, and maybe I shouldn't, if all I'm doing is offering my body to a man who only wants that. I talk a good talk about living for today, having fun, learning from each experience. Let's be honest for one frigging minute, shall we? I want someone to love and respect me and treat me well AND give good loving! I don't have that, and I won't find it as long as I let men treat me like dirt. I'm a beautiful, sensitive, strong, intelligent, funny, kind and loving person. I deserve nothing less than the best. This is a test, and I'm so scared I won't pass. Because I'm so lonely and alone. I don't feel so strong right now. I feel pretty sad and want to be comforted so badly. Why do I have to be all alone? I don't want to be alone anymore.

10/19/01
Weird day—low tide with my biorhythms. Felt low energy and mildly depressed. Going to the gym didn't help at all, it just drained me. My head was full of negative thoughts the entire day and of course, much of it centered around my imagined rejection by Michael. I haven't heard from him in several days, and am resolute that I will not email him till I hear from him. I imagined all kinds of scenarios where he simply stopped corresponding with no reason

given; I imagined what I'd say in an email, letter, or even on the phone to let him know how it hurt, being treated this way, even if he had made it clear we had no future. I was so down on myself, wondering why men always leave me, and how lonely life was going to be when I can't find one decent man.

I finally decided to review the last email from me and the last one from him to see if there were any hints that he'd grown tired of me or I'd said something that could have been misconstrued. You know what? There weren't. His last email was fine, regular, still mentioning our planned rendezvous. My response was not demanding, whiny, or bitchy in any way. There is no reason to think he's stopped emailing or gotten sick of me. I bring these thoughts and feelings on myself. I have had so many negative experiences that I have come to expect men to grow sick of me and to leave without explanation. I can't blame myself for this line of thinking, but it is faulty logic to assume Michael's doing the same thing. I'll just wait and see. It will be VERY hard to do.

I am still on the fence about whether I want that weekend to take place. It could be really awesome or suck really bad, depending on my outlook at the time. How can I NOT want to feel that good again? He is so good at making love and just so present in the moment...how can I not want to do it? Yet I feel nervous and scared, too—like it's some kind of a test for me. Can I just be in the moment that whole time and not worry about what comes next? Can I help but think about some way to sweep him off his feet so he totally digs me and can't stand to be without me? I've never tried to capture a man's heart before, and it seems silly to start now. Still, I can't help but imagine how lovely it would be to have that kind of man in my life. To have that kind of bliss bestowed on my body and mind—don't I deserve it?

This is really distressing! I want to "go with the flow," but I also want to make it happen! I want to live for today, but I keep dreaming about tomorrow. I want to be independent enough not to need a man, yet I ache to have one worthy of me in my life.

10/21/01
Feeling better I guess. I realized what negative thought processes I was engaging in and stopped! Good for me! Had a fun time videotaping myself Friday night with the original intent of sending it to Michael as half-joke, half-way to

turn him on—well, it is not very sexy, but it's certainly funny! I was silly and I have thought of more to add, but maybe I'll just keep it for myself. I mean, shit, who knows what will happen next!

In the sermon yesterday, there were some messages that hit home with me. She was talking about how any place where you're seen and heard can be a holy place, and it got me to thinking that, in my eyes, that is what being with Michael felt like. It felt holy. I was seen and heard and appreciated in a way no one's ever done before. I was completely in heaven, and now, I can only imagine it falling short of my expectations. I've got to stop HAVING expectations. I'll set myself up for disappointment.

Later...I finished my videotape. I don't care if I send it to him or not. It was so much fun just to make it, it was worth the time! I'll wait and see if I hear from him and what tone he takes before I decide. Besides, I MIGHT want to copy it onto VHS, send a copy to him and keep the original. It's a hoot!

The video fades in to the sound of heavy breathing, moving past. The first shot is of a dimly lit, rectangular room, a brick fireplace at the end, a pottery lamp on either side of the raised brick platform in front of the fireplace. A wooden mantel sits above it, crowded with framed photos and knick-knacks. More photos, of the studio variety, adorn the wall above the mantelpiece. To the right, a faded, spongy, powder-blue sofa; to the left, a large black television sitting on a small wooden TV stand that faces the sofa; in between them, on the neutral colored carpet, lies a purple yoga mat. A hula hoop is leaning against the sofa. The heavy breathing is from Victoria, who runs past, obviously just having turned the camera on herself. She is wearing a sleeveless red tank top and black stretch yoga pants, slightly wider at the bottom. She stands with her legs spread, one foot to either side of the yoga mat. Facing away from the camera, she bends over to stretch, legs straight, derriere facing the camera. After a couple stretches to either side, touching the ground beside her feet with the opposite hands, she stands and turns. As if it were a pleasant surprise, she notices the camera. "Oh!" she exclaims. "Hello. I'm in training! I gotta get ready for a big weekend coming up. Gotta get ready for Michael!" She reaches over, picks up the hula hoop and steps inside it, bringing it to waist level. She begins circulating the hoop with big thrusts of her hips, knees slightly bent, arms raised up like a goal post. She continues to smile and talk.

Expressions

"Gotta keep moving, get some hip action going!" Then she puts a finger to her chin and looks up toward the ceiling, a query on her lips. "I wonder what kind of woman Michael likes? Is she more classy and sultry? Or more of a wild and wacky woman? Or maybe he prefers sexy and hot...or what about just some kind of a kick-ass, rock-n-roll woman?" She removes the hula hoop, still puzzling, and walks toward the camera saying, "Hmmmm...I wonder..."

Camera fades to black momentarily, then, with the awkward sound of rustling paper and clicking buttons, the image fades back in. This time, an 8-1/2 x 11" piece of paper, held horizontally by a hand, is directly in front of the lens. On it, in all caps, written with crayon, are the words "CLASSY & SULTRY." The paper is held there for a second or two, then is yanked down from view. A brief view of an empty, square room is seen. It has a wooden floor. The back wall of the room is all window, covered with cheap vertical blinds. A multi-colored long-haired cat weaves in between the slats of the blinds, exposing dark patches of window. The recorder clock says it's 11:37 p.m. To the right of the room, a darkened doorway leads off to another room. An electric chandelier hangs from the ceiling, cobwebs obvious on some of its curved arms. The sounds of applause and a piano beginning a sad and doleful tune are heard. Victoria saunters into view from the right in a long black evening gown. It has spaghetti straps, rhinestone décolletage, and a slit up one entire leg. She is bedecked in rhinestone jewelry—earrings, necklace, bracelet—and she has on red lipstick and a glamorous air. She begins lip syncing to a song that a seductress would sing. She tells a tale of disappointment, from the letdown of the circus to the lackluster anticlimax of love.

Victoria plays the part, tongue in cheek, of a lounge singer with her ballad, dramatically lifting an invisible glass and swaying to the music, raising her hands in exasperation with the lack of expectations met. As the applause closes the piece, she saunters off screen.

The camera jerkily fades out, then back in again. This time, the paper held in front of the camera reads, "WILD & WACKY." A wrist, this time with multiple jangling bracelets, reaches to an unseen tape deck and pushes play. The second song begins. It's Rick James singing "Super Freak." From the dark entryway to the right of the room, Victoria emerges, this time in a beige, tight-fitting mini skirt, a hot fuchsia, 3/4 length sleeve blouse with a wrap-around waist and deep-cut neckline, and platform shoes with black soles and wide white straps. She begins moving around the room, shaking her booty, shimmying, bending forward as she jerks her body to the beat, again mouthing the words to the song. Her arms move wildly but rhythmically, sometimes criss-crossing in front of her face or snaking above her head. She bends her knees and lowers and raises her body. Her head bobs and juts to the music, and she twists, turns, and boogies through the entire song, exiting with an Egyptian-style movement.

 "Super Freak," by Rick James and Alonzo Miller

Fade out, fade in. An out-of-focus paper this time, moving away from and toward the lens as the focus tries to grab onto it. Finally, the paper is legible. "SEXY & HOT." Madonna's "Justify My Love" starts its slow, hypnotic, erotic beat. A leg and hand emerge from the dark doorway, toes pointed, then half a body. She is wearing a maroon lace teddy with long sleeves, off-the-shoulder neckline, and matching panties, evident because the teddy appears to be about 3 inches too short for Victoria's long frame. She writhes her body against the doorjamb, looking at the camera with heavily lidded eyes. This time she moves more slowly, finding the rhythm and undulating with it. She profiles herself, back arched, buttocks out, one leg bent at the knee, hands on her knees and face turned toward the camera. Again she sings along, but only some of the words this time. She points at the camera, mouthing the words. She walks slowly toward the camera, then away. She looks back over her shoulder as she places her hands on her butt cheeks, visible as the teddy rides up, exposing the high-cut panties. She rotates her hips in a move that cannot be mistaken for anything but an invitation. Her body is not perfect. Her chest is flat, her stomach pouches out a bit, but her legs are firm and long, her movements silky and smooth. The only thing betraying her seriousness is the constant tugging at the teddy to pull it below crotch level. The song ends and Victoria swims out of the picture with one more hug to the doorway.

 "Justify My Love," by Lenny Kravitz, Ingrid Chavez, and Madonna

Another piece of paper, this time reading, "KICK ASS." The viewpoint is different this time. The camera is pointed at another wall. An off-white, balloon-style window treatment hangs over a large picture window, decorated with small dots of color—flowers, perhaps. Below the curtain sits one arm of an L-shaped sofa in dark greens, burgundys, and blues. In front of the sofa is a large square cherry coffee table with a black wooden base. On the matching end table to the right of the sofa is a lamp with a green metallic vine as its base. A framed photo sits on the table. Above the lamp is a shallow cherry shelf with a ledge that holds two similarly framed photos. As a long wail of electric guitar begins, Victoria jumps into the picture and onto the coffee table. She is dressed in brown suede bell-bottoms and a paler brown faux-suede top with a scoop neck and 3/4 length sleeves. Her feet are bare. As Van Halen's "Ain't Talkin' Bout Love" begins, with its hard edges and gritty rock sound, Victoria begins a pounding dance that includes air guitar solos and wild tosses of her head. She is clearly having the time of her life. She jumps, turns, tosses, shakes, and grinds through the song. The grand finale as the guitar licks wind up and then down includes a badly timed jump from the coffee table to the floor where she intends, but doesn't quite succeed, to disappear beyond the camera's view.

 "Ain't Talkin' 'Bout Love," by Michael Anthony, David Lee Roth, and Eddie Van Halen

Cut to final scene. The camera opens to Victoria, now in black jeans and a long-sleeved, berry-colored scoop neck top, walking from the camera to a chair directly in front of the camera. The cut of her shirt is wide and low, exposing her collar bone and showing off her broad shoulders. She is in a different room now. She sits at a barstool-height table set in the corner of the room, small and round with a wooden top. The chair has a metal back that outlines two chili peppers. On the peach-colored wall, a red telephone rests just above her shoulder. A second chair sits empty on the other side of the table. Above it hangs a calendar. In an overly affected voice, Victoria introduces herself as a movie critic. She uses cliché Hollywood lingo to describe the video up to this point. After tearing apart its overall disastrousness, from shabby editing to juvenile graphics, she breaks down the video into its separate features, criticizing each installment. About the first, the classy and sultry one, she teases that the dress would be better suited to a cruise ship, and that the singer clearly didn't rehearse the words enough. Regarding the second segment, she critiques the dancer's hair, saying it looks like something out of the movie Something About Mary. She does, however, compliment the dancer on "having her moves down." As to the third piece, her first comment is, "Sexy and hot, it's NOT." She makes judgments left and right about everything from the ill-fitting teddy to the overly long performance.

Finally, regarding the "KICK ASS" segment, she mentions that the dancer did appear to be having fun, though her air guitar was extremely cliché and out of date. In sum total, the movie critic feels that the video would probably not even make it onto America's Funniest Home Videos. Then she signs off. She walks toward the camera, and as she fumbles for the off button, a throaty laugh is heard, and the throat and chin still in view vibrate with the laughter.

10/22/01
Checked my emails today, but no word from Michael. But it's early yet. If I don't hear from him today, I'm sure I'll be bummed, but what's to be done about it? Nothing. Going to call a friend and see if I can copy my tape at her house. I don't care if it's ever seen by anyone else, but I want to record it for all time!

Later... I never heard from him today. Trying not to get down on myself. Composed a brief civil email, but decided to wait till tomorrow before sending it. Still not sure about the video, though. Part of me imagines him receiving it and any doubts he's had about getting together are erased when he sees how clever and funny I am (haha). Then I imagine him with a girlfriend, and think, "WOW, that wouldn't be well-received." Whatever. He hasn't told me to go blow, so I shouldn't assume he plans to. I just wish I'd hear from him, one way or the other. But I'm not going to get down on myself. I'm a lovable, beautiful, smart, caring, clever, funny, creative, sensitive, talented person. There's nothing about me to reject, and nothing wrong with me. I just haven't found a good match yet. Good sex does NOT equal good catch.

From: Vicki Woolfrey [vickwool@aol.com]
Sent: Tuesday, October 23, 2001 11:36 AM
To: Michael Bellamy
Subject: Hey you

Hey Michael. Hoping all is well with you. It's been about a week since we last "spoke," and I'm just wondering how you're doing. I'm doing fine. Been enjoying the warm weather with long walks, trips to the pumpkin patch, and yard work (for all the good that did...the yard is already covered with leaves again!). Hope you've been able to get out and breathe. Miss talking to you.

Victoria

Expressions

From: Michael Bellamy [MB@ka.org]
Sent: Tuesday, October 23, 2001 1:17 PM
To: vickwool@aol.com
Subject: Re: Hey you

Hello Victoria –

Yes, it has been a while since we last "spoke" – no worries, everything is generally fine. I have been working out of the office quite a bit the last month or so, much more than usual, so that is the reason for the slowdown of exchanges. (Yes, I'm still into the reunion weekend!) And as I have yet to purchase a home computer, I'm relegated to the office e-mail.

Good news – my dad is home from the hospital and re-gaining his strength. I was fairly scared there for awhile, so when I was finally able to talk with him, it was a relief to hear his voice at home. I've had a bit of a cough lately and have been hopped up on cough syrup with codeine – some mornings are very hard to shake the cobwebs if I've taken it the night before, but truth be told, I'll live. Not like this crazy anthrax shit. I so despise whoever is doing this...

Was able to get outside this weekend and enjoy the terrific weather as well. I would always try to coax my dad into waiting for all the leaves to fall before raking, but it didn't work. I know all too well the devious tricks the wind can play!

Please tell me about your children when you can – sounds like you guys all have fun together, at least outside. As you know, I don't have any children but have lots of nephews and nieces – 14 in all, so you can bounce a few stories by if you care.

Hope you are staying well – in a holding pattern about the weekend you mentioned, Nov. 17? Work has been busy enough of late that I might take you up on your offer to play travel agent, if the offer is still on the table. Tempted to schedule that weekend right now, but please bear with me a few more days. Think I'm heading to see my folks in two weekends so that should be OK, but will let you know ASAP, OK?

Take care, Michael

From: Vicki Woolfrey [vickwool@aol.com]
Sent: Tuesday, October 23, 2001 4:08 PM
To: Michael Bellamy
Subject: RE: Hey you

Michael, so glad your dad is home. That is great news! Also glad you're still standing, though sorry about the coughing. It's the time of year. The whole anthrax thing is very distressing. I know 3 people who work for the postal service, and it's really scary.

You're right about the raking. I should just wait. It's just so overwhelming when it's a foot deep...

I had mentioned the weekend of the 10th, not the 17th! Oh no! I have my kids the 17th. So the 10th is when you're seeing your folks? What a bummer. I guess we'll have to keep trying to find a common time. I could try and switch weekends with their dad, if that's the only way. I really want to see you! Let me know, okay?

As for my kids, what would you like to know? Chloe (my daughter) is almost 8. She is in 2nd grade. People say she looks just like me. There are some photos of me as a kid that do look a lot like her. We have similar personalities too (sometimes that's good, because we understand each other's humor or whatever; sometimes it's bad, when we're both particularly moody). She is into gymnastics and art right now, and she is wacky. Very brainy too. I thought she was a genius when she was a baby (I think that's pretty common...). She spoke her first word at 9 months. It was "cat."

My son Connor is 5. He is in kindergarten half-days. It is the first time in my life (as a parent) I actually have a little time without my kids, between them spending time with their dad and being at school every day! I have really come to enjoy that space of time, and it makes me such a better mom for them when I'm recharged. Anyway, Connor has unbelievable blue eyes (which neither of his parents do) and a great smile. He is very sensitive and charming. He is also very silly. I have a lot of fun with him playing cars, Rescue Heroes, and so on. We all enjoy reading books together or making up silly songs (this is one of my hidden talents. It actually has a name: "filking"...that's making up songs to another pre-established tune).

I have a kazillion nieces and nephews too, and I did dote on them quite a bit before I had my own kids. I love watching them grow into adults (as a few of them have by now). It's so weird to remember them small and then see them driving and dating and going to school or work and being grown-ups! The one saddest thing that has come out of the breakup of my marriage is not getting to see my nieces and nephews from that side of the family as much. I miss them a lot. How often do you see all yours? Are they nearby? You said you're the youngest of 5...what are the other siblings (sisters, brothers, ages, etc.)?

Thanks for getting back to me. Keep your eyes on the mailbox...

Victoria

10/23/01
Happy to report I finally heard from Michael today, though I emailed him first, just a casual hey-how-are-you. He claims to still want to get together, but now he's got the dates screwed up and who knows if or when this will happen. Well, it's fun to imagine, anyway. I copied the tape today. I'll mail it tomorrow. Hope he likes it. In his email, he asked me to tell him about my kids. He keeps surprising me. I don't even want to think this, but, God, I think I could fall in love with him. I may hate having said that...one day when I look back, I may think myself quite the fool. But it won't be the first time, and it certainly won't be the last... anyway, I responded with a rather lengthy email with way too much information in it, but shit, he asked. It seems his dad is home from the hospital, which is good news. I can't help wondering if I'll ever meet his family. I can't help wondering if I'll ever see him again. It could so easily go either way. His job is over as of the new year, and then where will he go? It isn't within my control, but I'm having a hard time thinking about him just being gone. Who knows, maybe we'd stay in touch, maybe I'd see him next summer if I went to Star and if he ended up in New England. I can't think about it.

10/24/01
Pat came over for dinner. As usual, we had great conversations about parenting, men, being single, church, and every other thing in between. Drank a bottle of wine too. Feeling just fine! Never did hear from Michael today, but I was feeling so fine about mailing the video to him that I didn't care that much! Wonder when he'll get it? Not tomorrow—maybe Friday? Who knows. Hope he appreciates my ridiculous humor. Pat made me feel really good about him. She is the only one I've truly confided in about any of this, and even so, I didn't share that much. But she was talking about the whole "you have to kiss a lot of frogs before you get a prince" theory (a little cliché), but I felt all of a sudden that THAT was it—he IS the prince. The timing is just wrong, the place is wrong. But she said keep that door open, that maybe he IS the one and to just

let time take care of it. I don't know...hard to make any assessments, but I feel good just knowing there are possibilities.

10/25/01
I think I was a little tipsy when I wrote yesterday's entry; still, I enjoyed the feeling. I fell asleep laughing because no matter what else happens, Michael will see my silly video and hopefully it will make him laugh. It sure makes ME laugh! No word from him today, but he says he's been working out of the office a lot lately.

Later...I keep thinking the video should arrive tomorrow, or certainly by Saturday. I keep wondering how he'll react. I guess he'll tell me eventually. I just hope he finds it as funny as I do.

From: Michael Bellamy [MB@ka.org]
Sent: Monday, October 29, 2001 2:36 PM
To: vickwool@aol.com
Subject: WOW

Good afternoon, Tina!! (as in Turner)

If you could have seen my jaw drop when I saw the videotape mailer with your address on it...I popped it in and my jaw remained open for a half hour! Thanks! I never expected a videotape greeting. That has to be one of those things you bring to the post office and pause before you drop it in – then you let it go and know that once it's on it's way, there's no going back, that you've done something potentially crazy...so good for you! Now don't expect a video response on my end, I don't look nearly as good as you in slim, tight-fitting wardrobes. And I can't dance as well, but I've got you beat on the Van Halen jump thing. Got to work on that timing, Victoria!

It really blew me away! No worries, I won't blackmail you with this, but it's really good ammo! No videos in Maryland though! And I did think the critic at the end of the video was a bit harsh...like SHE would ever have the guts to dance in front of the camera!

Well, you've set the stage now! I think that date is OK, will let you know by Wednesday. This weekend I'm in Denver working, my last big assignment for the KA, photographing and videotaping a National Dog Agility Championship. Will be back next Tuesday.

Will be around the next two days though, so let me know what the sequel will be.

Hope you're outside a little bit today!

—Michael Lee Roth

From: Vicki Woolfrey [vickwool@aol.com]
Sent: Monday, October 29, 2001 3:30 PM
To: Michael Bellamy
Subject: RE: WOW

Michael, I'm glad you enjoyed the video. You're right, there was this moment where I could have just not sent it, but I thought, what the fuck?! I have been laughing ever since, knowing that no matter what, it would make you laugh. I've watched it a couple times just for grins.

Well, Denver is a cool town. I have very fond memories of Denver. Will you get to play at all, or is it all work? Do you travel a lot for your job? I used to travel so much for this one job, and I saw a lot of cool cities. There's still some more I want to see, though! Never been to New Mexico, so I'm going to Albuquerque next October for my 40th to see the hot air balloon festival. Always wanted to ride in a balloon. But Denver...yes, I liked Denver.

I must go now, alas, it's time to meet the school bus. My kids are really excited about Halloween. Spent part of the weekend making their costumes (no, I'm not a seamstress, but creative). Chloe is going to be a pirate and Connor a sea monster. My personal favorite costume I ever was, was a tree. I won a contest and everything. What about you?

Well, talk to you later. And you'll have to demonstrate your jump for me some time...

Your Private Dancer Tina

10/29/01
Got an email from Michael, which was good, but again, couldn't get excited about it. He got the video, claims to have watched it with his jaw dropped the whole time. Whatever. He mentioned that "the date sounds good" but now I don't know if he means the date he thought it was, or the one I originally suggested and reminded him of. He won't actually commit to doing it, and frankly, I'm losing my enthusiasm. It's been over a month now, and due to the

decreasing enthusiasm he's shown and his decreasing attention, I sense it becoming less of a goal for him. My perceptions are shaded by how I'm feeling today, so it's not a good day to assess how I feel about it.

At this moment, I feel like it would be just fine if we ended it here and now. I am back in my world, and I don't have the energy to imagine things any different than they are now. I don't know how he feels, but it's all pretty weird. I've lost sight of why I wanted to do this. Yeah, great sex. But is it worth the risk? I mean, the whole birth control thing, and just the whole frigging inconvenience. I'm tired just thinking about it. And then planning it—the logistics, reservations, blah blah blah. I'm not into it right now, as you can tell. I'd rather stay home and not worry about how I'm going to look the morning after and if my razor stubble will gross him out, and whether I'll snore, or if we'll tire of each other before the weekend is up. It's all too weird. The spontaneity of our first meeting can never be recaptured. I don't know about this. All that shit about him being the prince, it was bullshit. I don't even know if I believe in that crap. Without much interest from him, it's hard to say. I'm not thinking straight. Any other day, wouldn't days and nights of great sex with a young, hot lover sound great?! I'm just tired, bloody, crampy, and out of it. Give me a week.

10/30/01
Felt a little better today, but not hearing from him made me feel ticked off, like if he can't even take a minute to write, then fuck it. I don't feel particularly like going now. I feel like it's a bad idea, and I really want it to go away. Course, I'm feeling fat and zitty right now too. Had a good workout at the gym after a marathon of activity. Took a brisk walk on a GORGEOUS day, then let my trainer kick my butt with back and biceps. Felt good, felt like I looked good. Felt as if there were promise and hope. Now I feel gross, and I feel a little—what? Used? I don't know if that's quite it, but somehow I feel like I'm just there waiting for his go-ahead, and then I'll be some sort of love slave for his pleasure for a weekend, and then I'll never see him again. In other words, yeah, USED. What's the point? I mean, he's not interested in me—not the way I had hoped might happen. I should let it die. One great memory would be better than one BIG REGRET.

On the other hand, I hate to pass up the chance to see if that chemistry I felt was REAL or not. I hate to let it slip away without ever knowing.

Expressions

From: Vicki Woolfrey [vickwool@aol.com]
Sent: Wednesday, October 31, 2001 2:32 PM
To: Michael Bellamy
Subject: Happy Halloween!

Hey Michael. BOO! I thought maybe I would have heard back from ya by now, but let me email you before you're out of the office again and say that if we are going to really get together, it might be easier to discuss it or plan it over the phone than by email. If you want to, you can call me at home tonight, maybe after 9 (I'll be dealing with trick-or-treaters till then, I imagine). I just want to know one way or the other what the plan is and whether or not to keep that weekend open. I was really looking forward to it, but I think I'm sensing some ambivalence on your end, and if that's so, just let me know. If I'm completely wrong, let me know that too! If our one night is all we get, it'll go down in my personal history book as one of the best, most fun nights of my life; if it's meant to be that there are more nights like it, or even better, then that would be a bonus. Personally, I think we really connected and I'd love to try again, but I'm not going to push myself on you (unless you ask R E A L nice), and I feel kind of silly thinking about something so much that may not even happen. I am rambling, so I'll say adios here and hope to hear from you. Adios!

If you want to call, my number is 777-555-2286. HAPPY HALLOWEEN! (^^)

Vicki

10/31/01

I sent an email today guaranteed to SCARE off Michael! Hahahahahahaha-ha!! I said I wanted to know if this was on or off or what, and that I sensed some ambivalence on his part, but I wasn't bitchy (I don't think), and I made it clear I was still interested. But I also said if it didn't happen, I'll have no regrets. I enjoyed our night together, and if it's meant to be, it will be. Now I feel like I sealed my fate...he's got the chance to back out if he wants out, or he can salvage this with reassurances. Or he can totally blow me off. I guess whatever happens is, at this point, out of my hands. I feel some anger, some regret that we may not see one another again. I am so pessimistic...it beats being disappointed. And then I can stop the fantasizing and live in my reality, which really isn't bad. Just a little cold at night sometimes. And a little empty, but I am full of love for my children, my family, and friends. I must sustain myself on that. I just wish I had a photo—he is the best. My mind's eye will have to keep him there. When I'm 85, will I give a shit about this? Will I even be able to remember it? Probably not. Will it sustain me through the cold and lonely nights? I am not down—just wondering how this fits into the scheme of my life. What purpose did it serve? What did it show me? Was it just to give me hope? To comfort me? To be a joyful time? To remind me that I'm alive and beautiful? Will its purpose ever be revealed to me? I just want to believe it had a reason. It must have, because I can't handle that it was meaningless. That I can't do. I guess its meaning is whatever I make of it. It may not have the same meaning to him, and it may not have the same meaning to me in times ahead. Maybe it just WAS.

Later...A quick note before bed...HE CALLED! Wow, he is so damn CUTE! He's going out of town tomorrow, but said he'd call when he gets back. I think we're on. Oh man.

11/1/01
HAPPY HAPPY HAPPY. That's how I feel today. I'm so glad he called. Hearing his voice and just talking to him, it made all the difference. Yeah, it was a little awkward, but I felt reconnected to him in a way email just wasn't doing. He sounded like he's having a tough time with all the changes coming up in his life—his job ending and trying to find a new one and maybe moving, and his dad being sick, etc. etc. We talked about music, my silly video (he said it turned him on), his siblings, my impending sale of the house, the leaves, etc. But there was one thing I found a little off—he was not comfortable planning the weekend until he comes back from Denver next week. He kept saying he wanted to get together, and that the weekend I was talking about was good, but something was clearly bothering him that he didn't want to talk about. I hope it isn't some other relationship he's involved in. God, don't let it be his old girlfriend. He had told me that she'd been in touch with him after September 11th to see how he was doing. Sounds like there's still a connection there. I'm just going to ask him. Geez, I don't want to be in the middle of that. It's kind of silly to surmise from just his tone of voice and distractibility. I really hope that's not it, but something's bugging him. I tend to imagine the worst—if it's that he's still trying to resolve feelings for her, I don't know what to do. Give him space and time to figure it out, I suppose. He's definitely hedging. We'll see what happens on Tuesday. Supposedly, he'll be calling from work.

Great—kids are home that day for election day. That should be amusing. If this happens, it could be really great. If it doesn't, I guess it's back to the drawing board. I like the idea of him and me, but I don't feel like there's any real hope of a future.

I was out raking the leaves, and thinking about him telling me he loves to rake leaves; he wishes he had a big yard. I think the joy of raking is severely diminished once you have kids, though they sure have a blast jumping in them. They undo what you've done. Somewhere I lost the joy of raking leaves. Maybe it's because no one ever helped me. Max never helped. I hated doing it alone, but then I did so many things alone. He would do it with me. But that's just a dream.

11/5/01
Supposed to be hearing from Michael tomorrow, but I have a lot of errands to run. Hope I don't' miss his call, but if I do, oh well. Feeling like the likelihood of getting together is pretty small right now. I have two theories about his reluctance to commit to this weekend: (1) his old girlfriend of 8 years is trying to get back together with him (or he with her) and that makes our "relationship" risky; (2) with all the changes in his life right now, he is feeling vulnerable, and doesn't want to be in a position where feelings might actually occur. Well, whatever his deal is, it's not about ME, it's stuff HE has to deal with. As long as I remember that, it can only be disappointing, but not painful.

FALL FROM GRACE

From: Vicki Woolfrey [vickwool@aol.com]
Sent: Tuesday, November 6, 2001 1:59 PM
To: Michael Bellamy

Michael,

Some advice for the future: women would much rather be told the truth than have some attempt at placating them by "letting them down easy." This is going to sound harsh after you were so sweet, but I think you know I'm not stupid. Choosing a 10-year-old's birthday party over getting together with me sent a clear message. I only wish you would have felt comfortable enough to just say you didn't want the weekend to happen, especially before it got as far as it did. You have your reasons, and I can respect that. I can only guess they had to do with not getting tangled up with someone when you have so much up in the air right now. I'm trying not to take it too personally, though let's face it, that was a pretty obvious rejection. The fact that you didn't even try and come up with an alternate date said to me that this is not going to happen, and that I was really the only one interested in meeting. I feel pretty foolish now. I'm not looking for an apology and I'm not trying to send you on a guilt trip. All I want is for you to know that your actions affected me, and I'm really angry and hurt, probably just the things you didn't want to deal with. Actually, I guess you really don't have to deal with it. The likelihood that we'll see each other again is pretty remote. I really enjoyed our time together, and I really enjoyed thinking about the possibilities of a second meeting.

Take care. Don't drag this out by trying to stay friends if you're doing it out of guilt; that would really only make it worse for me, and probably for you. That makes it sound like I wouldn't enjoy being friends, and I probably would. But again, if you stay in touch just so I won't feel bad, or so that you won't feel bad, that's not a very good reason.

Victoria

P.S. Please respect me enough to not show that video to anyone or make a joke of it. It was done in fun, but I think you can tell it was personal. I'm not sorry I made it or that I sent it, but boy I feel a little stupid now realizing that you weren't into this as much as I was. I guess, in retrospect, I saw that coming, but I didn't want to believe it. All I really wanted was to feel as good again as I felt the night we met.

 *"Somebody Kill Me," by Adam Sandler*

11/06/01
TODAY SUCKS. I feel so much ANGER and HURT. I am so rejected, and I feel so STUPID for letting myself believe it MIGHT be possible to actually find happiness, even in small doses, with a man! They are all the SAME. Sex is all that matters and commitments OF ANY KIND and HONESTY—too tough of concepts for their puny brains. I got the call, can you fucking guess?? He is blowing me off for his 10-year-old niece's bday party, but that's not what's so AWFUL, no it's that he knew that when we last spoke, and he didn't mention it but he wouldn't even commit to a weekend of SEX?! What is up with that? It's just too much trouble. And it's not like he apologized and it's not like he tried to make up for it—no, didn't try to even make a different date, which would have been disappointing enough. It's the same old story, they can't just SAY what they mean. They either don't say anything, or they lie, or they have some lame-o excuse that is so transparent, but they're trying to be NICE to let you down EASY. Well FUCK YOU. To let it get this far? It was potentially going to happen in a matter of DAYS—why put off the conclusion? Because men are too CHICKEN SHIT to own up to an actual DECISION.

I was numb, and then immediately hurt to the core. I threw the phone across the floor and cried so hard it almost hurt to cry. It felt good to pound the floor and my head. I am so angry with myself for letting myself FEEL again. It is so painful to be torn down after being built up. He did that! He made me feel SO GOOD and made it sound like I was SO SPECIAL and BEAUTIFUL and SEXY and HOT. Right. I'm NOTHING to him, not even a good enough piece of ass for him. I feel like shit. I feel worse than shit. I wanted to kill him. I wanted to beg him to reconsider. What a fricking psycho men can make you. I can't do this anymore. I can't keep opening myself up. It's just too much. And I blame MAX for being the JERK who got this fucking ball rolling—how dare he promise to stay with me forever? How dare he leave me alone and dealing with this CRAP that keeps suffocating me. Keeps making me believe, then all the air blows out of the balloon. Party over.

And I'm mad at myself for believing, if only marginally, that this would really happen. There were PLENTY of signs it wouldn't—his early reluctance via email...on and on. I feel like such a FOOL.

Mean Little Boys

Like an old used balloon, she lay crumpled in the corner

Deflated, bereft of oxygen, empty of life

She lay there a long time, not seen or noticed, certainly not attended to

She remembered once having been inflated, though not to her full capacity

She remembered having been tethered to someone's wrist, a boy's wrist

Colorful, floating in the sky

She belonged to someone and her presence made them happy

But like an ornament, it was her decorative qualities, not her soul

That made her desirable

When she wasn't fully inflated, when she had wrinkles or bulges

When the string became frayed and she lost her bounce

When the string became cumbersome and got caught on things and slowed the boy down

Her worth became less, and soon she was discarded

She landed in the corner. She didn't shrivel up completely

Just enough to lack life's luster, just enough to go unnoticed
One day she opened up and let some air in. She had to suck very hard
She couldn't completely fill herself, and she wasn't sure she could keep it in
But she had enough air to bounce along the ground and go places
She could let the wind blow her and take her and that gladdened her heart
She thought maybe, just maybe, this would be enough
Sometimes little boys picked up her frayed string and held it briefly
Sometimes they blew enough air in to extend her life, give her hope
But the air seeped back out, the string was dropped or forgotten
The wind blew her into New York City
A boy picked up her string and wound it around his wrist, but didn't tie it
He liked the balloon—her color, her shape, her bounce
He liked balloons, to play with, to handle, to admire
He blew lots of air into her. She inflated more fully than she'd ever been before!
She flew above the clouds and danced between the sunbeams and felt the wind
She knew a happiness she hadn't known before, and a freedom that was new
She was so full, she was nearly bursting, and she began to believe she was beautiful
But the string slowly began to unwind
She held on as tightly as she could. "Don't let go!" she cried
Suddenly, a sharp pin entered her soul
All the air went out in a burst and a pop
Pieces of her lay scattered
The boy wanted to go to a birthday party
Maybe he would find another balloon.
11/7/01

11/7/01
Not feeling much better today. I feel as though a light has gone out. He lit something inside me when he touched me and told me I was beautiful and I believed him and I believed it for a long time. I was beginning to enjoy seeing myself in the mirror, imagine that. I was walking taller thinking someone, SOMEONE finally saw something in me worth loving. I had an inner warmth thinking of being in his arms again and how good that would feel, no matter for how short a time. Now the light is out, extinguished by the total rejection I feel. It is so painful. And I feel cold all the time. And I hate looking in the mirror. I don't like the person I see. She is old and depressing and too needy and she can't command respect and she is ugly and undesirable. Bad breath, bad skin and nails, too tall. Not attractive or amazing or wonderful. I thought maybe those words had started to describe me.

I thought about dying yesterday. Not in a suicidal way, and yet not in an abstract or philosophical way either. I felt like maybe a part of me was dying and I thought about how I felt like maybe it wouldn't be so bad to let the rest of me die too. My self-loathing and confusion are great today, and it's hard to keep going, but my kids and my other responsibilities are there beckoning me and keeping me just on this side of gone. I would think about going to see my therapist, but I think she would try and put me on anti-depressants. I don't want that. I know this will pass. It has to.

And the SICK thing is, I'm still entertaining fantasies that he'll show up on my doorstep, or send me flowers or some action to prove he gives a shit, yet I know he doesn't. He might feel bad for a while for having had to hurt me, but he won't care about how it's affecting me.

Later...I've made a therapy appointment for tonight. It depresses me even more that after all this time, I feel the need to go. My head is so foggy I'm not sure what I'll say. I feel so bad right now, and I don't know how to get out of it. I think I'm starting to go a little numb. It is too painful to keep feeling like I do, so I'm just starting to go numb. I don't even know what hurts right now. I can't remember everything I was feeling. I'm outside of myself trying to get away from my hurt.

She lay her head down on her bed where she'd been writing in her journal. The cat lay next to her, lazily purring, eyes half shut. Victoria thought that maybe this hurt even more than the marriage ending. It was hard to believe, but she thought maybe her heart was even more broken this time. Or maybe it just hadn't had time to heal yet, and so this blow was too much to take. She loathed herself for being so weak.

She had finally called the counselor she and Max had gone to at the end of the marriage, the one person she'd felt had listened and understood, and been instrumental in bringing her back from the brink. She hadn't wanted to believe she felt bad enough, but the numbness was affecting her ability to function. She could barely work up the energy to meet the bus or make meals for the kids, or read them stories before bed. She felt cold and zombie-like, as though she were walking through thick fog. Everything sounded muffled and looked blurry. The colors seemed to have drained out of her world.

Victoria had woken with a headache, the kind you get when you cry too much. Her nose was stuffed up, her eyes were puffy and red, and she felt horrible. She dragged herself up out of bed, splashed some water on her face, and made a simple breakfast of juice and cereal for the kids. Then she lumbered down to the basement where the computer was. She sat a long time in the red office chair, the one Max had brought home from work when his company was in the midst of replacing furniture. She had made frantic, last-ditch-effort love to him in that chair, fulfilling some need to make him look at her instead of his computer screen for just once...now she sat there in her pajamas, mouth sticky and cottony with morning breath.

She knew that, despite how absolutely horrible she felt, she could not remain angry at Michael. She could not live with herself if she cut him completely out of her life. She realized, as pathetic as it was, that she would rather have some tenuous thread of a connection based on anything, anything at all, than nothing. She re-read the email she'd sent two days before. It was harsh, fueled by her anger and her rejection. She'd lashed out, wanting to hurt him back, childishly flinging her pain at him in words as sharp as knives. She began typing.

From: Vicki Woolfrey [vickwool@aol.com]
Sent: Thursday, November 8, 2001 10:10 AM
To: Michael Bellamy
Subject: An Apology from me

Michael, I wanted to apologize for blasting you in my last email. It wasn't fair to you; I was reacting in pain and anger. There's a lot about me you don't know, and one of those things is how fragile my relationship with sex has been. You were a big turning point for me because not only did you take care with my body, but you took care with my emotions. Not only was it the first time I'd had sex at all in over 2 years, but the first time in my life that I felt that kind of connection to a lover. You touched something deep inside me, and you made me feel beautiful. I felt seen and heard, and I have never had an experience like that EVER and it was a big deal to me.

I don't expect you to have known that, and I don't expect the experience to have been as big for you as it was for me. I guess I wasn't 100% honest when I made it sound like I was so modern and progressive and that getting together again was no big deal. I wanted to be that blasé about it, but the fact is, it WAS a big deal to me, and I unfairly took it out on you when your own life was going on. I don't like the way things were handled, but I had no business trying to dictate what your priorities should be.

Please accept my apology. You have been nothing but sweet and kind to me, and for what it's worth, I have appreciated our attempt at trying to get to know each other better. I'm not sure what your motivation was; I'm afraid mine may have been a little selfish, hoping somehow to make it all into more than it was.

Michael, I said I didn't want you to stay in touch because it would be too painful. But truthfully, staying in touch with you would be nice. I care what happens to you, and your dad, etc. If you still want that, I would cherish the friendship. If this has all been a little too intense, I would understand that as well. Sorry for putting words in your mouth and assuming what you were feeling.

Victoria

Victoria solemnly pressed the SEND button. She didn't expect to hear back from Michael. After having breathed fire on him the last time, she wondered if he wouldn't just thank his lucky stars he hadn't gotten any more involved with her than he did. But she knew she couldn't leave things the way she had...that her last words to him couldn't be ones said in rage. She wanted him to know that he'd meant something to her...he still did. She wasn't going to deny that anymore. She wanted him to know that it hurt, but she also wanted to tell him that it was hurt bred out of feeling.

When she sheepishly checked her email within the hour, she was surprised to see that he had written back. At first, she felt a cold shock, as if knowing that what it contained had the potential to destroy her even more completely, were that possible. It could hold words of critical and hurtful origins that would rip her apart. It could send her down into the blackness out of which she wasn't sure she had the strength to climb back. She got up from the chair and paced in circles around the room, agonizing over whether or not to open the email. Like Pandora's box, she worried that evil nightmarish ghouls would fly out with unstoppable force, dooming her. She cried in short bursts, more afraid than grieving, more disturbed than hurt. Did she dare expose herself to more pain?

After about ten minutes of torturing herself relentlessly, Victoria sat back down in the chair. Her heart was beating wildly, as if trying to escape. Her palms had a cold slick of sweat as she numbly reached for the mouse. She clicked open his email, his response that held her very near future.

From: Michael Bellamy [MB@ka.org]
Sent: Thursday, November 8, 2001 11:02 AM
To: vickwool@aol.com
Subject: Re: An Apology from me

Hey Victoria—

Thanks for the note, a little easier to digest than the last one. I wasn't sure how to respond to the other either. I certainly accept the apology as I would like to continue to remember our brief time together in a positive light. Although the circumstances were unusual, the result was a memorable, special and unique night. Revisiting it could have played havoc with our emotions, at least me. Regardless of that, and although we probably aren't going to be seeing each other for a while, I would like to stay in touch periodically.

I would like to think that we could have pulled off a rendezvous casually, with no more emotions getting involved. But I did sense both from you and myself that maybe it would get a little deeper than either of us need. I think you're a beautiful woman, inside and out, from what I've seen and heard in the past couple months, but I was concerned that we might be biting off more than we could chew, to separate the physical from the emotional. We're both dealing with lots of shit and it could have made things even more confusing – at least for me. Then it would have been hard for me to treat our rendezvous as strictly casual; I'm not the type of person who can easily or conveniently separate the two as black and white. Our encounter was genuine in that we treated each other with care and respect during the evening we shared. I'm still glad we had that night together. I was concerned another get-together could have gotten things more confusing than you or I were ready for.

I apologize for not being more forthright with you about this; your intuition was ahead of mine. I'm sorry your emotions got yanked around as a result. At the onset, it felt like you and I both thought we could be rock stars and just have a wild and crazy romp, no strings attached. That part of it sure would have been fun (as it was before), but the other stuff concerned me. It just wasn't readily apparent to me.

Again, thanks for your note. Looks like we'll have some big changes coming up soon, where to live, jobs, and I'd like to hear how you're doing. Who knows where I'll be and what I'll be up to...

Please take care in the meantime. I sincerely hope and wish the best for you and your kids.

—Michael

11/8/01
This chapter is over. It feels so strange. I emailed an apology to Michael this morning. I couldn't live with how bad I was feeling, especially about totally blaming him for everything. I think it was an honest message. I told him how much that night meant to me and why. I told him I hadn't been honest when I

said it was no big deal us getting together again. I told him it was a big deal, and while I didn't like how it was handled, I couldn't fault him for choosing what he wanted to do with his time. I also told him I did want to stay in touch, if that was okay with him. I made no reference to trying to get together in the future. I don't believe it will happen.

Surprisingly, he emailed back pretty promptly; I was afraid to read it. I cried and worried for a few minutes before I could bring myself to open it. I finally did, and it was honest and true. He basically said that we had both been fooling ourselves by making so light of a rendezvous. He mentioned several times his own emotions being confused if it had happened. I guess he could have blasted me back, or not responded at all. That would have been so awful. But this was pretty damn sad. It felt like goodbye, though he says he would like to stay in touch. I don't believe this has all happened. I don't believe I can feel so strongly for someone I only met and knew for a few hours. I don't believe how much it hurts to be unable to see him or touch him. My heart feels broken. I can't believe I'm going to go on. I can't believe other things are still going to happen in my life that might even be good. I am in turmoil over this. I am wondering if I will ever, ever hold him again.

At therapy, she asked, "Do you think you fell in love with him?" I started to cry AGAIN and said I thought maybe a piece of me had.

I feel like a light has gone out, like the bounce is gone from my step, the light is gone from my eyes, and the life is gone from me. Why does this have to feel so bad? I want to throw up and rid myself of this feeling.

I'm sitting in the car in the parking lot at Kidsports. I couldn't deal with making chit chat with the other moms. I feel lifeless. No color, no light. No love.

 "Give You Back," ©1999, by Matthew Scannell

Victoria put the headphones on and stretched her calves and hamstrings, her quads, using the station wagon parked in the driveway for support. It was another cool morning, but not too cold for a walk. She felt, more than ever, the need for physical activity. It didn't erase the pain, it didn't cover the wound, but it helped, in small ways. It kept her moving, kept her from sitting still and stewing, thinking of nothing but the betrayal she felt.

She began briskly walking down the sidewalk, taking her usual route past the bus stop, then around the corner following the sidewalk up a hill, turning into a court, taking its perimeter, then continuing around the rather awkward multi-sided block that made up her neighborhood. She passed cars and houses and yards, one person walking a dog. She had her music on loud, listening to something upbeat, to keep her moving, to distract her, if possible, from remaining forever focused on the one thing that seemed to be the only thing she thought about these days: Michael.

She moved quickly, pumping her arms and breathing rhythmically. She thought of every walk she'd taken this fall so far. She thought of how things were before she even knew Michael existed. How her life had been empty, but she had remained ignorant of all the possibilities. She thought of how things had changed once he'd entered the picture. Her thoughts were brighter, happier, more hopeful. Her anticipation of life had grown and become fun again. And now, it all just seemed a chore. She was just going through the motions, trying to survive each day. How long would it last? And thank god she could still take walks and keep moving.

Walking in Autumn

Looking forward

Leaves drifting slowly down, journeying

Air cool

Sun warm on my back

Breathe in, breathe out

The smell of asphalt and pavement

One foot in front of the other

Pacing off the distance

Arms pulling, propelling forward

Marking time with seasons

Looking up
Fiery red and orange and yellow leaves
Outlined against a depthless and clear sky,
Flawless.
How crisp and lovely the breeze!
Swallowing delicious air
Filling my lungs, my soul
The smell of dryer sheets and chimney smoke
Moving with purpose
Arms outstretched, embracing
Skipping amidst fathomless beauty
Looking down
Leaves, brown and crumpled
In drifts against the curbs
In front of my feet
The path obscured
Wind, raw and fierce
Lung-piercing oxygen
Tears streaming down
The smell of trash and ashes
Pounding pavement
Arms closed tight, holding in, keeping out
Outrunning the resolve of winter
11/9/01

11/9/01
I feel such sorrow over what could have been, and the realization of how crummy things were for me with men in the past only makes it all sadder. I'm glad to have had this experience, but everything else now pales by comparison. How will I ever find that again? My mind hurts from all the feelings. I've got to get some sleep.

Saturday Morning

Today was the day.
I was going to touch him again.
I was going to feel his heat
His kiss
His touch on my skin.
I was going to clasp his hands and breathe into the warm hair of his chest
And feel the roughness of his chin against mine
And his tongue in my mouth, my ear, all over me and in me.
Tonight was the night I would sleep in his arms,
His breath on my cheek,
His body warm against me, safe and protecting and loving.
Our sweat would mingle
Our saliva
Our bodies merging and tasting and loving.
My body was going to tingle and hum and vibrate
And my breathing would quicken to gasps and moans.
My heart was going to beat right out of my body
As I arched and moved with him.
My head was going to fill with the sounds
Of the music and the lovemaking.
I was going to explode into a thousand sparks.
I was going to wake tomorrow and not have to go.
I was going to smell him on me and not have to shower.
I was going to move with him again and again
Until we both had had our fill.
And my heart was going to be full.
It feels so empty here
Alone on the edge of my bed
In my robe and slippers.

11-10-01

11/10/01

I've tried to think on this. What have I learned? I've learned there IS good loving out there; I've learned never to settle for less because I DESERVE it. I've learned to do a better job of picking partners. Geez, look back at some of the losers I've allowed into my body. I am making better choices. Somehow, that isn't quite consoling me, though.

From: Vicki Woolfrey [vickwool@aol.com]
Sent: Sunday, November 11, 2001 4:45 PM
To: Michael Bellamy
Subject: Reflecting on it

I'm not going to do this all the time, but I just had to let you know that I woke up this morning (it's Sunday) thinking I should have been in your arms right now. This is really tougher to process than I thought it would be. Everything you said in your last email was true and honest and I agreed with all of it. It's a relief to hear that you had some emotion invested in this too. You could have been a real jerk and blasted me back or not written at all or gone ahead with this whole weekend thing knowing I had these unexpected feelings, and you could have just taken advantage. But you didn't do any of those things, and strangely, as saddened by the whole turn of events as I am, that makes me think more highly of you. You are truly unique. Maybe that's why not getting a chance to be with you again is even harder to deal with.

I attached a poem I wrote in October, and another I just wrote Friday. This second one is broken up into three pieces that represent before meeting you, after meeting you, and after we decided not to meet a second time. Well, you DID ask to see some of the poetry you inspired. There are more, but frankly, they're more intense. One of them could make a sailor blush with its language and sexual content. Poetry writing has always been a good outlet for me.

Looking on the bright side, at least I didn't have to worry about shaving or my breath all weekend. Keep me posted on your job situation and your life and your miscellaneous thoughts.

Victoria

11/11/01

Feeling pretty low. I am aching inside. Why does this hurt so bad? Is it the broken dream, or do I really have authentic feelings for this person? Is it that I feel hopeless about ever meeting anyone, or helpless because this person isn't in my life? How do I know the difference? How do I gauge it? Why do I want to run to him, find him, and hold him without letting go? If I open my eyes wide enough, will I see the big picture and realize it isn't him, but the experience that meant so much to me? How do I sort it out? By letting time pass? Excruciating days on the calendar.

I spoke to Pat tonight. She really helped me see things in a way I could deal with. She validated me, helped me accept that this would have been too intense for either of us. I mean, really. Where did I actually think this was heading? My life is here, with my kids, and while that may limit my social life and all but snuff out any love life, it is, in fact, my reality. It would have been nice to just meet and have great sex for an entire weekend. But that isn't what was going to happen. I was going to get even more attached. How healthy would that have been? I can't just go have sex—that's not me anyway, and I would have felt cheated or used or less than me. I respect Michael so much for figuring this out and being honest and true. He could have taken real advantage of me, but he didn't. I guess I'll have to take that as a good thing. Pat was right. We seem to care about each other, and that has made a casual rendezvous all but impossible. This is helping me quite a bit. I think I may be on the road to perspective here.

I hope I don't end up regretting having sent the email I wrote to Michael today. It may have been a little too honest. I attached two poems I'd written which maybe were too intense, but I don't fucking care. He doesn't have to respond. I just wanted to show him what he inspired in me. One was in the midst of all the excitement, post "glow;" the other was more of a philosophical look at my ability to change my moods with the onset and demise of hopeful fantasy—well, reading it, you might not quite get that from it, but it doesn't matter because I know how I felt. I have printed off all the emails and poems and some day, it will be a historical account of what it was like going through this monumental experience which has so many facets to it. I also left a phone message and email for Deena to see if she had any pictures of Michael from the wedding. I need to have just one to remember him by.

11/12/01
Deena emailed back. It doesn't look too promising re: the photo. The photographer didn't take any pics at the reception. Some other folks did, but she hasn't gone through them all yet. I may have to ask him again, but not just yet.

I felt a little down again today. I know it will pass. It feels less bad every day. But I was supposed to have gone away this weekend. I felt so weird. It didn't work out. Honestly, I don't know how I feel sometimes. It seems like he was the only one thinking with his head in the end. What was I thinking? Casual sex and maybe again some time in the future? Who was I trying to fool? And these fantasies in my head—what were they about? Was he going to magically be part of my life and fit in perfectly? Or I his? That isn't at all logical or realistic. But where does that leave me? Do I never get to have a relationship because of my obligations and commitments? Is that how it works? Am I alone or lonely for the rest of my children's years at home? WOW. I hate this.

11/13/01
It has been difficult at times today. It's so weird—I read through my journal last night, and I always had reservations about the whole thing, but in my mind, I still managed to build things up. How is that possible? Was I trying to talk myself out of it, but still harboring fantasies about it? Which was the real way I felt? Is it possible to have felt both ways at the same time? All day I've felt up and down, even as much as I feel I've accepted it. I felt good on my walk, strong at the gym. But there were moments when I wanted to just lay my head down and stop having to push through this routine. I am staying busy with school stuff all this week and next—trying to immerse myself in my other doings. I just don't feel very motivated. And finances are bringing me down and the thought of the holidays are making me blue. I feel twisted up inside, and confused. I can't believe how easy it is to just end whatever it was that all that WAS. Was it anything? Am I not supposed to email anymore? Am I not supposed to expect to hear back ever? It's so fucking weird.

11/15/01
Still having conflicting feelings about Michael. Of course, I haven't heard from him. I am planning to try again next week before Thanksgiving with a casual "hello, how are you?" and weekend update. On the other hand, I want

to tell him to go fuck himself for cutting off like this, though in many ways, it makes perfect sense that he did. I have this need to stay connected in some remote hope that something may exist in the future. That sounds pretty silly, but it is how I feel.

I had a dream last night that I went to retrieve emails and this long list of hundreds of emails kept scrolling by. I saw "Michael Bellamy" in the list, but it was moving too fast, and it seemed maybe some of the emails might have been viruses, and I had to be careful about opening any of them. I never did find out if it was a new email from him and what it said. I have LOTS of fantasies about him, though they're no longer of a sexual nature. They involve seeing him under some extravagant measures, like I've somehow scored some backstage passes to a U2 concert and I get to take him and watch how happy and excited he gets; or I meet up with him accidentally and we just can't help but want to be together.

It really isn't all that comforting and it doesn't make me feel that good to imagine these things. I keep wondering if he thinks of me at all anymore, or if it was just the greatest relief to ditch me, or if he is working hard to distract himself enough to avoid thinking of me. That's what I keep trying to do, none too successfully. Yesterday moved too slowly.

11/16/01
I wish I could get my mind off of him, but I can't. He is so beautiful in my memory and I still am making believe there is something there. I fantasize about contacting his Aunt Amelia, the one who encouraged me in the first place, just to get her take on it. But why would I do that? What am I hoping for (even now)? It's some kind of dream with pretty much no basis in reality.

Is it even possible to fall in love in so short a time?

And why do I reject that question only moments after writing it? Because it sounds so ridiculous!

11/17/01
I am so sick of having Michael as the only focus of my writing and thoughts, but I have this ache inside me that won't go. I only wish I could see him in person and see if this feeling is real—if there's really anything there, and if he

responds to it. I have it in my head that maybe me and the kids will go to Sandy's for New Year's this year, and that maybe I could somehow hook up with him for brunch on New Year's Day. I don't know if he'll still be in NYC, or if he has plans, or mostly, if he'd agree to see me. But it would be daytime and in a restaurant, so somewhat safer than an empty bedroom in the middle of the night with wine in me. I wonder if he'd agree to see me under those conditions. And what was it again I was hoping to achieve by doing this? Oh yeah. Staying in touch. Right. What am I really hoping would happen? That he couldn't handle the mere proximity of me and would grab us a cab and maul me in the back seat? What REALLY? I won't even follow through with this line of thought. It's pretty silly.

TENTATIVE

From: Vicki Woolfrey [vickwool@aol.com]
Sent: Monday, November 19, 2001 9:16 AM
To: Michael Bellamy
Subject: Checkin' In

Hi there. Hoping you are well and wondering what you're up to. Did you go see Bare Naked Ladies this past weekend in Maine? If so, how was it? I hear they are coming here with a bunch of other bands for some big radio-station-sponsored deal. I have been busy with school stuff mostly... "Muffins with Mom" in my daughter's class, teacher conferences, volunteering, etc. I'm helping with a Thanksgiving feast on Tuesday in my son's class as well. Had our annual church auction Saturday night. It's always a hoot. People get so excited! There are always good things to bid on, like fancy dinner parties and nights out at the theater. I offered up 3 things this year as donations: an apple cider pie fresh from the oven, and two "Vicki's Diner" meals—one for adults, and one for kids. It was quite embarrassing as the auctioneer (a friend of mine) kept adding things I would do if people would just bid ("C'mon folks! Vicki will wear a mini skirt while serving the meatloaf!"). I plan to dress up as a sassy waitress and take orders off a daily special menu. It should be fun.

I bought some good stuff too (an invite to a sock hop, a stack of cool greeting cards, etc), but my favorite thing was bidding on the chance to cut this guy's hair. His hair was down his back to his rear end. He'd been growing it for 6 years. He and his wife are going to donate the hair to "Locks for Love," which makes wigs for children with cancer. Anyways, I got to cut off half his hair, helping two causes at once. Sunday I took my kids to see a local children's production of Aladdin. My daughter has been doing theater camps the last 3 summers, and hopes to try out for a production in January. Thanksgiving promises to be special. It is the last one I will host in this house. Only my parents and my brother and his wife are expected. Everyone else that's usually here has other plans this year. I am looking forward to the smells of the food, though will try not to overdo with the eating this year. I have been on a special diet since I've been with my personal trainer that is high protein, low carbs so I can get bigger muscles. Halloween was really hard with all that candy around, and I DO plan to have pie and ice cream after the turkey, but hoping to ease up on the mashed spuds, rolls, etc. Are you going to your brother's? Have a wonderful time! Oh, and I have been raking a lot of leaves, but trying to be more zen-like about it and enjoy the moment rather than obsess about the overall task. The weather has been kind (warm, dry and not windy), and I actually did both the front and back yards in just two days!

Take care Michael.

Vicki

She hoped the tone of her email was just right...not too personal, but not chilly. She hoped it had just the right amount of upbeat information and questions, without prying or sounding too intimate. She hoped that by sending it, she wasn't dragging out an ending that should have occurred long before.

From: Michael Bellamy [MB@ka.org]
Sent: Monday, November 19, 2001 3:44 PM
To: vickwool@aol.com
Subject: Re: Checkin' In

Hey Victoria—

Just got back from the Maine weekend and hope to end up there someday, laid back and unpretentious, unlike NY. NYC is the greatest city in the world in my opinion, but that doesThe 'Ladies were fun! Highly recommended as a live show, very funny between songs. Good mix of people too, lots of families there. Good way to spend a couple of hours, so assemble some friends and go!

Cutting hair that long must have been fun — I would have bucked up for that too. A sassy waitress? Don't forget the hairnet and to call everyone "hon." And for all the ornery folks, you can tell them to "kiss your grits."

Sounds like a quiet Thanksgiving for you too. I'm heading up to my brother's where they celebrate on Friday so all his in-laws can travel a bit more leisurely and he can take his time with food preparation on Thursday.

Victoria read the email again. The first paragraph had such an abrupt interruption in the flow of what he'd been saying, she assumed he'd pushed SEND too soon and some piece of information had been erased or he'd been about to write it differently and hadn't. She tried to guess what it might have said. Might he have been saying, "...but that does not explain why it's so loud or dirty."? Was he about to say, "...but that does not excuse some jealous terrorists for crashing into its two tallest buildings and killing innocent people."? Or maybe he had something completely intimate and personal to say that he'd almost sent, then realized that she could completely have misread it and misinterpreted it and that it would only further entangle them both. Could it have been something along the lines of, "...but that does not explain how meeting you there was the most surreal night of my life."? She sat musing in front of the screen, a piece of her addictively set on the missing fragment of sentence, when suddenly another email from him appeared in the inbox.

From: Michael Bellamy [MB@ka.org]
Sent: Monday, November 19, 2001 3:55 PM
To: vickwool@aol.com
Subject: Re: Checkin' In

Whoops! Somehow sent that out by accident...

Well, trying to resume after that, think I was saying NYC is not my cup of tea, and a place like Maine is, is essentially what I was getting at.

A much better approach to raking leaves, don't you think? Part of the circle of life, to borrow from the Lion King. They should all be on the ground now; this is the time to get 'em. I actually look forward to raking and getting damp and dirty picking 'em up. And the smell. Ahh...Plus they're fun to pile up and jump into!

Time to wrap up for the day...thanks for checking in. Glad to see you and your children are doing fine and having fun together! Wishing you and your family a very happy and safe Thanksgiving!

—Michael

Victoria re-read both emails from Michael. Something about the way he'd sent out the second one in such a hurry after realizing he'd made a mistake sending the first one made her feel a twinge of love again for him. He still cared, didn't he? Somehow, he still cared. She was sure of it. Why else would he have gone to such trouble to make sure she knew he'd sent it by accident, and how was it he could continue to be so chatty? It almost felt like he didn't want the connection to end. And yet, their conversations were few and far between, and very civil. What did it mean? Anything?

11/19/01
I sent the email I composed on Friday today (Monday) to Michael. It was friendly, chatty, and no mention of sex, love, guilt, or any other remotely intimate feelings or terms. I made myself NOT check emails till tonight. He actually wrote back, and was equally FRIENDLY. I am trying not to be bummed. It's better than not hearing back at all, I suppose. Why can't I stop hoping? It only makes me unhappy.

I can't express any of this the right way. There doesn't feel like a right way TO express how I feel. So lonely and sad and disappointed and broken.

11/20/01
Just sitting here regretting, which is never good. I keep telling myself, if it had been meant to be, it would have been, and if it is meant to be some time down the road, then it will be. Why can't I accept that and go merrily on my way? Merry is the LAST word I'd use to describe myself right now.

Later...Is it just that I am more keenly aware of how completely lonely I am? Is it that Michael made me realize how true happiness has evaded me time and time again, and the stark contrast between his open, giving love and the empty, dark, and cold existence I have the rest of my life and the rest of the time is just too big? I can't even comprehend the distance between the one perfect experience and the reality of my lonely soul.

11/23/01
I fought the urge to call Michael today and leave him a message. I knew he wouldn't be home and I guess I thought it would be safer to call if I didn't actually reach him. But I didn't call. I got so bummed I had to get up off my ass and get out quick. I went to Blockbuster and rented 4 movies and bought 4 more. One is for Michael. It's Almost Famous which I had recommended to him. I am thinking of trying to get hold of 2 copies of Go also—one for me and one for him, since we both got the reference he made. But I'm nervous to remind him of that night, though that's rather silly since that's really all we have between us. Well, the two flicks I watched tonight (Clerks and Chasing Amy) were great. Both by the same guy, with some of the same characters in them. Good laughs. Too tired to continue.

11/24/01
I'm lying here in bed wondering if I've completely imagined EVERYTHING about my so-called feelings for Michael. I don't know how to find out the truth either. I keep wishing I could see him again to just see if there's anything there aside from physical lust and total gratitude for having given me the best sex of my life. I mean, I keep thinking, "He's the one" and "I think I love him" and yet, what? I'm down here, he's up there, and there's no current plan to ever see one another again. Oh sure, I keep thinking up ways to try and see him. Some are a little sneaky, like just showing up at his door. That could be dangerous. Some are more planned, like going to Sandy's for New Year's and trying to get together with him while I'm up there, just to meet for lunch or something, even with my kids—no plan to rendezvous in a cheap motel. Or to see him over the summer (still so far way) if he moves to Maine and I'm up that way for Star Island (again WITH the kids). Is this all just fantastical wishful thinking? Why can't I move on, and should I let it go at all when he could in fact BE the one? Does he have any feelings for me? If so, why hasn't he expressed them? If not, why would I want to put myself through this? It's all a little too confusing. But I imagine him here beside me and my heart feels full.

From: Vicki Woolfrey [vickwool@aol.com]
Sent: Sunday, November 25, 2001 2:57 PM
To: Michael Bellamy
Subject: So how was yours?

Hi Michael! How was your Thanksgiving? Did you spend the whole weekend with your brother and family? We had a really nice time here. All the food turned out great, and everyone was in good spirits. My 22-year-old nephew (son of my older sister) turned up at the last minute, which was such a nice surprise. He played with my kids a lot, and even did dishes! My brother and his wife ended up spending the night with us, which was also a treat. I got to go for a walk Friday morning to try and walk off some of those mashed potatoes, and my kids got extra time with their aunt and uncle. Also had a visit from a dear friend and her kids that afternoon, which we all enjoyed. Over the long weekend, I went to see Harry Potter! It was great! Have you seen it? Read any of the books? I thought it might be too scary for my kids, but they enjoyed it quite a bit. We're reading the book aloud together too, which is fun. I make good voices for the characters. Also rented a bunch of movies. Have you ever seen any of the Kevin Smith films? I rented Clerks and Chasing Amy, both excellent. Also got a little xmas shopping done. Do you shop for all your nieces and nephews, or what? I am only buying for my own kids this year, as well as the two little ones I watch. Bought myself a couple things too. It's nice to have a few presents under the tree from Santa when the kids get so many! I am framing a poster of chili peppers I had bought a few months ago. It was too big to fit in a frame I could buy already made, so I'm sinking some big bucks into having it professionally framed to hang in my chili pepper kitchen. Can't wait to hang it! Well, I'm talking your ear off, so I think I'll head out to the gym one last time before the kids get home from their dad's. Hope you had a great time with your family!

Vicki

11/25/01

Sadly, the fantasies continue. I emailed him today to ask about his Thanksgiving and tell him about mine. I also emailed Sandy and Deena about possibly going up to NJ and visiting NYC at New Year's. Kids have off from school the week between xmas and New Year's, and I have them that weekend and on New Year's, so I thought, what the heck? Visit with Sandy, possibly hook up with Deena, and yes, maybe see Michael. I started the ball rolling, so we'll see what happens. I dream too much. I'm embarrassed for myself, some of the things I imagine. Driving back from the gym, I was imagining I was in love with him (again). I really don't know if I'd recognize "in love" if it happened. I can't tell what it is I feel for him. Gratitude? Mind-blowing awe of his sexual expertise? Is he just some object for me to focus my attentions on since I have no one and so desperately want someone in my life, and he was nice to me? I just can't get a handle on it at all.

...Just watched Go again just so I could see the scene where they talk about getting tantric. I love that. I love that night. And a part of me does love that guy.

From: Michael Bellamy [MB@ka.org]
Sent: Monday, November 26, 2001 3:45 PM
To: vickwool@aol.com
Subject: Re: So how was yours?

Was quite fine, thank you. Was spent entirely in New England with friends and family. Did a bit of hiking, eating, playing with the nieces, eating, and...uh, eating. I have lots of hiking to undergo to burn this past weekend off. So much running around visiting everyone that I crashed a little bit ago. The old head bob at work – probably for 15 minutes right after lunch when I was good and full. (more eating again) Happy to hear your weekend had some pleasant surprises! Very nice. Borrowed the first Potter book from a friend so will read that first before seeing the movie. Heard the movie is quite good. Can't stand that kid in interviews though...

Have seen Clerks and Chasing Amy (I think), peculiar movies but entertaining in that they're off-center.

Are you a Red Hot Chili Pepper fan too? And do you like jalapenos and habaneros? This is a real thing with you...

Is it really X-mas time now? I want to go back to Halloween again, do T-Day again, then maybe I'll be ready for late December. Lord and Taylor here in NYC was already cranking out X-mas tunes 2 weeks ago! There are no more off seasons! Of course, I'm kidding, I'm happy for all the little guys who start to get wound up, inc. my nephews and nieces.

Fly to SC to visit my folks on Wednesday for 6 days — looking forward to it, a bit of much needed R and R, I hope.

Glad you and yours are doing well — will talk soon.

—Michael

From: Vicki Woolfrey [vickwool@aol.com]
Sent: Monday, November 26, 2001 5:35 PM
To: Michael Bellamy
Subject: RE: So how was yours?

Glad your Thanksgiving was good too. I am ashamed to say that I still have so much food in the fridge that I am thinking of throwing some of it out! I don't like to do that, but the jeans are telling me that I need to cease with the apple pie and ice cream. I am having a really hard time typing because I have two band aids on my fingers. Just went to give blood, but I didn't pass the iron test, so they rejected me! I hate that. I kind of knew it would happen, but I wanted to at least try. I did successfully give blood last spring for my nephew who had heart surgery. I ate a lot of red meat, greens, and beets beforehand, though. Oh well.

I've never seen the actor from Harry Potter in an interview except in a magazine. The girl who plays Hermione (Potter's friend) looks so much like my friend's little girl that it is uncanny! Apparently lots of other people think so too and are starting to call her Hermione at school. Weird. In Monsters, Inc. (did you see that?) the little girl Boo looked just like another friend's daughter. Something VERY weird is going on.

As to the chili peppers, it has indeed become a theme for me...at least in my kitchen where they grace dish towels, pot holders, the walls (ceramic and real ones dried), and are also present in my salt-and-pepper shakers, napkin holder, soap dispenser and even dish drainer! As for the group, I like a lot of their stuff, but they're a little hard core for me.

And I couldn't agree with you more about xmas coming so soon. I love this time of year, and also despair at it too. People rush around so much they get mad when they can't find a parking space or have to wait in line, and they spend like crazy. It seems to lose the spirit somewhere. However, I'm trying to make an attempt to decorate the house with lights, etc. BEFORE the week before Christmas this time, so maybe I'm getting into the spirit of it after all. I got my first xmas card today in the mail, and I'm mailing mine out this week. That is one habit I can't seem to break myself of. I really enjoy getting pictures of people's families and letters and so on, so I started mailing them to everyone I know as a result.

Well, I think I've touched on every topic possible, so here ends it. Have a terrific time with your folks! Hope they are well. Using up that vacation time, I see. Any word on the job situation? Or might you take some time off before hitting the want ads? Talk to you soon.

Vicki

11/26/01
Heard from Michael today. His emails remain friendly and talkative. I am really adoring him at this moment. But as I said to Sandy today, I never can tell when I'm imagining or reading into things, or when it's real. When I'm at the bus stop in my sweaty gym clothes trying to figure out what to make for dinner and wondering if I'll be on time to give blood and worrying about making cookies and xmas ornaments for the family fun night at church, well, it seems a little ludicrous to be imagining anything else in my life. But damn, he's cute.

11/28/01
I am 100% aware of how little Michael and I fit into each other's lives, and at the same time how desperately I wish he were in my life in more than some email friendship. I feel like it was all a dream, though I have some proof it wasn't. I wish someone would send me a photo of him. I would very much like to put that piece of my life into perspective and be able to look at it without being submerged IN it.

12/2/01
Feel a new peace with my existence. I'm so immersed in the activities of a domestic mom that I keep reminding myself of where I am and who I am. I can't even fathom being with a man now. I have put away the frivolous thoughts and fantasies and am dealing with the here and now and it's damn busy! I have no time for games or dreaming. I am comfortable just letting my belly hang out and my face look zitty and pale. I just want to be me. I'm not sad or disappointed anymore. Just really tired.

12/4/01
I've been raking—a lot. Got entire back yard (including plant beds) done yesterday and today, as well as walking and going to gym both days, so have been getting quite the workout. Raking of course makes me think of Michael. I went ahead and mailed him the two videos I bought him for xmas. What the fuck. I'd already ordered and paid for them. So what. Also talked to Deena today about seeing her over New Year's, but doesn't sound like she'll be around, so my chances of seeing Michael are now close to nil. Can't decide whether to mention to him that I'll be up that way. What's the point? He doesn't want to see me, and I'm not so sure anymore that I want to see him, so maybe not. I'm going to see Sandy, not him.

12/6/01
Had my first REAL dream about Michael. Dreamt I was with Deena and she finally had her wedding photos. Strangely, in them I was wearing the bridesmaid dress I wore back in 1986. Also, my glasses. We looked at a lot of pictures (ones that never took place at the wedding), but I was anxious to see the group shot taken in Central Park. When we finally came across it, it was like a mini movie—almost like an enchanted picture where all the people moved and talked, as in Harry Potter films. I spied Michael at once at the back of the group with his video camera to his eye. But he put it down, and I found that if I angled the photo, I could get better views of him. He was wearing different clothes too. He circled the perimeter of the group to the right and came right up to where I was. The group was beginning to disperse. I checked him out as he passed in front of me. He then turned to walk through the center of the group, so that his body actually touched mine as he walked past. (Of course, none of this actually ever happened). In my dream, though, it was apparent we were attracted to one another from the start (while in reality, I know I didn't even notice him till we were seated at the same table at the reception). It was a cool dream.

Later...So guess what arrived in the mail today? THE PICTURE!! The same one I'd been dreaming of! I had this joyful moment of satisfaction or something when it arrived. There I was in the front row (sans pink dress, T.G.) and there, off to the left, was the real Michael. It was a pretty clear picture of him, though it didn't look much like I remembered. I felt happy to have it. I don't *expect I'll ever get a good pic of him. He certainly isn't likely to come up with one, and none of the Cashells have stepped forward with any.*

From: Vicki Woolfrey [vickwool@aol.com]
Sent: Friday, December 07, 2001 1:08 PM
To: Michael Bellamy
Subject: Your answering machine sucks!

Yo Michael, just tried to leave you a message, but I can't even tell if I did, and I got cut off before I finished babbling, but hey, I WAS babbling. What I was saying was, got the group shot from Deena's wedding (which is way cool), and there you were! Question: Were any other pics taken of you that day that you recall? I am doing my photo journaling and I am going to do a page about that wedding, and it would mean so much to have a photo of you (preferably taken that day). It would have been great if the photographer had taken shots of each table. Oh well. If you don't know of any (and I've already asked the Cashells), please, please, please try and find a relatively recent one, or at least ask someone to take a mug shot of ya and send it my way! Hope all is well. I'm doing great.

Vicki

PS I planted 100 bulbs day before yesterday! I'm a gardening goddess!

From: Michael Bellamy [MB@ka.org]
Sent: Friday, December 07, 2001 3:12 PM
To: vickwool@aol.com
Subject: Re: Your answering machine sucks!

Yo Vicki—

S'up? (street slang for "Hello, how are you?" if yo ain't down...)

Sorry 'bout the machine, it's chock full of stuff I need to delete, so hence the cutoff. There are numerous messages I want to record on my camcorder before I delete them, just haven't done it yet. But I'll look forward to it tonight. Heading up to Boston to see old college buds this weekend. A cool city, even if it is so damn milky white.

I'll look for that photo from Deena in the mail. And I'll see again if I can dredge up a decent photo, as long as you have noble intentions with it. Noble, yes? If you really, really, really want one, I'll see what I can do. Thanks for the shot of you and your kids – you are a beautiful family. Sincerely. You're lucky to have 2 shining stars like you do...

Setting up and nervous about my post-KA job – the major pre-occupation I have these days. Jobs aren't growing on trees in NYC these days...

Again, thanks for the holiday greeting from you. I enjoyed hearing about your children and their endeavors – budding movie stars, it sounds like.

Got's to wrap up, so I'll bid you adieu for the weekend.

We'll talk next week...

—Michael

12/8/01
He did email back. Who knows, maybe he'll send a photo. Stayed up entirely too late last night re-reading "our story" (puke)—all the emails and poems. It's rather sickening. Sometimes I still fancy that he's "the one" and that we'll have some Hollywood ending where we run down a crowded street trying to find each other before it's too late and live happily ever-fucking-after. Then I get grumpy and think how ridiculous that seems. Then I get bummed out because I feel lonely and pathetic resorting to fantasy followed by angry bitterness.

12/9/01
In and out of my love fantasy today once again thinking of Michael as some chosen one, then thinking about the cat box or gymnastics or church crap and he seems the farthest possible thing from real.

From: Vicki Woolfrey [vickwool@aol.com]
Sent: Sunday, December 09, 2001 9:06 PM
To: Michael Bellamy
Subject: Got tired of the other subject line but couldn't think of a new one

So, define "noble". I am not planning to use your picture for dart practice, if that's what you mean. My photo journaling of Deena and Todd's wedding simply wouldn't' be complete without you, though. SO PLEASE, YES, SEND A PHOTO! Thanks!

Tentative

What do you mean record messages on your camcorder? I don't get it.

Hope you had fun in Boston. I go up there usually once a year (Quincy) to visit my friend who lives above a funeral home. The hair place across the street is called "The Hair After". Get it? HAHHAHAHAHAHA I did some xmas shopping this weekend and got a massage. Nothing too earth shattering. Rented 2 more videos: Diary of Bridget Jones and Legally Blonde. Both fun, and oddly, both involved scenes where the main character showed up at a costume party in a bunny outfit, and no one else was dressed up. Isn't that weird?

Have you looked on the internet for jobs yet? Surely your skills are in demand, though it might not be in NYC. Thought you wanted to get out of there anyway...? What is your title, anyway? I looked on Monster.com under "videographer" but that doesn't appear to be a job title. Speaking of NYC, the kids and I are going to be up that way the weekend before New Year's, in Lawrenceville. Was hoping to see Deena & Todd, but doesn't sound like anyone will be in town. We'll be going into the city one day...my kids haven't ever been. Maybe see FAO Schwartz, or perhaps a horse and buggy through Central Park? Haven't figured it all out yet. It's my friend's daughter's bday too (the one who looks like Hermione—how's the Harry Potter book coming?), so party one day, and of course there's New Year's Eve when they always serve lobster. I wish I could have scored some Lion King tickets, but they simply aren't to be had. Will you be around, or do you even know? Is lunch on New Year's Day a possibility? That's when we're heading back home. Actually, I suspect we will all be recovering in one form or another, but it seems a crime to be that nearby and not at least attempt to say hello.

Well, as Tigger says, TTFN (ta-ta for now). (My slang isn't as "down" as yours, I guess, WORD UP!)

Vicki

And sing this mantra over and over:

All I want for Christmas is a brand new fuckin' job,

A brand new fuckin' job,

A brand new fuckin' job

NOTE: Your assignment is to answer ALL questions posed in above email.

Releasing the Dove

From: Michael Bellamy [MB@ka.org]
Sent: Monday, December 10, 2001 8:46 AM
To: vickwool@aol.com
Subject: Here's a new subject line...

a. define noble – yes, a non-defaming use of a picture. A picture of osama bin laden as a dart board is acceptable however...

b. I have several very entertaining messages on my answering machine that I would like to preserve before deleting. A way to do that is simply hold a camcorder close by to record the sound.

c. Yes, I get it. Gallows humor...

d. Yes, it is weird. And ironic as my friends and I also rented Legally Blonde – not too bad, huh?

e. Yes, have posted on Monster though no serious bites.

f. Do want to get out of NYC...but not just yet. Want to leave on my own terms, so a bit longer.

g. Producer

h. your call – probably depend on the weather, though. Too cold for a buggy ride?

i. haven't picked it up yet – got a few books queued ahead of it

j. don't yet know, Boston, Florida, CT or NY

k. that's right, don't even know, see above

l. yes, it is a possibility, but could very well depend on the previous two and hangover intensity, but maybe it could work.

You think I'm not down 'wit, TTFN ?? Remember the nieces? And nephews? If not from my own childhood, all the little guys keep me young..."The wonderful thing about Tiggers, ..."

Lion King on Broadway is AWESOME! Have been twice, most recently with 6 members of my family last May. Waited over a year for the show after getting tickets though...but still worth it.

Amen to the job song, can you get Adam Sandler to sing it for me?

Tentative

From: Vicki Woolfrey [vickwool@aol.com]
Sent: Monday, December 10, 2001 9:33 PM
To: Michael Bellamy
Subject: This subject line lacks creativity

Thanks for so dutifully answering all my queries. Geez, I didn't actually expect you to give me your recommendations for where to take kids in NYC, but thanks! I tend to agree with you on the cold part. I need to take them up for like a few days and see all the cool stuff some time. Maybe in the spring...

So is there any criteria one must meet to rate a permanent record on your answering machine hall of fame? I'll have to think of something creative. A song perhaps? Sung in the voice of a lounge singer, and slightly off key? I'll give it some thought.

Okay, what's in Florida? Besides sunshine.

I can't believe you've seen Lion King twice. One of the advantages of living around the city, I suppose. Well, how many times have you seen Rent? I know I asked you this before, but I don't remember. Well, I'm going for #6 some time this coming year. It's an addiction, I'm sad to say.

Tomorrow is my very last training session at the gym. I feel there will be a period of withdrawal. Who will force me to do "just one more" and embarrass me to no end announcing loudly that my armpits need shaving? But, I ran out of dough. I'll have to try and keep up with it on my own. Well, once again, the bus stop beckons. So I'll bid YOU adieu! (So impressed you could spell that).

Vicki

From: Vicki Woolfrey [vickwool@aol.com]
Sent: Monday, December 10, 2001 9:33 PM
To: Michael Bellamy
Subject: Oh, I forgot

Ooops, meant to mention I mailed you a package...now don't freak out! It's harmless! It's a Christmas gift I HAD to get you, and it's perfectly innocent and okay to open in public. And don't feel weird about the whole "Oh, should I get that person a gift since they got me one?" thing...no, not necessary! I just felt the urge, and I did it. Put it under your tree, though! HO HO HO!

JUST FRIENDS

12/11/01
Well now, THERE was the type of dream I thought would have come a lot sooner. Dreamt I was on Star Island and who should be there but Michael. He approached me and within a few minutes said something to the effect of, "What are we going to do? We're so in love," and I said, "You mean YOU feel that way?" and he nodded his head yes, as if of course. We kissed and embraced a lot. Then we spent a lot of time lounging around in each other's arms trying to make decisions. We listened to some man read Harry Potter aloud in some room; we talked about job possibilities for Michael; we tried to decide what to do with the rest of our day; we missed all the meals because we couldn't bear to leave each other's arms; we talked about going out on the rocks to kiss. Somehow, he communicated that our ill-fated weekend still shouldn't have happened.

Anyway, there was more to the dream, but the basic theme was my true love and the place I love the most—together. What could be better than that?

Later...No response yet to email stating I'd sent an innocent xmas gift. Well, fuck it. I'm loving him, or at least the thought of him. It's kind of pleasant, in an abstract way.

From: Michael Bellamy [MB@ka.org]
Sent: Tuesday, December 11, 2001 4:38 PM
To: vickwool@aol.com
Subject: Re: This subject line lacks creativity

Have seen Rent once, which is enough. Now before you list "5,635" reasons why it is so great, I guess my rationale is based on the fact that Taye Digges wasn't in it...very brief today, it's train time...but 6 times? Phew! You undoubtedly have the soundtrack.

More later...

From: Vicki Woolfrey [vickwool@aol.com]
Sent: Wednesday, December 12, 2001 8:42 AM
To: Michael Bellamy
Subject: RE: This subject line lacks creativity

Dare I admit I can practically sing the entire show (rather badly)? Yes, I have the soundtrack and have listened to it too many times to count (possibly 525,600 times...that is the actual number...sorry, but had to mention that). What's weird is Taye Digges is on the soundtrack, and now whenever I see him in a movie, I can hear the Rent character, Benny. It's funny and annoying at the same time ("Hey you, yeah, move over/get your ASS off that Range Rover!"). He is a talented guy. And another annoying fact: my sister-in-law, my brother and I (they've seen it several times too) cannot help but quote it ALL the frigging time. Other people don't know what we're referring to, and it distracts from whatever the situation is, because then we start to laugh and sing even more of it. Example: say the doorbell rings. We say "The door" in the same way Roger says it (see, unless you've seen it that many times, you wouldn't know what I mean) and then follow up with the words that come after. It's rather endless.

Uh oh, Connor's stomach is rumbling (as is mine), so time to make some breakfast. Bye!

From: Michael Bellamy [MB@ka.org]
Sent: Wednesday, December 12, 2001 2:34 PM
To: vickwool@aol.com
Subject: RE: This subject line lacks creativity

Hey, I'm actually impressed my guess at the number was as close as it was! I coulda won the Price Is Right with that approximation.

Check out imdb.com, if you haven't already, for info on every movie and star out there, inc. Taye Digges from Rochester, NY, etc...

I'm the same way with certain movies and my friends are the same – Trainspotting, Swingers, Go, First Blood, Jaws, etc...something happens and it cues a line. And half the time at least, no one else knows what you're talking about. Happens all the time!

Are you an Ally McBeal fan? I'm not really, but I know Taye was on the show at one point...plus House on Haunted Hill, etc.

all on imdb.com

more later,

Michael

From: Vicki Woolfrey [vickwool@aol.com]
Sent: Wednesday, December 12, 2001 9:48 PM
To: Michael Bellamy
Subject: Blah blah blah blah blah blah blah

Yes, but what gift would you have WON on Price is Right? That estimate actually kind of sucked! I would like to win a new car myself.

I loved Swingers! That's the same director that did Go! Did you know THAT? (I have a feeling you did know that). I rented those two back-to-back a couple weekends ago. Haven't seen Trainspotting or First Blood. Wait, is First Blood Sly Stallone or Jean Claude Van Damme? I love Jean Claude (but clearly not enough to know what movies he's in). I also quote Terminator. Haven't seen that one in a while, though...I'll have to dig it out! I used to watch Ally McBeal, but it got too weird or something. I've seen Taye in the movie "Best Man" and I keep meaning to rent "Stella's got her groove back" or whatever it's called. Maybe I'll have a Taye night some time. He is so hot!

I listened to the Rent soundtrack again after that email. I love it so much! Sang right along. Another favorite sequence of lines: "This lot is full of mother fuckin' artists!/Hey...Artist...you...got a dollar?" I don't know why, I just like it.

I'm so tired. I'm going to bed now. Have been spending all week trying to find out what to do with Chloe and gymnastics...long boring story, but we've been out every night at one place or another either trying a class or checking out a new place, or whatever. Also have her bday party this weekend, so have been busy THINKING about what I still have to do, but not actually DOING it. And then there's our big Christmas Choir Concert on Sunday (just got home from practice). I have to wear a long skirt. I prefer short. It's no fair. Okay, GOOD NIGHT!

12/13/01
Had a horrible night. Should've been good. Got an email from Michael that was pleasing and responded. Planned to go to bed early and go to gym this a.m. But I tossed and turned all frigging night and of course blew off the gym, which is distressing. I'm really tired. Thinking ahead to our weekend in NJ and visiting with Sandy for a few days. That will be such a relief. I know the chances of hooking up with Michael are probably one in a million—he sounds as though he'll be off somewhere—but I look forward to emailing him till then. After that, he doesn't even have a job lined up, and hence, no email. Don't know how we'll stay in touch. Guess a phone call once in a while, but certainly not this daily or even weekly communication. I think that was the crux of my sleeplessness. I feel that our time is coming to yet another kind of end, and it is supremely bumming me out. He may move or just fall out of touch, and what can I do but let it be known I'd like to stay in touch? Keep the door open, Pat said. Oooh, but it gets mighty drafty.

From: Vicki Woolfrey [vickwool@aol.com]
Sent: Thursday, December 13, 2001 9:18 AM
To: Michael Bellamy
Subject: Daily Affirmation

When you look at that face in the mirror each morning, just say with conviction, "You are SO Money!"

Signed,

One of the "Babies" who thinks you are

(meant to tell you this in last email, but was brain dead; am even more so after a completely sleepless night. Remind me next time not to list all the things I have to do in an email to a friend just before bed)

12/13/01
My latest fantasy involves the fact that he quotes movies, one of which of course is Go which I recognized when we were together , another of which is Swingers which is made by same director and I recently rented it with Go and I quoted it to him in my last email. My fantasy is this: he has made a deal with his friends, who also frequently quote this movie, that if a woman ever said those words to him, that if he (or any of them) were told they were "money" by

a woman, that that would prove she was "the one" and they'd have to drop everything and be with her, maybe even propose. I am clearly lacking sleep and brain cells, but that is where my dream world is taking me today. Like he'd just show up and tell me I was the one and he couldn't live without me! (Cinderella complex at work here, no doubt!) Why do I sometimes feel like I'm totally in love with him, and then having written it or even thought it, I think it's a ridiculous notion? And sometimes the idea of finding a man who totally "got" me is so good, and I want to find that man and, like, bear his children; and then I slap myself and say what I NEED is a man who can handle that I'm my own person, I'm DONE having kids, and I don't WANT to get married ever again! Schizo. That's me. Purely schizo.

From: Michael Bellamy [MB@ka.org]
Sent: Thursday, December 13, 2001 4:28 PM
To: vickwool@aol.com
Subject: Re: Daily Affirmation

I was thinking just that! OK, Victoria is tired, she's telling me she's tired, but she's still writing!! Why doesn't she get some sleep? Oh well, hope you get some zzz's tonight...

We use Swingers often, just today, Vegas baby! Vegas! became Philly baby, Philly! as we're off to see college friends. All the New Years ideas are from high school or college friends located all over – will see what pans out.

First Blood is the first Rambo movie – best of the lot, which might not be saying much, but it is decent. Trainspotting is heavy duty – not a pick-me up – deals with heroin abuse. You're right – Ally has gotten kinda weird.

Taye movie night could be fun – for all the ladies of course. Yeah, he's a good looking dude, be sure to get House on Haunted Hill for the scary installment of the screening... silly, but creepy.

all right, "hey, artist, got a dollar?" – shutting up shop to go get some sleep.

More later – ps that osama dick is a real mofo if that tape is authentic – disgusting excuse for a human

From: Vicki Woolfrey [vickwool@aol.com]
Sent: Friday, December 14, 2001 7:44 AM
To: Michael Bellamy
Subject: RE: Daily Affirmation

Young man! Watch your language! "dick" and "mofo" in the same sentence... well, I guess the situation warranted it. I agree wholeheartedly. Yes, I wonder too about the authenticity. Isn't it always so perfectly orchestrated? I sometimes can't really believe any of what I see on tv.

So now you're off to Philly! Question: do your neighbors know you exist? You are gone every weekend! Have a blast!

I got z's last night, but they were not the "sleep like a log" z's or "sleep like a baby" z's. They were so weird! Had many strange dreams last night. Think I may have taken acid instead of Sudafed yesterday...just kidding. Love that scene in Go when the guy has taken 2 ecstasy's and is having the head trip at the supermarket...and with the cat! That was so fucked up! Oh, and speaking of dreams, I forgot to tell you that the day the Central Park picture arrived, I swear, I dreamed the night before that I was looking through all the wedding photos (which of course I haven't seen) and was anxiously awaiting seeing that one, and when I did, it was so cool! It was an enchanted photo (a la Harry Potter, which you haven't read yet!) and the people moved. One strange thing: I was wearing the pink bridesmaid dress I wore to a friend's wedding in 1986. Must be that acid again.

Well, have a great weekend. The clock is ticking for you, and I don't mean till New Year's. Will your last day of work actually be December 31st? That's pretty f—ked up, if so. Wish me luck singing in my choir thing (it WON'T be "Sodomy/ it's between God and me!"...) (That is another favorite line from Rent). (Excuse me, it's early and I'm groggy, and it's FRIDAY)

Happy Friday!

Vicki

From: Michael Bellamy [MB@ka.org]
Sent: Friday, December 14, 2001 10:56 AM
To: vickwool@aol.com
Subject: Thank you!

Hey Santa —

Couldn't wait until X-Mas, had to open the presents! Thanks! Go and Almost Famous, which, honest to God was on HBO? last night...very ironic

so, will watch it in its entirety very soon — autobio. about Cameron Crowe, right?

Go, I know all too well, so will use for brushing up on lines...

"what are you guys doing in here?"

"raping small children..."

"yaht, yat, yaht!" Taye Digges utters this fantastic cutaway laugh in the Vegas hotel room — such a subtle yet effective shot to include

Many thanks again for the tapes! A very nice and appreciated Christmas gift!

Good luck with all the dancing and singing this weekend...try to stay off the acid, at least the brown variety. I heard that's a bad trip, man.

Off to the company holiday party in an hour, (big yeah) then on to Philly where the chances of having more than 2 beers are considerable. Good to see the crew together. I'm quite sure my neighbors think I'm CIA at this point...

signing off —

Special Agent Michael

From: Vicki Woolfrey [vickwool@aol.com]
Sent: Friday, December 14, 2001 3:08 PM
To: Michael Bellamy
Subject: Top Secret***For Your Eyes ONLY

Special Agent Michael,

Taking a quick breather between my kazillion errands and making homemade xmas ornaments for all 12 teachers involved in my children's education...before baking bday cake, wrapping presents, etc. Oh, yes a short breather...glad you liked the present. Couldn't wait? Geez! What were you like as a child? Hope you never did what my sister and I did once...sneak down early, open some gifts, then attempt to re-wrap them and replace them under the tree. No,no,no, Almost Famous is not about Cameron Crowe (at least I don't think so). Just watch and see. Talk about acid trips! (I...AM...A GOLDEN GOD!)

Take it easy on the egg nog, but yeah, go for it on the beers! Talk to you next week. Oh, and don't ride in the trunk on the way to Philly.

—99

From: Michael Bellamy [MB@ka.org]
Sent: Friday, December 14, 2001 3:23 PM
To: vickwool@aol.com
Subject: Re: Top Secret**For Your Eyes ONLY

I...AM...A GOLDEN GOD!????? What did I miss?

you'll love this present snooping story...

about 8 years old and I found where my mom was stashing some of our presents — under their bed. So, I look around, no one is watching and I stick my arm underneath and pull a few gifts out. None for me, damn, so give it another go...all of the sudden, hot sharp pain all over the underside of my forearm! A damn wasp is repeatedly stinging my arm! It's guardian-attack wasp for the presents! I got out of there ASAP...

guess I had a relapse last night! Thank god you didn't arm it with guard bees!

From: Vicki Woolfrey [vickwool@aol.com]
Sent: Saturday, December 15, 2001 9:30 PM
To: Michael Bellamy
Subject: RE: Top Secret**For Your Eyes ONLY

Thanks so MUCH for the laughs! Needed desperately today as it was exhausting and had an ill-fated ending. Here's the Reader's Digest Version:

Chloe's bday party. Ahhhhh. Every year a new challenge. 10 kids, downtown Manassas, crossing busy streets, entering room with many breakable things, teacher of pottery class with absolutely no sense of humor or enjoyment of kids, kids who don't WANT to make a mug, kids who would rather play with the clay than actually make something with it, kids who are thirsty and when get no response from teacher, start to ask her, "Do YOU ever get thirsty?" then "What do you DO when you're thirsty?" followed closely by "WHERE do you get the drink?" The teacher never even got a clue. 10 kids back across busy streets, back home for pizza, cake, presents, chaos. A couple hours of respite where my kids play and I clean mess from party, then out to dinner with family. All this captured on throw-away camera cuz film I bought for good camera is wrong kind for my camera and won't go in, and thankfully I HAVE a throwaway camera. Topped off by leaving camera at restaurant, calling restaurant, and them telling me they do not see it. SO BUMMED. Entire day is on this camera. Entire fucking day.

Came home to go to bed essentially, but had to send email via pager to ex to see if he knew where camera was, so saw emails, and luckily got yours! Loved the story! Were you ever discovered? What did you tell you mom re: stings?

As to the golden god, you'll just have to watch the movie. Hope you had (actually, currently, as I write this, you most likely still are HAVING) a great time with your buds! You are so lucky to have a circle of friends as you do! I don't have friends...from college, that is! Went to local school, very big, didn't meet anyone new. Just a few friends I already had in high school! All my friends now are post then pretty much, sort of.

Good night! I shouldn't be trying to make sense at this point! And, re-reading this email, I DON'T!

12/16/01

Have had Michael on my mind, as usual. Read an email last night he sent Friday afternoon. It was a funny story from his childhood. At times like that, when he's sharing something personal with me and making me laugh, I feel so close to him, and I believe I love him. But only an hour before that, as I got kids ready for bed and felt so crappy, it was easy for me to think, "Eh, why bother emailing at all this coming week? What do we have?" It keeps coming down to hopes and dreams on my part, though it seems a tentative friendship has arisen from the ashes of our passion. Where it will lead, if anywhere, is anyone's guess. I know what I wish (sometimes), but that isn't usually a good predictor. I have to get up and start getting ready. Today is our big choir concert.

From: Vicki Woolfrey [vickwool@aol.com]
Sent: Sunday, December 16, 2001 1:27 PM
To: Michael Bellamy
Subject: Footnote

Connor put the camera in his dad's coat pocket. It is now in my purse and ready to be developed! RELIEF

12/18/01
I am feeling a little—not down, exactly, but as though the future stretches out too long before me. I sometimes see parenting as putting off all the rest of my life. I put 110% into being a mom, and all other areas disappear, from intimate relationships to careers to personal pursuits. I try to look at it as a "phase" of my life, but I keep thinking, by the time they're gone I'll be 50 or older, and I can't see a romance or career STARTING then…it's such an odd place to be—on hold, yet experiencing something I treasure and that not everyone gets the opportunity to experience. I want to absorb it, enjoy it, learn from it, grow from it, make the most of it, give it my all, etc., etc. But it breaks my spirit sometimes to have to pass up other things. Wanting to have been settled into a relationship and a home at this point in my life, and neither of those areas is secure. The future is so unknown. I guess it's only a trick we play on ourselves ever believing we KNOW what's ahead, but the changes that come are so unexpected, and sometimes so unwanted. I feel so unstable right now with nothing certain—my place of residence this time next year, the state of my separation, the possibility of working, the chances and risks I'll take. I want to have some sense that it will all turn out okay, and I just don't have that right now. I wish so much I had someone special to support me through this. What is the likelihood I'll have someone in my life anytime soon? I'm so lonely. I live for my emails from Michael, soon to end. I can't rely on him or email to fulfill this emptiness.

From: Vicki Woolfrey [vickwool@aol.com]
Sent: Thursday, December 20, 2001 10:15 AM
To: Michael Bellamy
Subject: Stay in touch, you!

Michael,

Decided to have my Taye Diggs night last night. Watched "How Stella Got Her Groove Back." IT SUCKED SO BAD! Not even a nakey shot of Taye could save this loser! Bad acting, stupid and predictable story line with melodrama thrown in where it should have just stayed light and sexy, and the acting was horrific! Sorry Taye, but YEAH, it was bad. Have "House on Haunted Hill" lined up, but I must confess, I'm not a fan of scary movies, so don't know if I'll get up my nerve to actually watch it. Maybe I'll fast forward to parts with Taye.

This week is wrapping up quickly...I can't believe it's only a few DAYS till Christmas! Geez, I still have so much to do! Next week my kids will be home all week, so don't know how we'll fare...that can always go either way...having fun staying in pj's all morning can quickly change to fighting over who's turn it is to pick a video.

Been thinking you will not have email access soon...should we switch to letters or phone calls or telepathic messages? I'll miss these conversations with you. Perhaps at your next job you'll have email again...you really SHOULD get a computer for home! What's the job status, anyway? Any bites?

Have a terrific Christmas and New Year's! If you end up in town New Year's Day, give me a call! Otherwise, have fun! AND STAY IN TOUCH!

Victoria

PS Oh yeah, I forgot...just heard Opera Man singing at a benefit for NY firefighters and police (on a tribute cd), and he was so funny ragging on bin laden, etc. Have you heard this?

From: Michael Bellamy [MB@ka.org]
Sent: Thursday, December 20, 2001 10:33 AM
To: vickwool@aol.com
Subject: Re: Stay in touch, you!

Hi Victoria —

Can't say I've seen "Stella" but your review is the latest I've heard to stay clear of it, so thanks for the warning. "House" is no Academy award winner mind you, really falls into the teenage gross out movie category, but it's kinda fun. But has a few weird and nasty scenes in it, so watch it in the afternoon!

Work stuff sucks right now; I'll just leave it at that. Combined with a late charge into the X-Mas foray = stress, and lots of it. Just got Deena's picture of the wedding you had mentioned — pretty cool shot! They got you with your eyes closed, oh well, but it still is pretty unique.

Up to CT this weekend to be with most of the family there — inc. a nephew in the Marines who is home for a few days, so that's extra special. Could be overrun by all the little ones on X-Mas Eve, but it's all fun because of the excitement in the air.

I'm working on a home computer set-up which would have e-mail so we'll see what Santa brings this season. Got your number as back-up too. Have a wonderful Christmas with your family and a safe and Happy New Year's!

—Michael

PS Haven't heard the song yet, sounds very promising though. I'll look for it on the radio!

12/20/01

I feel a chapter has closed (again). I don't know why, but inside of me I feel that there is an end at last to this constant interruption in my boring existence. I emailed Michael what I feel was one last time today asking him to stay in touch, knowing he likely will not. His job ends next week, so unless I made an effort to contact him another way (email contact won't happen after this), I don't believe he will make an effort to stay in touch. I was upbeat and happy in my message, but after I pressed SEND, I knew I wouldn't be initiating anymore. He emailed back and it felt final. He said he'd be getting a home computer soon, blah blah blah. He has my number, blah blah blah. I'd bet money I never hear from him again. And I guess in a sick sort of a way, I'm relieved—wanting this perfect misery to end. I'm tired of hoping something may develop over time. I think I may yet again have been making it true in my mind when no evidence points to it at all. Big surprise. I feel the emptiness of single parenting stretching out ahead of me endlessly and it's really made me sad. It'll be a blue Christmas.

1/3/02

Wishing I had someone in my life, but realizing how ludicrous that is. Missing the idea of Michael. No word from him, and I don't really expect any. Pining away is a waste of time. Sorry to have him on my mind; the memory isn't keeping me as warm as I'd hoped.

1/20/02

I called Michael Saturday and sang a song to his answering machine—same song Harry sings Sally in that flick. I feel kind of foolish now, but it doesn't matter really, since he's not calling back.

1/24/02
...Well dip me in shit and call me brownie! Who fucking called this afternoon? MICHAEL. I couldn't fucking believe it. He was home sick (well, guess he's always home these days). He's been out of town with family. So there was a reason. I blabbed nonstop, but so did he. I love him, I tell you. I love him.

1/27/02
Almost midnight. Can't fucking sleep. I think it has more to do with the brownies and chocolate chip cookies I ate before bed than anything else, but that hasn't prevented me from obsessing for the last 2 hours about calling Michael and telling him how badly my body is screaming for his touch. I can practically feel his hands on me. I have fantasized about him coming down here or me going up there, or even just having phone sex for Christ sake. I am really horny and really unbelievably out of control where he is concerned. Logic tells me NOT to call or write or anything and NOT to reveal these feelings. He seemed so uncomfortable with any mention of feelings the other day. Men and feelings! Why can't they fucking handle them? It's all mixed up in my head with all his words so filled with promise back in October when hope was still part of the equation, when I still could believe something MIGHT happen.

Why can't I let go of this? How hard have I really tried to let go? And yet, if I get myself involved with someone else, how authentic will it be if I'm still secretly desiring some unattainable dream man? Now listen, Michael isn't the one. He can't be or he'd be here now with me. He'd pursue this. He's not. He hasn't instigated any communications, hasn't ever said or done ANYTHING to indicate he is looking for some future with me. I need to leave it ALONE.

THE LAST EMBER

Floating. Lighter than air, bobbing effortlessly on a pinpoint of light that carried her over peaceful waters and through gentle mountains where chill breezes never reached. Completely free of inhibition and fear, her body a loose, fluid, amoeba-like blob as one with the earth and sky. No thoughts. Only breaths. In and out...in and out...in and out. Drifting into oblivion...

She sensed more than saw or heard the change. It was the lack of sound rather than its presence that woke her. The voice that had led her down the silent meditative path had ceased its monotone, and the interwoven pattern of background sound (part quiet new-age music, part water trickling over stone) had also stopped. She heard muffled rustling nearby. She actively commanded her eyelids to open. In the dim light of jasmine-scented candles, she could just make out the three other figures shrouded in woolen blankets. She rolled to one side and slowly sat up, crossing her legs and wrapping her own blanket around her legs. They were already breathing together, preparing to ohm. The low, sonorous sound rose slowly and vibrated through the scented air. She added her own voice to the others. Then, as if communicating in some other way besides vocally or visually, like ants or bees, they all bent at the waist, their hands in prayer at their chests, and said, "Namaste" in unison.

On the drive home from yoga class, Victoria slowly let all her intruding thoughts resurface. She knew she was not yet a master of meditation. She generally fell asleep during the relaxation period at the end of yoga class, and then had to rouse herself enough to make the drive home, by which time the effects of said relaxation were all but gone. And once a week could hardly be labeled a "practice." Still, the brief reprieve from the constant bombardment of obsessive thoughts and images of Michael was welcome, and she was beginning to wish she could join a Buddhist monastery and stay in that calm and thoughtless state all the time. She could feel the shift, too, that was her pattern. She knew she would soon move toward action in the face of all her futile dreaming and pining.

2/19/02
Oops, I did it again (to quote Britney Spears)

Yeah, I did. I called him. I don't know why, I just felt like it. I wasn't mushy, I wasn't angry; I was just telling him about the house and talking. He made the conversation flow—it's not like he was trying to get off the phone. I mean, we talked a long time. He told me stuff he'd done in younger days, we talked about the Olympics, found out he has a sister in Tucson too, and at the WAY end, I mentioned again that I'd be in NYC soon, but I didn't press him to join us, just told him to call Deena if he wanted details. That was good, right? He is so damn easy to talk to. My head keeps telling me to hang it up already, to let this go! I mean, I tried so hard to just leave it alone. But I couldn't do it. I couldn't. This is going to sound so stupid, but if he is the one great love of my life, I am so doomed! I mean, I don't know what the future holds, but I am so sure it would be wonderful if he were in it. I'm sick that I said that, but why pretend that I don't feel it, even if it makes him uncomfortable to hear me even mention an actual feeling?

❧

Six months ago, she'd been in this city. It was the same air she'd breathed with him, the same roads they'd walked down in early morning before anyone else could witness the time warp that shimmered off the streets in the dawn light as they moved in a timeless bubble. But now she walked alone.

Victoria was in New York with her brother and his wife. They'd come to see Rent one more time. This was the final time, Victoria was sure. She had finally outrun the course of this obsession. One down, one to go...

Victoria was currently heading on foot from Penn Station toward Deena's apartment. She'd parted ways with her brother and sister-in-law after the show, them heading back to Sandy's where they were all spending the night. Victoria was meeting Deena and Todd for drinks, then maybe dinner out. The only unknown had been, did Deena call Michael and invite him along? Had Michael called on his own and invited himself to join them, knowing Victoria would be there? The chances were slim to none, yet a breathless hope was settling into her chest and a fluttering in her abdomen had begun. Just the chance he would be in the same city at the same time in the same space was pumping adrenaline through her body and sweat through all her sweat glands, despite the chill in the air.

Inside the alcove to Deena's apartment building, Victoria pressed the elevator button, her heart knocking furiously inside her ribs. She stepped in, doors sliding reluctantly shut. She popped a cinnamon Altoids in her mouth and ran her ring finger under her bottom lashes, removing any traces of smudged mascara. The elevator ascended to the top floor, the old door sliding open right into Deena's living room. She and Todd greeted her with hugs and smiles. Victoria stepped in over the threshold. She hugged back, kissed cheeks, and smiled her most dazzling smile, but no other eyes looked on. No one came out of the bathroom or looked up from the sofa. No one turned around from the bookcase where he'd been browsing books; no one stood up from behind the tiny kitchen island having just cleaned up a spill on the floor. No one else was there.

Victoria buried her disappointment and made small talk as they decided where to go to dinner. They settled on a small but crowded Korean restaurant Todd and Deena knew of, and took the subway, Victoria happily letting the native New Yorkers navigate. Once they were seated and drinks had been ordered, the three settled into a comfortable catch-up conversation. Eventually, the topic of the wedding came up. So, how was married life? Were they planning a family? Had the wedding photos been developed yet? And wasn't the reception such a good time? Then it happened.

"So...," Deena began, leading Victoria into the question, "...what happened with you and Michael?"

Victoria felt both their eyes on her as her face flushed. "Well, what do you want to know exactly?" she asked coquettishly, looking down at her soup broth. She suddenly became aware of the other patrons and shyly wished they were in a much noisier restaurant.

"Well, did you guys DO IT?" Deena blurted out.

Victoria laughed nervously, a little too loudly. As she caught her breath, she thought about the fact that it was sort of an embarrassing question, but she considered it a good ice breaker as she hadn't had the nerve to bring Michael up on her own.

Todd shushed Deena and said, "Vicki, you don't need to answer that..."

Victoria took a big breath, sighing it out as she gathered her courage. "Yeah, we 'did it,'" she admitted, looking up at Deena.

She wasn't sure when she opened her mouth if the words would come out at all, or what feelings would resurface and spill out when she accessed that stormy sea, whether salty drops would spray her face, or trembling limbs would rock their less-than-sea-worthy boat of a table. But if she gave away how much she was shaking, Deena and Todd didn't notice, or at least pretended not to.

"Well, good!" Deena responded, leaning back in her chair. "SOMEbody should get laid at a wedding!"

They discussed Michael some more, Deena asking if Victoria had been in touch with him since then. She did her best to answer without sounding too attached to the outcome. She wished desperately that her emotions weren't so close to the surface, that it wasn't so blatantly obvious that she was totally bowled over by him.

Deena and Todd commented that Michael was young for his age, describing various encounters, one in which he'd drank till he puked from the top of their apartment building. Victoria was starting to agree that he was a little immature, though it didn't seem to lessen much the magnetic pull she continued to feel toward him, to his powerful forcefield.

On the train ride back to Hamilton, Victoria stared out the window recounting the conversation and dinner. She had been disappointed that he hadn't been there, but not totally surprised. It felt rather that he had given her his final answer. His absence or his presence, either way, would have been the sign she'd been looking for. She weakly promised herself not to write any more cards or letters or make any more phone calls. She didn't completely believe she had power over it, but she knew she had good intentions, anyway.

3/6/02
I was watching NYPD Blue last night, and at the end, a female character said to Sipowicz, with whom some undefined something was beginning to exist, that she didn't want to label what they had, just be in each other's lives somehow. I guess that is what I held onto—some hope that we'd remain somehow connected, without calling it "lovers" or "friends" or any other name. But I'm letting that go. It's time to say goodbye love, goodbye. Hello solitude. And I mean inner solitude—no one else inside my heart or mind but me and my kids. It needs to be enough. I have to believe in it being enough. Then it won't feel so bad.

3/18/02
I had a REALLY weird experience today. I was driving home from the store and this song came on. I felt everything else block out...no sounds, no thoughts...I felt like it was speaking to me, through me, about me, of me, and I had this sexual reaction as if Michael were there in me—okay, I said it was

weird. I don't mean I felt like I was actually HAVING sex, but my pulse got quick, and my breathing, and I felt like I was starting to climax or something, only it was really sad. I was overcome with a feeling of loss because he's not in me, he's not near me, he's not ever going to be. It was a profound and odd experience. I am so NOT over him and yet resigned to the fact that there isn't going to be anything. I guess it doesn't help that I'm incredibly horny.

🎧 *"Save Me," ©2001, by Gregory Slay, Cinjun Tate, Shelby Tate, Jeffrey Cain, Cedric LeMoyne*

Salt trails
Etched down my face,
Familiar paths
Whose origin is plain and empty pain

3-23-02

4/4/02
Last night, I did the strangest thing. I picked up the phone, and it's like my hands had no connection to my brain. They dialed Michael's number even as I cried out to myself, "Don't do it!" I didn't want to debase myself, I didn't want to give in to the silly fantasy, I didn't want to act out of drunkenness! But I called, and he answered right away, knowing it was me (caller ID). Believe it or not, we spoke for 3 hours—that's till 2:00 a.m.! I couldn't believe it. It was the most straightforward conversation I've had with him. I said a lot that I had never planned to say. The basic gist is, though, that it seems he's still attracted to me too, though with lots of caution evident. I was pretty flipped out. I basically admitted I've never stopped thinking about him, that I have very strong feelings for him, and that I'd like very much to see him again (thanks, alcohol). But I felt like I was in the act of convincing him this would be a good idea, and I don't want it to be up to me, my decision. I know what I want. He's the one that's stuck. He did say one sort of hurtful thing about wishing I were younger, no kids. I took it as his ideal—but he may not be able to look past that. In any case, we agreed that right now, distance and timing wouldn't allow for much of a steady or consistent relationship. Still, there was talk of getting together (and I'm not holding my breath) and my own personal feeling is that we shouldn't

overanalyze it, or try to define what exists. But I don't want to ignore it either. I want to be with him so badly I can hardly stand it. Why shouldn't we get together when it works for both of us? The thought of touching him again—God, I hope he doesn't run away again, but I think I'll be more prepared for it this time if he does. We left it that he'd call next week. That in and of itself would be a miracle if he really does. I'm not really expecting him to, though I'm praying he will.

But wow! We had a real conversation and it wasn't all in my head! He conceded that it was definitely more than random good sex. I just felt happy to have been able to express that and for him to have validated it. Now I KNOW it was real.

Victoria retraced the steps she'd taken yesterday that seemed to have led to this new development. She'd started the day out the normal way. She'd taken Chloe to the bus stop, as usual. She'd had the same conversational small talk she always had with the grandmother who always waited there too with her granddaughter, a rather chubby fifth grader who seemed to like Victoria. She liked to search for four-leaf clovers, and today she'd found one, and in the sweetness and generosity that only children seem to truly possess, had given it smilingly to Victoria.

Her day had gone on as usual, nothing out of the ordinary. It had been a Wednesday, Max's night to take the kids. She'd gone to choir practice, just like every other Wednesday night from 7-8:30. Afterwards, Victoria had gone across the street and had a few beers at the tavern with two friends from choir. Victoria had felt tipsy, but not entirely drunk.

Still, upon returning home, and even though it was nearly 11:00, she had gotten it in her head to call Michael. She argued with herself aloud (no one was home, after all), and it seemed she'd known it wasn't such a great idea to call. Yet, all the same, she had retrieved his number from her purse where she'd been keeping it on a post-it note she'd stashed in her wallet and dialed. She had physically felt herself trying to stop herself, but it was a losing battle.

And he'd been home, and he'd been willing to talk, more than willing. He'd answered the phone, "Hello Victoria," not the least bit surprised or caught off guard. She couldn't quite get over that they had talked for so long. Was he maybe working out his own demons too? Did he have a constant argument inside his own head, a conflict that wouldn't drop, as she'd had? They had been so honest with one another, and he'd sounded almost as if he'd wanted her to convince him that they should get together. He'd hedged, he'd waffled, he'd paused. But he hadn't said "no."

The next morning, hung over and working on only three hours of sleep, she got up to go to the gym early, making use of the rarity of no kids. It was a cold, frosty morning, and she shivered in the car. She drove to the gym trying to believe that it could still happen; they could still, just maybe, have a future.

Charms, Prayers, and Omens

Yesterday:

At the bus stop,
The fifth grade girl with the glasses and violin case
Handed me a four-leaf clover.

Last Night:

I picked up the purple phone and dialed the number
on the crumpled yellow post-it from my wallet
while I pleaded with myself, "Don't do it!"

Today:

Magenta petals peeked out from tulips closed to the spring morning chill.

Dizzy and yawning, I drove at dawn
while U2's "Beautiful Day" played on the radio.

4/4/02

"Beautiful Day," ©2000, by Bono, Adam Clayton, The Edge, Larry Mullen Jr.

HOPE LEAKS ETERNAL

4/5/02
Have been in too good a mood today, as though I believed I would see Michael again. I've fantasized about being able to lay eyes on him, lay my hands on him. God, to touch him again. I have sent my silent prayers into the universe for him to please not be scared to touch this sacred chance, to allow it to just be, to play itself out. I feel this strong pull and it's not clear what the source is. I hate words like "fate," "destiny," or worse, "God's will." I don't know that I believe any of them.

Victoria put down her pen. Was it really possible that Michael might reconsider all the doubting and hedging and really think it through, and if so, was it possible he would decide it was okay to see her after all, that it might even be a good thing? She couldn't believe that he was even open to talking about it, and to her, that meant he wasn't yet 100% convinced this was over.

She started imagining again what it might be like to get together with him, to meet up somewhere and have a chance to maybe sit and talk in a quiet restaurant or diner, sitting close enough that their thighs were touching, touching hands and feeling the electric shock run through each other, looking into each other's eyes. She let herself imagine again what it might feel like to kiss him, to have his mouth on hers, his arms around her, her hands in his hair.

Then she sighed and got back up off the bed to finish the project she'd started; she was in the middle of repainting the master bathroom. She'd been slowly changing her personal space ever since Max had left. It had started with removing his dresser, which was a heavy dark wood and only served to remind her of everything from folding his laundry to seeing both their reflections in the mirror attached to it. She wanted to lighten up the room.

She'd repainted the bedroom a pale lilac and rearranged the furniture. She'd purchased new sheets and a comforter to try and transform the bed from the cage of disappointment it had come to represent. And with the house going on the market, she'd needed to update things anyway.

So, now she was repainting the bathroom, a complimentary yellow to the shades of purple in the bedroom. She'd bought new towels and bathmat, and taken down all the coffee art that had decked the walls, yet another reminder of a past she no longer took part in. He'd been the coffee drinker, not her, and the cute porcelain knobs hand-painted with coffee mugs that she'd found were removed.

She shook the can of paint, only half-full now, opened it with the paint can opener, and stirred it with the already yellow stick. Then she poured the cake-batter-colored paint into the tray and removed the plastic bag she'd wrapped around the roller to keep it from drying up. It was time for a second coat. She rolled paint onto the roller, then rolled off the excess and stood to begin the second coat.

As she stood up, she caught her reflection in the mirror. She was wearing torn denim cutoffs, already spattered with several colors of paint from previous jobs, and an eggplant-colored t-shirt that read "Welcome Home" in white script over the left breast. She had not bothered to shower yet today, knowing she'd only get sweaty and speckled with yellow pinpoints of paint, so her hair was unstyled and hung limply over her pale face. She'd foregone the makeup too thus far, and so looked drawn and puffy and tired.

She smiled feebly, reminding herself that, if by some miracle, he wanted to try again, if by some grace from the angels he actually came through this time, she would need to do something about her appearance. She sucked in her stomach, straightened up her posture, and tried to imagine herself as sexy. Then she began a second time to make new and beautiful what had become so hard to look at.

 "Making Out," ©2001, by G. Stefani, T. Kanal, & T. Dumont

4/6/02
5:30 a.m. Can't sleep anymore. I can't stop thinking about him and feeling this doomed feeling that I won't hear from him again. All I do is imagine how it would feel if he were to touch me again, hold me, kiss me, make love to me. It's almost torturous—I feel a growing despair based on my belief that he will get a case of nerves and not be able to go through with it. I know he has so many worries, but the exact nature of them, I'm not sure. It's almost as if he is afraid not that I will fall in love with him, but that he will fall in love with me, and that it will somehow ruin his plans. Men and their plans! They think they have it all figured out, and then they reject any other possible combination of factors. "She can't be the one. I pictured a 30-year-old, single, professional woman, not a 40-year-old, married, stay-at-home mom." Well, hey, I didn't imagine a young, somewhat inexperienced, unemployed guy with doubts—I had in mind an older, similarly backgrounded man, who knew he wanted me (and my kids) and for Christ sake, who lived somewhere in the vicinity! Can we tell our hearts what to long for? Can we decide who they will seek out or yearn for, once discovered? I'm not sure it is within our ability to control that. I'm not sure I want to control that. It seems a miracle to me that he and I met at all and that circumstances seemed to bring us together—circumstances, by the way, that we could not have predicted. It further seems a miracle that our bodies seemed to know exactly what to do with each other. It was magic and I don't think it should be tossed aside. What are the chances of finding that kind of synchronicity? This is some glorious gift, and we shouldn't refuse it. I think it better to focus on the possibilities, not the consequences. Am I hoping for too much? I just think it could be a beautiful thing, us being together –in whatever

way we're meant to be together. But we ARE meant to be together, one way or another. That, I believe.

And still. Still I have this hopeless fear that is really more of an acceptance about how life isn't always fair. No matter how good we could be together, no matter how much we both might deserve the kind of happiness that being together might bring, there seems to be this doom factor. I pray he has the strength and courage to listen to his heart, not give in to fears.

4/6/02
Wow, now I don't feel at all sure about what I wrote this morning. What am I thinking? If he is half as schizoid as me (and more likely, he's twice as), he'll never think it's a good idea to get together, and right now, I'm fine with that. After spending a day with myself, running errands, having my car die on me, packing boxes, watching kids, then going to a church function, I felt like, yeah, THIS is my life. It has NOTHING to do with being with him or any other man! I was me, and I was "mom," and I was Vicki the caregiver, and Vicki the party girl, and Vicki the membership chair. I definitely wasn't Vicki the lover or partner or any other description that had to do with a relationship. It's too complicated and too messy and too fucking unlikely. I don't even expect to hear from him, and I know I'll be disappointed when I don't, even knowing how freaked out I've made myself today. Where was I thinking this might go? He isn't PART of my world, and I'm not part of his! I was thinking I'd like to meet his family. I was thinking I'd like to meet his friends. I must be INSANE. I'm going to bed.

4/9/02
Waffling between the urge to call and the urge to hide my feelings in food and television and music and anesthetize myself against the pain of another rejection. Unable to decide how to handle this—unable even to discern my own feelings day-to-day, hour-to-hour. Absolute certainty that we should be together, and that I should fight for it—then the pendulum swings and this is all a dream, a fantasy, and it needs to be left behind with all my other childish longings. Then back I swing—shouldn't I indulge my inner child? Don't I deserve a lovely fantasy to come true? Back and forth I go.

The phone rang. She heard the ring, almost began sweating before the first ring had finished. Her heart raced and she held her breath as the second ring began. In those split seconds, Victoria prayed out loud and inwardly and realized every possible outcome. Not unlike one's life the instant before death seems imminent, every possible scenario seemed to flash before Victoria's eyes.

It could be a friend calling to set up a play date; it could be the plumber calling back about the backed up sink in her bathroom; it could be a telemarketer; it could be him...it's got to be him. He is calling to say goodbye...OR he is calling to say what the hell and let's do it! Or maybe he is calling to continue the drawn-out process of processing this aloud, to tell her in his hemming and hawing way that he does have feelings but he isn't sure they should pursue this. Or he's calling to say let's just be friends. Or it's the wrong number.

4/10/02

Officially Over. His honesty was blunt. His logic was sound. He's not coming here, I'm not going there. There's no future for it, and no point therefore in going through with anything that would only further entangle us. It makes sense and all, so why the fuck does it hurt so much?

After a healthy cry and then a healthy workout, I'm still pretty bummed. I feel reasonably sane, though. It really wasn't such a big surprise. I knew he'd ALWAYS had reservations, and if he didn't come willingly (pardon the pun), what would have been the good of that, in the end? How much heartache would we both have suffered before realizing it must end? He's just ended it before it could begin. I see the reason in that. But it is so difficult for me to control how I FEEL about it, which is this: I somehow believed we were such a good match, we would find our way to each other. To have even considered it seriously, on his part, was, I have to admit, pretty amazing. And he says he did consider it. I believe he has feelings for me, which he isn't allowing to surface, which he is shutting off to avoid getting hurt. I can't really blame him. I'm about to go into that mode myself. I can't stomach the idea of chancing my heart again. I do appreciate that he admitted to still being attracted to me and having feelings—it makes it not all seem for nothing—the experience was really good for him too, and I'm happy it wasn't just some roll in the hay, though I never really thought it was. I guess what still baffles my heart is how close we came to actually touching and maybe even holding on to something true.

> Sweeping up the pieces
> before they've fully broken
> Taping over conversations
> before they've yet been spoken
> Analyzing potent dreams
> yet to be remembered
> Choking off the silent screams
> never uttered, yet unrendered
> Accepting all the logic
> while unproven and unwritten
> Swallowing the pride,
> Tempting apple yet unbitten
> Gathering back the caution
> that so elegantly scattered
> Putting back upon the shelf
> the things that nearly mattered
> Shouting at the mirror
> in tight-fisted humiliation
> Reflections of what might have been,
> tears of lonely expectation.
> 4/10/02

CALENDAR

Victoria awoke to the feeling of being watched. She stifled a yawn and rolled over to the nearly inaudible breathing of Chloe. Chloe stood silently next to Victoria's bed, balancing between a hunger-induced urge to wake Victoria and a fear-induced reluctance to disturb her.

"Hey Sweetie," Victoria hoarsely croaked as she opened eyes still glued shut with sleep.

"I'm hungry," Chloe stated matter-of-factly, the same as every day before.

Victoria swung her legs over the side of the bed, yawning and rubbing her eyes with one hand while the other searched blindly for her glasses on the bedside table.

"Okay, okay, let me just go pee," she mumbled as she crossed the room to the bathroom.

"Now there's an interesting look," she said half to herself as she caught her reflection in the mirror on her way to the toilet. Her hair was sticking up straight as if frozen into place by an icy, arctic wind. She sighed as she relieved herself, then she tried to focus as she flushed, briskly washed her hands, and flicked off the light, heading to the kitchen.

She poured juice for Chloe and Connor, placing their cups on the dining room table. She tossed vitamin tablets next to each of their cups, and then pulled out the milk, bagels, margarine, and bacon from the refrigerator. She pulled apart a bagel, sticking one half into the toaster. She grabbed a frying pan from a cupboard beneath the counter and put three slices of bacon in, turning the heat to medium. She poured a bowl of Cheerios for Connor, adding the milk and a spoon to the bowl, and placed the bowl on the table. She checked the toaster to see if the bagel had burned.

One of the few variations in the daily routine was how brown or black the bagel would be, and if she could scrape off enough of the burnt crumbs to satisfy Chloe's picky sense of perfection. Luckily, it was a golden brown, and she plopped the bagel down onto a paper towel and buttered it, then brought it into the dining room. She came back to the bacon, turned it with a fork, and walked over to the wall calendar.

The white boxes outlined in black stared back at her. It was a fresh calendar page, the first day of June. She had put a diagonal pencil line through each day as she'd counted off the days of April and May. Every day felt like marking time with nothing to look forward to, Victoria felt like she was simply counting down the days until...until what? It all ended, not even with a bang? It seemed so pointless.

For almost two months, Victoria had been able to reasonably move about her days and nights without completely obsessing about Michael. She tended to her children, worked out at the gym, and immersed herself in volunteering at the school and the church. But it was almost mechanical. The routine was the same, day in and day out, and each day looked like the one before. She had gotten into the habit of writing down not only things like doctor's appointments and play dates and teacher work days, but the boring and vapid details of each day, if only to prove that she was actually doing SOMEthing every day.

She'd written down when the kids went to Max's, though it was the same schedule week in and week out; she'd been writing down when she was going to the gym and to choir practice and when the choir was singing, though going to the gym was surely not something she needed to remind herself about. She went whenever the kids were gone, and she didn't need to stop and try and remember if there was something she should be doing. Choir practiced every Wednesday, same time, same place. And they sang every second and third Sunday.

But having nothing at all on the calendar, it just seemed so bare and empty and devoid of meaning. Still, she filled up those squares, filled up her mind with meaningless details and kept track of them meticulously, crossing them off, sometimes checking off individual items on any given day, just to give her some kind of focus other than him. But sometimes, without her bidding, the thoughts and memories would come upon her in a surge that she couldn't ignore.

6/1/02
I remember now riding back in the cab with him from the reception to the B&B. We drove by so many pictures of victims and candles lit all up and down the sidewalks, and he pointed down a street where you could just make out the search lights. I was so distraught, and thinking back, I think sharing that moment with him had much to do with the connection I feel—felt. My heart aches for the victims of that day, and the loved ones they left behind, and my heart is broken because I am not with someone to share that wrenching gulf with. I felt I found something–someone—so special in Michael, and I felt that feeling returned. It is heartbreaking that circumstances, fears, doubts, logic reared their heads and prevented us from reaching out toward one another for a more solid connection. I am torn apart by his absence in my life. I felt we enriched one another. But I can only speak for myself. God I miss the thought of him. And I am having a really difficult time crowding out thoughts of how he felt physically.

6/14/02
I feel somewhat wasted—here I am, this loving, caring, sexual being, and no one to share it with. I don't ache for him as much anymore—unless I really think about it too much. Does that mean that the part of me which he re-awakened is going back to sleep? Will I become numb again to protect myself? It should at least be scientifically interesting to observe.

It was written on her calendar. July 7th. This was Michael's birthday. She wasn't sure when she had acquired that piece of information. Perhaps one of their phone calls during which she had rambled endlessly, doing anything to keep the lines of communication open as long as possible. But there it was. His birthday. Should she do anything about it?

She wondered for the hundredth time if a card was in order, or if she was supposed to leave it alone. So, she sent nothing, but instead wrote a poem commemorating this day, even though he would not know she had. She followed this with letters she never sent either. She felt a desire to express how she was feeling, but felt an even more powerful warning not to continue to pop up in his life, all feelings and emotions on her sleeve.

Birthday Wish

Thirty-three (three times eleven)
Years ago, a gift from Heaven
(on this day, July the seven)
To your parents, full of joy,
Their fifth and youngest, baby boy
This day (now, then, in between)
From boy to man a change was seen
How full of pride they must have been
A loving, caring man is he
Though searching with his soul he be
A parent's wish upon their son
For laughter, love, fulfillment, fun
And courage, wisdom to find the one
To share his life and fill his heart
And make whole what was once a part
6-22-02

Birthday Wish II

Thirty three (three times eleven)
Years ago, on seven seven
You came to be
What joy for me
Happy Birthday
7-6-02

THIS LETTER NEVER SENT July 6, 2002

Dear God, I wish I could somehow have made you see. Made you somehow realize that love is impossible to plan or shape, that it chooses you, you don't choose it. And somehow, somehow make you hear my heart talking to yours the way they spoke to one another the night we met, when bodies, minds, hearts, and souls were one in a cherished act of love. I wish I could have eased your fears and misgivings about doing something that wasn't part of the plan, wasn't the way you pictured it, to let go of preconceived notions of what a relationship has to be, must be to work, and kept you somehow from dwelling on a future that wasn't set, couldn't be foretold. I wish your eager, searching heart could have listened to itself beating, and not be quelled by doubts and cliché misconceptions about age and time. Our hearts are ageless, and when one heart recognizes another, there are no physical boundaries of color, time, size, or shape. I wish I could have somehow shown you how to see not baggage and obstacles, but experiences and challenges that make a love grow stronger and a body wiser and deeper. I wish I could have taken your hand and shown you one possible future, where partnership and caring and like-mindedness and mutual respect and pure passion made the foundations, not some societal rules for matching and meeting some perfect standard, some idea of perfect that isn't based on perfect love, but perfect setting and timing and physical characteristics. I wish I could have shown you that space and time can be overcome with love and endurance, and that when two hearts share themselves, no distance is too far. And I wish I could have made you see that as a positive thing.

To say I wish I could have made you love me doesn't begin to say what I mean or intend, but only simplifies my desire to have made your eyes somehow open wider and your mind somehow open up to more than one narrow view of what love could or should be. I will never believe that I imagined what passed between us. I nearly convinced myself it wasn't anything more than some wildly divine but singular experience, and that it should be, if not forgotten, at least placed upon the shelf like some trophy or memento of a fabulous trip. I nearly succeeded in forcing my mind to stop its focus on the electrical connection, and instead talk itself into casual appreciation of one of many experiences still left to be had.

What passed between us cannot be categorized, because it never happened before, and it can never happen again. Not with another person, anyway, and not in the exact same way. The theory of one perfect person, one soul-mate, one ultimate match is not a convincing one. And yet, if that theory were true, if, as you guess, there is a lightening bolt that strikes, that is closest in description to what I felt, that is what I experienced; you are who fit better than any person or situation I could have imagined, and being with you, imagining some undefined future with you in it, that made me more alive than I've ever felt. It isn't that I didn't have my own ideas of what I needed and still think would make a more logical match, but I contend that my heart is wiser and my instincts a better guide than some list of characteristics I may have conceived to find a good mate. The crossing of our paths awakened in me every thing that had gone to sleep, and some parts of me I didn't even know were there. And now my greatest fear is that they will fall back into the shadows and recesses of my being, untouched and forgotten; and for your sake, I fear that you may not have the good sense to listen to your heart and instincts when they don't tell you what you expect to hear.

We do not get to choose where our paths take us in the end, but we get to make choices along the way about how to accept where our paths lead us, whether to rejoice or grieve; whether to embrace or reject; whether to pay attention to or ignore completely what we encounter as we go; and we get to choose, to some degree, with whom we'd like to travel. We can invite them on the journey, though they may not choose to go, and even if they do, they may not finish in the same place we do. It is an uncertain business, this life journey, with few guarantees. Still, I wish with all my heart that you would join me, even not knowing where we'd end up or when; but I can promise that my heart is open and joyous with you in it, that my love is pure and true, and that my flaws and weaknesses are inseparable from my gifts and strengths, as are yours. I accept and love you for all that you are and may become. There are no boundaries or conditions where this is concerned. I am asking you to be in my life, in maybe a way that as yet has no name or description. Connections with other human beings are too precious and beautiful to ignore or set aside. I believe we were given a gift, and I believe it was intended to be more than one solitary encounter. It may not be as either of us anticipates, hopes, believes it to be. But can we throw it away based on misguided expectations?

These letters, so powerful, went unmailed. Victoria realized that, as true and honest as they were, they might not be received with the kind of enthusiasm she felt while writing them. So she squirreled them away, perhaps as historical records of this journey, for whose benefit she knew not. Maybe her own? Maybe someday this would all make sense. Until then, she opted instead for a no-nonsense, friendly, chatty style she wouldn't be embarrassed to send.

July 16, 2002

Dear Michael,

Thought I'd write just to let you know how things are going down here. My move was successful, and we're all settled in. Lots of friends helped me out with the packing, and it was a smooth, easy transition. I even drove the moving truck! I really like owning my own home and I had a good time furnishing it and am already making plans for painting and decorating as time and money permit. It's just the right size for us, the kids are happy, and I feel comfortable and safe. What more could I ask for? (Okay, maybe a shaded parking space would be nice...)

Our summer is going well so far. We joined a pool, and have been spending a lot of time there. The kids are turning into total fish. They are finally old enough to swim alone while I look on over the top of a book or magazine, soaking up some sun. I also enjoy jumping in on a hot day and swimming a few laps. It's a good place to have cookouts and invite friends, so we've been doing that too.

We took a couple weekend trips so far that have been fun. We went to Rehoboth Beach, DE, with one of my friends and her two kids. Cramped hotel quarters (two double beds and six people...my kids refused to sleep on floor in sleeping bags, so I got to get squished between them on a bed that was about a foot too short for me!), but great weather and lots of fun playing in the sand and waves, going on rides, and eating boardwalk junk food. Also had a great camping weekend on the Chesapeake Bay with two other families. One family had a hobie cat, so we did a lot of sailing. I even got to sail at night, which was both thrilling and relaxing, staring at stars, listening to the skipping-stone sound of flying fish, and feeling the breeze on my face. I think I'm in love with sailing now. We all agreed to do more camping more often. It's such a fun way to spend time with your family and friends, and now that I'm more confident with the camper, I feel I can travel just about anywhere with it. I'll be heading up to Boston this weekend to see friends, and then on to Portsmouth, NH, to spend a day on Star Island (think last year's xmas card) with my dad, who is going for a whole week. We'll be scattering my mom's ashes. Yes, she passed away in May. Not totally a shock, but very sad and still slowly feeling the aftershocks. I did most of the planning of her memorial service, which turned out beautifully, and has resulted in me reconnecting with some people from my past that I dearly missed. I'm spending a lot more time with my dad now, who is actually experiencing guilt from his sudden freedom to travel and get out now that he isn't tied to spending all his time caring for my mom.

I'm doing great with my training and working out. I feel better than ever physically, and actually have been wearing two-piece bathing suits for the first time in about 20 years! People had to put their sunglasses on when my belly was first exposed, it was so white! Other than that, nothing to report but, as the card says, missing you. Can't help it.

Hope you are well, and that your job situation has improved. I think of you often and wonder how you're doing.

Victoria

July passed, and then August, and there was no answer from Michael. Victoria had foolishly hoped that her innocuous letter would get some response. But as the warm, liquid days of Virginia summer plodded by, she lost hope in her optimism. It seemed ill-placed. She tortured herself, berating herself with euphemisms regarding her inability to let go, her obsessive behavior, and, in general, her complete failure to move on. She felt it was time to really, this time, cut the ties. She wanted him to know, too, that this was what she was doing, and why. She penned another letter, this time intending it to be the last...really.

August 31, 2002

Dear Michael,

It's so hard to believe that almost one year ago, the world so dramatically changed with 9/11. And it is equally hard for me to believe that less than two weeks after that, my world so dramatically changed when I met you.

I have been thinking a lot about mortality. With the anniversary of 9/11 coming up, I am recalling how I felt that day. I thought so much about the people I cared about and what I should say to them before I die, and just trying to focus on each day of living...you know, carpe diem. Then, with my mom's death, I once again thought about how I wanted to leave this world, with my accounts settled, so to speak, and all the things said that I needed to say. Now, as my divorce is about to become final, I am working on a will, which is a requirement of my property settlement agreement. I was faced with the decision of what to do with my children should I happen to die, and their dad should happen to die too. Morbid, yes, but necessary to decide. Surprisingly, it wasn't as hard a decision to make as I'd thought. Still, once again, it made me think of my short time on earth, and how uncertain it is.

Because of these intersecting events that have all made me consider my own life and choices, I felt there were some things I needed to say to you. It's not that I think I'm going to die or anything as dramatic as that. I just realized that these things should be said, if not for your sake, then for mine.

I felt terribly hurt when, in our last phone conversation, you told me you wished I were younger and didn't have children. That I can't change either of these things, and wouldn't want to if I could, isn't even the point. The only difference between our ages is that I have had a couple more years of experience in life, which neither makes me wiser nor better than you, but has given me more to reflect on, and possibly an inkling more awareness of what I want. I know that you are still struggling with what you want. For all your talk of looking for "the one," I don't really think you were ready to find her. I, on the other hand, knew almost the moment I met you that I had found all the things I was looking for... well, except for the one obvious missing element: it was not me that you were looking for.

As for my children, well there's probably nothing more damaging to say to a mother than to wish her children didn't exist. I'm sure you didn't mean it quite like that, but with the instinctual protectiveness that goes with the territory of mothering, I felt on some level a desire to attack. My children are truly amazing people, and they are the biggest part of who I am. By wishing them away, it was like wishing me away too, and that really hurt.

Those are the most important things I had to say. Other than that, I wanted you to know that, of all the incredibly stressful events of the past 6 months (moving and buying a home, my mother dying, getting a new job and career, and my divorce finally going through), none of them caused me as much distress, anguish, and deep sorrow as I felt when I believed you no longer wanted anything to do with me. I wanted you to know this because it is important to know in our lives that we are loved. For the time I spent believing in the possibilities, you were loved...by me.

I apologize if telling you these things made you uncomfortable in any way. I will not initiate any further communication with you. Please just know, I have no regrets where you are concerned, except perhaps that I didn't say these things sooner, and as long as I live, I believe you will always, for me, be "the one."

Good luck to you always. You are a treasure for whomever finally catches your heart.

Victoria

A Poem for You

He smiles and laughs, breaking bread with the elders

He listens and looks, encouraging contact, connection

He touches and strokes, sparking fire and passion

He caresses and holds, offering warmth and protection

He lingers and strolls, stretching time and space

He ponders and considers, baring mind and soul

Vicki walked briskly down the sidewalk to the corner where the mailboxes were. The kids were already in the car, and though they were running late for an appointment, she thought she had better check the mail first. It felt as though she may have ignored the mail these last few days before school was going to start, what with buying supplies and new shoes for the kids and preparing herself for her first year of teaching. She was feeling overwhelmed and harried and buried beneath a hefty weight of errands and tasks.

She inserted the small brass-colored key into the narrow metal door and pulled out the stack of envelopes and advertisements. She shuffled through the stack as she walked back towards the car. It was mostly bills, credit card offers, a dental appointment reminder, the usual. And one off-white envelope, handwritten. She didn't recognize the handwriting. Her eyes jumped up from the middle of the envelope to the upper left-hand corner, to the return address where it read, in all capital letters, "Michael Bellamy."

She felt her heart skip a beat, and then she said, "Fuck!" How could he have just sent a letter? She had just sent a letter. A dying-swan, goodbye letter. Which he could not possibly have already received and responded to. Which meant this letter was not an answer or rebuke to her goodbye, but a response to her earlier letter from July, her friendly, no-talk-of-an-us letter.

And as she was just receiving this letter, she imagined that he too was just receiving her second letter, maybe even today, maybe even at this very moment, opening her envelope, laughing at the fact that they had passed each other in the mail, or confused that a response in the form of a second letter had come so soon. And maybe he was reading it and absorbing her sober message, and maybe even feeling disgust at her saccharin message of love and farewell, and the poem! Oh geez.

Before she even read a word of his letter, she gazed toward the sky and laughed bitterly. She climbed into the car, threw the mail onto the passenger seat, and slammed shut her door. The letter could wait. She didn't need to have the irony strike her any harder at the moment. It was enough to realize that once again, their timing had been completely and breathtakingly off. She laughed and rested her forehead on her hands, which gripped the steering wheel, muttering, "Unbelievable!"

"What's wrong, Mom?" Chloe asked from the back seat.

"Nothing," she answered, laughing under her breath. "Nothing's wrong. Life is just SO strange."

She threw the car into reverse and backed out, feeling ever so slightly hell-bent on destruction.

Hi Victoria –

Firstly, I apologize for the length of time it's taken me to get back to you. For someone who still is not working full time, I've been pretty busy trying to get that elusive job, taking care of health matters and traveling with friends and family. More on all this shortly...

I'm very sorry to hear of the loss of your mother. I can't imagine how much it... well, sucks. It must be a hurt I can't even imagine, and don't want to. My condolences to you and your family.

Keep knocking on wood or whatever, but my folks are doing pretty well. Enough so that they came to visit for the first time in years. It's alarming the number of medications my dad is taking on a daily basis, but if they're helping stay ahead of all that ails him, then so be it. They both looked great and we visited with my siblings, even went to a Classica concert at Tanglewood in MA. Ever heard of it? Or been there? I didn't know, but Eric Cashell suffered a stroke some time ago...not sure if you knew. Didn't sound like he was doing too well either.

I had my 2nd procedure in July to correct an irregular heartbeat and so far so good, though I need to get back in shape and put it through its paces.

Trying like hell to get back to New England and almost made it to New Hampshire with a job opp. that apparently came down to the wire. Ugh. Working my Maine connections right now—was up there last weekend and so far, I'm hopefully optimistic.

Where else has my summer taken me? Let's see: June – Fishing in Maine; July – Cooperstown, NY, for a potential job and a baseball game; Lake Placid, NY, ESPN Great Outdoor Games; Montreal for Expos Baseball—got a foul ball!; August – CT and MA to visit folks; Ocean City, MD, college reunion for the boys; Maine last weekend for job stuff and to spend time with my vacationing brother and his family; AND, this weekend, off to Nantucket with a college buddy! Don't ask me how I can afford all this, I'm not even sure.

Glad to hear the new house is working out! And that the training is making you feel good! I could use some of your dedication in that regard. Hoping that this new great job I'm going to get is to be the springboard for me in so many ways.

Hey, your guys must be starting school right about now! New schools I presume? Either way, I hope it all goes well for them. Sounds like you had an absolutely super summer with them, doing all you did. Your weekend in Rehoboth, not far from OC, MD, sounds an awful lot like our "hairy man weekend" recently. Super cramped, short beds (which you know about!), no a/c, or too much a/c, etc. (I zonked out one night on the floor—my knee directly over an a/c vent—I love sleeping in meat-locker conditions, but my knee was numb with frostbite the next day!)

And you're quite the camper, now?! And how is life w/o the hot tub?

All right, time to wrap up and get some sleep prior to the long weekend. Hope yours is/was a good one despite a wet forecast...but hey, we do need the rain.

Thanks for checking in, Victoria, glad to hear you are well. I'm staying optimistic (it can be hard, though) and very eager to finally land on my feet and hit the ground running (I might have made that sound like a contradiction, but you know what I mean!)

Take care. Until next time...

—Michael

9/3/02
In a weird twist of fate (what HASN'T been weird about all this?), I received, of all things, a letter from Michael today! The strange thing is, he must've written it the same day I wrote mine, and they passed each other in the mail. I couldn't decide whether to laugh or cry when I saw it, addressed to me in his handwriting (the first time I've ever seen his writing). His letter was very

chatty and not too committal—but the fact that he even wrote blew me away. I wish I'd be able to close this chapter, but it won't close. Pat said it "meant" something that we both were thinking of each other on the same day. I don't know what to think. I just never have good timing with this man. We're connected, but off-kilter. I don't know what to say or do or think where he's concerned. My letter was so heavy and intense. Oh well! Oops. But I'm leaving it as is—not going to call or write to explain or apologize or comment on how weird life is. I admitted to the man that I loved him, and I effectively said I'd end it there, knowing he wanted nothing to do with me. Wouldn't be the first time I had no clue what he's about. Pat said let him digest it. I don't think we'll ever see each other again.

THE BOX

Victoria walked toward the closet. Her limbs moved stiffly, as if she were an automaton, incapable of thoughts or feelings, and yet she thought of the same thing, day after day, and felt deeply, intensely. She bit her lip as she pulled open the folding metal doors. She reached up to the top shelf, placing her hand onto either side of a cardboard box. It had thin sides and a flimsy top, and felt as though it would fall apart at any minute, as though the weight of what was inside would split the inadequate sides of the box, and the contents would spill all over the floor. The box was multicolored red, green, brown, purple, maroon, and white, with the word "STATIONERY" repeated in alternating white and black lettering. One letter different, and it could describe her lack of progress in moving forward.

She carried it over to her bed, one hand on the bottom to keep the box from falling open, and sat down on the edge. Her fingers ran over the box top, its smoothness feeling almost cool to the touch. She gently shook the bottom half out of the top onto her lap and laid the top next to her on the bed. She sighed resolutely.

At the bottom of the box lay a stack of white paper, 8-1/2 x 11". On top lay the invitation to Deena and Todd's wedding, still in its original envelope. Tucked inside the envelope too was the piece of paper Victoria had written train times on, sloppily folded into fourths, the hasty writing a messier version of her typically more controlled scrawl. The program from the wedding was also there with its list of hymns, readings, and participants.

Beneath its edges, the photo of the wedding party lay. Its monochrome inhabitants seemed to call from a great distance, begging to be remembered, but without true conviction. A cassette tape rested on top of all the papers like a paperweight. On the label was written, in thin green cursive, "My Experience of You." Next to it sat a small video tape, not much bigger than the audio tape. It was the original of the one she'd made for him, the one she'd poured her heart into, letting the thin brown ribbon absorb her very essence.

She lifted each cherished relic out of its sacred tomb, handling each one gently, lovingly, but perhaps a little cautiously, with a wariness that bespoke an intuition of darkness approaching. Like a bad addiction, she had become aware that she was spending entirely too much time with the box and its contents, reviewing every word they'd ever spoken to each other, every thought she'd had on the subject, reliving every ounce of proof that he had, indeed, existed.

She would take out the invitation and read through it once again. That was where this story had started, with naive innocence and joy. Then the picture, taken on the wedding day, the day they'd met. She would brush her lips ever so gently across his grainy black-and-white image, inhaling as she did so, imagining her breath could somehow capture some essence of him and hold it inside. She would mumble, "I love you," or just run her fingertips across his face, and stare hard into his indistinct eyes, trying to capture some spark or recognition.

She would lay these items down gently beside her. Then she'd put the audio tape into her Walkman tape player, don her headphones, and push the play button. Every song that she had come to associate with him, with her experience of him, was on this tape.

As she listened, sometimes she'd lie back on the bed, tears rolling slowly down her cheeks. Other times she'd laugh, especially at the Adam Sandler song and at how funny it was to include it. Through bitterness and despair, she had somehow found something funny, if tragic, about sharing sentiments surrounding being abandoned by one's true love.

Still, other times, she'd listen while she read. Every email they'd ever sent one another had been printed off and stored in this box. At the time, it had somehow been important to her to keep a paper copy of the emails. Admittedly, it seemed obsessive and slightly scary in retrospect. Still, these were her pieces of evidence, her assurances to herself that more had happened than dark, cramped, sweaty, random sex. It told their story so effectively, and she couldn't resist the urge to pick it up again and again, trying so hard to see if this time, perhaps, she'd gain some new insight, see some new logic as to what had happened and why.

Why? She could never get past the why of it. She would read for hours, straight through. Sometimes she'd pull out her journals and read them too, either before, after, or at the same time as the emails, trying to keep them in chronological order with each other. And the poems. The endless pouring out of her creative soul that had started not long after they'd met and had continued with the ups and downs of her moods, trying to express what it was this all meant to her, how it made her feel, what lessons it held for her.

Sometimes she'd cry after reading the poems, or become angry all over again, reliving the pain or the joy or the abject despair. She'd stay up too late, get a crick in her neck, sometimes fall asleep reading. It was becoming a more and more frequent pastime.

The video tape took a little more effort, and the right timing. It required a special case in which it had to be placed before it could be played on the VCR. And she could only watch it if she was alone, if the kids were asleep or gone. No one else could ever see her dancing shamelessly in lingerie. Just him.

And she had to be in the right mood. It made her laugh, most of the time. But sometimes, seeing how much effort she'd put into it, she would realize again that it had been meant as a valentine to him, a message within a message, the hidden, silent words screaming, "I love you so much! See how much I love you?"

Victoria had placed Michael's letter beneath the two tapes, knowing that it would become part of her ritual as well, that she would re-read that letter over and over, attempting to see if there was something to it that she hadn't gleaned at first, some unspoken message. Or just read it again knowing it might be the only thing she'd ever receive from him, have of his, that he had touched. She ran her fingers over his name, written in his hand, imagining his fingerprints, at least, touching hers. These mementos were all she had.

SINGLE-MINDEDNESS

9/10/02
Still fantasizing that Michael will suddenly see the light, have to drive down here in the middle of the night, show up on my doorstep, and not be able to live without me. But it feels different, like a game I play with myself to keep myself amused—more than some hopeful fancy. I am tired of men, of looking for them, of wishing they were smarter, of believing they could be real. They are such odd and unpleasant creatures, really.

9/14/02
Mostly, I'm still grieving over Michael. I know it's gone on forever, but ever since his letter came, I feel like he was reaching out—but I am not moving backwards. He is not interested in me or my life. I don't know what it is between us, but it isn't enough. I need more. Too bad my chances of finding it are so small. I have these "visions" when I lie on my red chair. I lie back and can almost see him leaning on the banister into the dining room, looking at me and smiling. It is such a warm feeling, and it also turns me on a little. Then I get depressed because it will never be. I keep reading the letter I wrote him, and the one he wrote me, and I think wow—the only thing he's ever given me to remember him by is this letter. And the last thing I've ever given him is a piece of my mind. How could our timing be so wrong?

9/20/02
I imagined what I'd feel like if I were marrying Michael. Now look, I know that isn't exactly "letting go"—on the other hand, I see it for the fantasy it is and

know I have let myself off the hook about ever contacting him again. Anyway, in my imagination, I can't even wait for the minute to say the vows—I just start hooting and shouting and jumping up and down in uncontainable joy in a white mini skirt.

9/22/02

It was a year ago, on a Sunday just like today, that I went to NY for Deena's wedding and ended up staying all night getting my brains banged out by a guy 7 years younger than me. I mean, it's hard to believe it's been a year now, and I should be over this. I feel like step-by-step, I'm letting it go, and it becomes less and less concrete—haven't seen him since, after all—not even in the much-coveted photo I kept asking for. It's been 5 months since we've spoken on the phone—9 months since we've emailed! And only a couple weeks since I got that letter that sounded like we were old buds—and the same couple of weeks since I mailed my farewell, serious and intense I-love-you-but-I-gotta-let-you-go letter. How weird was that, that we would write each other on the same day? I wonder if he'll think of me today or tomorrow. I wonder if he'll be smiling or sighing with relief that I am finally stopping with the hopeful attitude. I wish I could feel as free as I tried to make myself sound. I thought if I mentally let go, if I did something concrete to "end" the fantasy, it would help me to move on. I feel worse in some ways NOW. I have NOTHING to hope for or believe in. If that wasn't it, if that wasn't real, then there's NOTHING out there. I cried—almost—today, realizing all the things I have to do or can't do because I chose to be a mom, and I chose to be responsible and put my family first. I don't regret these choices, and I love my kids so much it can be downright painful. But at what price? Am I never going to have a relationship again? If it's not with their dad, then who is out there for me? It doesn't look too good. Michael gave me hope where none existed. He made me feel like it wasn't all for nothing, like I had something someone wanted, and wasn't it great that I felt that way in return? But now I see that it was fleeting, like everything else. No permanence, nothing I could count on. I still feel angry about that, though there's nothing he did or didn't do that was unfair or overtly hurtful. There were no promises made, no real plans for a future. I still think if we ever run into each other again, there'd be sparks, but that is all, and sparks aren't enough. They sure do feel good, though. I don't even feel hopeful about ever having sex again. It's so sad. Really sad. A whole year, and how long till I smile that way again? Ever?

Victoria felt as though her heart had become too heavy to lift. She felt that she'd somehow missed her chance, that she'd run out of turns to find her happiness. It felt very final and sad. She knew that deep inside, he was the only one she would ever feel this way about, and that with him gone, it would be a long and lonely road. She was so sick of friends telling her that she just had to wait for the right guy, that somewhere, he was out there, and that he would show up at the right time, when she was really ready to find him. She was sick of optimism and hope, and she could trick herself into it once in a while, but only as a diversion, really, because she knew, down in the pit of her bones, that he was it. He was the one.

On her weekends alone, in particular, when the house was quiet save for the purring of the cat, she'd sit at the kitchen table, chin on her hand, elbow resting on the table. She'd lose track of all time just staring into space, her mind running scenarios in which they'd meet again. Maybe in another few years. Maybe in a decade.

Maybe when they were old and stooped, they'd meet again, quite by chance, and though their eyes had become more wrinkled and their hair had grayed, and even with their memories faltering and their steps more cautious, their hearts would leap, even maybe before they'd consciously realized and recognized the other, their hearts would slam against their frail cages, eager to return to home, to the other. And all time would slip away and their eyes would shine with the memory and the recognition that before them stood the one true connection. And words would not even be necessary.

🎧 *"You Are the One," ©1985, by Michael Rutherford & Christopher Neil*

9/27/02

My mind is very occupied with thinking of missed chances. Why did I leave NY in such a hurry? Why was getting back here to a training session more important than sleeping longer and maybe getting closer to a man I was falling for? And missing out on an opportunity perhaps to have more mind-blowing sex? Why did I bolt? Was I scared of how great it felt? I had never really considered that, but isn't it possible? That so many wires have been crossed since then is no big surprise given the miraculous beginning. But why do I go on and on about this? I'm never going to see this person again—not that I can figure. And if I did, so what? He hasn't ever given me cause to believe he has strong feelings about me. But I guess I've interpreted certain things to mean, in fact, that he does have some strong feelings, but that he chose to shelve them, or ignore them, or run away from them. That's a choice, though. Why can't I accept it and be done? Will I ever be done? I'm so sad and lonely when I realize my life is going to go on much as it is—work, family, church. Nothing else. Nobody else in my life. It feels so odd. I don't have hope. That seems to be gone.

THIS LETTER NOT SENT October 29, 2002

Dammit Michael,

Every time I think I'm done thinking of you, spending my precious time daydreaming about you, wondering why and what if, every time, I once again get caught up in the memories of your skin and your body and your hands. I can hear your voice, your laughter, your whispers. I have tried to forget you. I have gotten angry and put you right out of my mind and sworn off you and any other men for that matter. I have tried dating and found myself horrendously bored, turned off, or scared. I have tried throwing myself into my work, my kids, my friends and family, and came up short every time because something was missing.

What did you do to me? What happened that I feel this strongly about you, that I'm willing to repeatedly make a total fool of myself, throwing my all into telling you every thought and feeling, when every indication says you have never had that much interest? Why set myself up for that let-down?

When I think back on conversations we have had, I remember times it seemed you had feelings for me...or the makings of them, anyway. When you said you wished I was younger and had no kids, yes, it hurt me, but what was behind that? Why did you wish that? If I didn't have kids and was younger, what would that have meant to you? Was there some sort of connection you felt to me that those facts seemed to obstruct? I can't get you out of my mind, and my body can't get you out of its physical sensation recall. That lightning bolt you mentioned, it happened to me. It was more like a hammer on the head, but it happened. NO one else has made me respond like you have, ever. Not when I've met them in a bar, not when I've had a chance run-in at a party or a friend's house, not when I was 20, 30 or 40, not when I was single or married. Not even my own husband ever made me feel so totally invested, body, mind, and spirit, in being with just one person so completely. How am I to "move on" when no one else compares even a little? How, when I've experienced total satisfaction in knowing who I am when I'm with you, can I ever feel the slightest bit satisfied with someone else?

I hate this feeling. I don't want it anymore. I'd rather go on indefinitely without anyone at all then be plagued with the knowledge that I was with someone who wasn't quite enough. I'm tired of being imprisoned by these feelings, and I don't know what to do with them. I want to rush to you and throw myself at your feet, or I want to punch your face in, or I want to run the other way as far and as fast as I can. Mostly, I want you to want me too. I want you to come to the realization that we have something important between us and that it shouldn't be denied, and that no obstacles like space and time and circumstance should ever prevent us from being together. That's what I want. I want to hold you and be held by you and feel the warmth of your body against mine again, and feel your hands on me, touching me or clasping my hands. I want to look into your eyes again and see your smile and taste your kiss. I want to speak with you at length about the world, our worlds, our lives, our thoughts and feelings. I want to connect with you again that way and in every way. I want to matter to you the way you matter to me, which is like no other person in my life. Only my children matter that much to me, but in a different way.

I don't know what it is you're looking for in your life. I know you think the right job in the right location will somehow bring all other rewards in their time. I just think you should know that our hearts can't be responsible for whom they choose, and no amount of planning and visualizing can prepare you when it hits you, when it's standing right in front of you beckoning to you. "I'm your future!" it screams, "don't ignore me!" If you turn your back on it, you don't know when it will return, or if. Did you not feel any of that? Did you not hear that call? It's hard to imagine it was so loud and clear and only I heard it...it's hard to fathom that a message so blatantly broadcast to me could be false information. And yet, here I sit, questioning it, for if it was true and real, wouldn't it be within my grasp? Wouldn't YOU be within my grasp?

Maybe it is only for the universe to know. Maybe in time, the message will be understood. Maybe, in time, the connection will be complete. Maybe it is time itself that I must wait on. Maybe someday, you will be there before me again and you will be listening and hearing it and seeing it and accepting it. Maybe one day the timing will be right.

11/17/02

I wrote a poem today about what else? Michael. This time it was about the constant image I can conjure of him in the room with me. Usually when I'm drifting off to sleep or alone daydreaming, he is there and he answers all my prayers. He is perfect, in my mind. He is everything and he has become that through my own devotion to the fantasy of him. I so wish it were real.

Spectre Staring

Spectre staring

Sleeping on my pillow

Sharing every dream

Saving this lonely heart from despairing

Still waiting for you

Slide beneath my covers

Silhouette in the dark

Settle this storm within

Sighing beside me

Saying all the words

Staying forever

Semi-conscious existence

Starlight and twilight

Singing me to sleep

11-17-02

12/8/02
I think I went most of Saturday (or was it Friday?) without thinking about him. I was pleased. But today he's there in double strength.

12/24/02
All I want for Christmas...evades me. All I've ever wanted since that fateful day is not possible. I've been obsessed these last few days—more so than usual, or at least more so recently than I have been in a while—with thoughts and dreams of Michael. I did it to myself last night—I listened to the tape again, looked longingly at my one crummy picture, read our last communications to each other with all the irony of the situation hitting me full force. I dreamt of him while I slept, of touching his beautiful face and body and having him near me. I've imagined every kiss and touch that ever was and many that I've only dreamed up. I had such strong urges to call him yesterday, or really and truly drive to him, which of course I reasoned myself out of. All I have to do is recall some of his less-than-perfect reactions to me, some of his less-than-encouraging words, and I know he doesn't want me in his life. How come it still hurts? How come I'm still not done with this? What can I possibly still have to gain from continuing to wish for something not within my grasp? How come every other man I've met has fallen so short of the mark, and can't begin to compete with someone who by now should be only a memory?

12/28/02
My biggest obstacle may very well be that there's no one else I want to touch me except him.

As the chill winter months passed, Victoria's escape became her poetry. She had no new experiences to describe or process, only the same tired refrain. But somehow, she kept finding new ways to interpret it, or feel it, all over again. She would sit on her bed and scribble out words, or at the computer, hands poised over the keyboard, small desk lamp burning into the loveless Saturday nights, passing judgment on herself or on him, or taking another look from another angle. These words formed pictures in her mind that either soothed or tortured, but always followed the same weary pathways. Strangely, she felt great satisfaction and even a little comfort in her musings. For above all else, she realized that she was tapping into a deep well of creativity that had been undiscovered prior to him. And if for no other reason than to keep it open and flowing, she remained in the shadow-land of memory and fantasy.

Reading the signs
Clearing confusions
Judging perceptions
Drawing conclusions
Following pathways
Making assumptions
Shaping the future
Allowing presumptions
Kidding yourself
Living in lies
Breeding false hopes
Unprepared for goodbyes
12/30/02

In passing,
Eyes locking,
Hearts pounding
Hands holding
Mouths searching
Ears straining
Hips meeting
Breath gasping
Smiles playing
Words saying
Thoughts wandering
Dreams awakening
Prayers seeking

Questions dangling
Promises breaking
Hopes dashing
Teeth grinding
Fists pounding
Tears spilling
Eyes swelling
Lips trembling
Memories lingering
1-15-03

How blurry now the lines of your face
How incomplete the sequence of events, the details
How vague the sensation of your touch...
And yet...
How clearly still I hear your voice
Saying shyly "I want to kiss you"
How well I recall the way your hands
Reached for my feet as I stretched,
Unsure you were, of touching me
And tenderly you brushed my hair
Off my neck
As you came up behind me
Your arms circling my waist
Your warm lips resting in the curve between shoulder and neck
How easily you held me in the hours before dawn
How unabashedly happy those days and weeks
Before reality took hold
How lovely the dream
Before the alarm clock rudely awakens
2/7/03

Releasing the Dove

❧

They entered the doorway, entered the past. The candy counter remained, as ever, an invitation to find a treat. Victoria's mind relived the many times she and her sister had skipped, walked, run, or ridden their bikes down the paths leading from their house to the plaza. This plaza, where their mom had worked in the small one-room post office, where the spring had brought crowds to enjoy the festival of music, food, entertainment, and paddle boating; this plaza, where Victoria and her friends had come to shop for earrings at the small shops, or buy hair products at the salon, or a sandwich and a coke at the deli; this plaza, that housed one of the oldest and enduring institutions, the Lakeside Pharmacy, where Victoria was now looking for a seat at the lunch counter.

And with her, her dad, Deena, and Todd. They were in town visiting the old neighborhood, Todd's first trip there. Deena was showing him all the old hangouts, the school field, the paths, the plaza. And now they were all sitting down to lunch. It wasn't the same as back then. Back in the "old days," you ordered onion rings and fries with lots of ketchup and slurpee-like drinks from the machine that churned them out day and night in blue and pink and yellow and green. You ordered BLTs and hamburgers and meatball subs.

Now the manager and his staff were Salvadoran, and the menu had items like papusas and chicken on a spit. They found a table where they could all sit and spread out, as Deena had brought along her wedding album. Victoria had seen it in her hands, had felt the adrenaline rush as she realized that she would see pictures she'd never seen before, that maybe one or two of the pictures might actually include Michael, perhaps from a distance, but maybe, just maybe close up.

But it would have to wait. They looked over the small, grease-smeared menus, then waited for the waitress to come take their order. Deena was telling Todd a story from when they were little, when she and Victoria had played out on the school field a game they'd invented called "Mother Nature." They would go out on a windy day and spin around in circles, pretending the wind was so strong they could not escape its grip. They would be tossed and thrown across the field, behind trees, into each other, screaming, and beg Mother Nature to not be so angry. They would promise her their service and loyalty and bow down before her mighty power. If only she would stop torturing them, beating them down. The two women laughed at the memory.

Victoria's father then began a long retelling of a story from a case he'd been handling at the courthouse. He was invigorated by the fact that he had a new audience, and particularly because Todd was a lawyer. He was a good storyteller, giving many details and dramatic pauses, his facial expressions animated and somewhat comical. Deena and Todd were patient and well-behaved listeners, with no eye-rolling or watch-checking as Victoria and her siblings had been known to do during a particularly long retelling.

The food arrived, and still they chatted on between bites of food and laughter. Finally the plates were cleared, and coffee was ordered. Deena and Todd announced that they were meeting up with some other old neighbors soon, so didn't have much time. For just a moment, Victoria felt a panic rise within her, accepting the possibility that she might not, after all, see the album. But Deena was too excited about showing it. She'd brought it along for just this reason, and now, as they waited for the coffee, she pulled it up off of her lap and laid it down on the table.

The photographer had used a technique where the pictures were actually part of the pages rather than affixed to them as separate photos. Deena went painstakingly through each page, one at a time, and since she was holding the book, Victoria pretended to nonchalantly admire each and every picture. Beneath the table, her right hand gripped her left, leaving fingernail imprints in her palm.

When Deena turned the last page, and the last mumbled compliment about her dress had been uttered, Victoria asked if she could take a second look through the album. She bit her lip and tried not to turn the pages too quickly. She had an urge to rip every page out and to fly through the album until she'd settled on the pages that held her interest, for there had been several. But she looked at each page, one at a time, feigning equal interest in each photograph.

But there he was. As the bride and groom turned to face their audience, just having been pronounced husband and wife, there, standing in full frontal visibility, was Michael, his legs planted firmly as he held the video camera to his face, filming the ceremony. Though his face was 80% covered by the camera and his hands, his body was completely in view. Victoria hungrily stared at him from top to bottom, reminding herself of his size, his solidity. She longed to run her fingers over his image, but dared not linger too long on any one photo of him.

And there again, in Central Park, at the Bethesda Terrace, a photograph of the entire wedding party, different but similar to the one Victoria had been sent in the mail. In this version, her eyes were open, her arm was not in front of her face, and Michael was clearer and seemed closer to the camera. He was smiling and Victoria felt herself flooded with emotion. The picture that had been mailed to all the guests had been blurry, had not been that flattering to either of them. If only Deena had chosen this version to send out instead! Victoria could not help but comment aloud.

"Wow, this is a great shot, Deena! I wish I had a copy of this one," and then realizing she would be giving too much away, added, "I don't have my eyes shut in this one."

She asked Deena if there were a way to order any of the pictures from the photographer. She knew that most photographers offered that option to their clients as a way to make more money. But Deena didn't seem to know, and didn't seem all that interested in finding out. Victoria asked again if she could check into it, because there were a couple photos she'd be interested in purchasing.

She almost asked if she could run to a Kinko's quickly and at least copy the pictures but refrained, knowing how desperate and pathetic that would sound. She bit back her desire to ask more questions about Michael, though they buzzed around in her head like angry bees (have you heard from him? have you seen him since then? does he ever mention me?). She also forced herself to close the album and return it, though not without regret, to Deena.

They drank their coffee, and she her water, and Victoria stole glances at the album as it lay closed in front of Deena on the table. She longed to take another look, to take it home and sleep with it, to add it to her collection. She shook her head to jar loose such thoughts and attempted, rather unsuccessfully, to return to the present moment.

2/24/03
I saw Deena this past weekend. She and Todd were down visiting. She brought her wedding album, and there were actually 2 different photos that had him in them. One was an amazing shot of the whole wedding party, much better than the one she sent out. He was looking directly at the camera. It was a good shot of me too. I have asked her if there's some way I could get a print of it. I would like to frame it. It is the most memorable day of my life and I want to always honor it. I didn't feel sad or depressed though. Just wistful. I think I am starting to let go of it. He really wasn't the one—he was just a damn good imitation.

3/13/03
I wanted to call Michael this morning (it's 6:15 a.m.) and say, "Ya know, I still compare every man I go out with to you. So, I want to thank you for giving me a standard, but I feel like cursing you for making it so frigging high."

Releasing the Dove

I figured it out,
After only a year
The gift that he gave me
The smile past the tear
I often have wondered
And pondered and wept
And kept the wheels turning
Long after I slept
What fine fate, what reason
Made our two paths cross?
And then just as quickly
Created such loss?
It never made sense
It never brought peace
It never allowed all the
Theories to cease
A glimmer sometimes
Of a blessing somehow
Perhaps to remind me
To live in the Now
Perhaps to establish
The level of joy
That I achieved loving
And being loved by that boy
Perhaps to unlock me
Mind, body and soul
From the frost and the frostbite
Gone out of control
Or maybe, more simply,
To slowly erase

Single-Mindedness

The tears and the sorrow
Etched deep in this face
But none of those reasons
Has satisfied yet
There's always the afterward
The why-had-we-met?
What kind of god
Would put him in my path
Then take him away
Leaving me aftermath?
I wanted him so much
I believed I would do
Most anything, anything,
To make it come true
But despite all my yearning
And longing and prayers
I discovered what I believed
Meant, no one cares
Not god, not the boy,
Not the strong winds of change
Not promises, practices,
Not the plans we arrange
No, none of it matters
And none of it stops
And nobody cares if
Another tear drops.
It took me a year,
As I say, as I write,
To finally see what
Brought all this to light.

It wasn't to please me
Or thaw me or teach me
It wasn't to finally have
Somebody reach me
No, none of those things
Was the answer I've sought
It came to me casually
Without too much thought
The reason he came to me
Loved me and left
The reason I got to feel
Full, then bereft
Was to give me a memory
Of passion and bliss
Of the last time I loved
Of the last time I kissed
No one should only
Remember the pain
Of rejection, of emptiness
Days full of rain
Much better to look back
And feel bittersweet joy
From the arms of a lover
A beautiful boy.
4/20/03

Seams

I only know the mem'ry,
Only whispers of the truth
Glances and sensations and

A tapping into youth
I only feel an emptiness
That nothing can replace
The ardour of his kisses
And the passion in his face
The pumping of my bloodstream
And the tingling of my skin
The crying of my heart's voice
"Open up and let me in!"
A part of me was born that day
Another part has died
Some parts of me remember
Potent potion trapped inside
Some days I can release it and
Forget it and move on
But days like this one haunt me
And consume me in their dawn
The night will be the longest
Restless pitching in my dreams
Darkness will enfold me as I
Unravel at the seams

5/9/03

5/11/03
Trying to decide about mailing a letter to Michael. Felt good writing it, but not sure how I feel now...it's sitting here ready to go, but not sure I'll mail it. What, after all, would be the point?

BAD DECISIONS

May 12, 2003

Dear Michael,

This letter may or may not get to you, since I don't even know if you still live in New York. In a way, I hope you don't, because that will mean you've found a job and moved, hopefully to New England where you'd hoped to land. Of course, on the other hand, I hope this reaches you and finds you in good health and spirits.

I suppose it may come as a surprise that I'm writing, based on the last letter I sent. In an ironic twist of fate, your letter to me arrived the day after I mailed the letter to you. I laughed bitterly at the time, thinking "Timing is everything." As has been the case with all our exchanges, the timing has played a role in either making them totally work or miserably fail. But isn't it odd that we basically wrote to one another on the same approximate day?

In my letter to you last summer, I said a lot of things. They were all true for me at that time. What I've found, however, is that despite trying my best to live my life without you in it in any form whatsoever, I just can't make it work. I still write poems about you. Yes, after all this time, there are still things I have to express. I still re-read all of the poems, and the letter you sent, the one thing you ever sent to me. I still listen to the tape I made of songs that, at the time I made it, represented to me all the feelings I was having. I have argued numerous times with myself over whether to share these thoughts with you. My cutting things off last summer felt to me like I was helping you out of a bind...how to politely, without hurting me, get me to leave you alone. You never said you wanted that, of course, but I always felt like I was a little obsessive where you were concerned.

So why write now? It's strange...mostly, out of curiosity. I just want to know where you ended up, and how things are going for you. How is your heart, I wonder? What job did you end up getting? Are you happy in your new home, assuming you moved? How is your dad? Did you hear about Deena & Todd's new baby? So many things I still want to know. I drove up to Lawrenceville last weekend for my friend's 40th bday, and the drive was full of reminders of my trip to NYC. Seeing the signs for Havre de Grace also reminded me painfully of how close we came to getting together a second time. I still wonder to this day what happened there. Something scared you off...I re-read all the emails we sent to each other and in retrospect, while I definitely pursued you, it was your idea in the first place to get together again! I always thought it was mine. It surprised me to read what you had to say back then. Somehow, you scared yourself, or the idea of seeing me scared you, or something. For the record, I scared myself as well. I was ready to do just about anything, and that frightened me. I think I would have entertained thoughts of moving to New England and having all your babies if you'd asked me to, despite what I may have said at the time about needing to stay here and being done with kids. Who am I kidding, I DID think those things! How's THAT for scary? I suppose it is ancient history now anyway.

I went to Ocean City this weekend with a friend, and was reminded of your letter where you told me you'd just been there with some friends. There isn't much that DOESN'T remind me of you, frankly. I wrote a poem recently that felt, at the time I wrote it, like I finally had figured out why fate put us together. I always need a reason, and I couldn't for the life of me figure it out. It puzzled me a long, long time. Why meet someone I felt so compatible with if there was no hope of a future? I tried on lots of reasons, but none of them ever satisfied me. Finally, it came to me one night that the reason was this: I shouldn't have as my last experience with a lover the memory of pain and emptiness (what I experienced with my ex husband); it should be beautiful and fun and exciting and happy. That I can look back at that and remember the kisses and lovemaking in a joyful context is so much better as a memory.

Of course, a week later, my thoughts rambled some more and now I'm stuck in Michael-mode again. What that means is I think of you very often and fight the urge to call. I don't want to intrude on your life, I don't want to hear in your voice anxiety over me getting in touch, which is what I fear. I don't want to risk feeling hurt again. It's so silly...I'm far too grown up for these girlish feelings. Still, there you have it.

Don't know how you feel about me contacting you, but here I am. A brief update: I started working this past September as a part-time kindergarten teacher. It was very stressful going back to work after so many years, but good to start getting paychecks again. In March, the school piloted an all-day kindergarten program, so now I'm full-time, yet another big change. My house is a mess (no time for cleaning), my time is at a premium, but all in all we are healthy and happy. Looking VERY forward to summer break. Contrary to what you thought, my kids did not have to change schools this year...I purposely looked for a house that was in a neighborhood zoned to the same school. That has worked out well. I'm now trying to get a transfer to teach at their school so life will be a little less complicated (i.e., no more running about getting them to various friends' and neighbors' homes for before- and after-school care). Not sure whether the transfer will pan out or not, but cautiously hopeful.

Other than that, life goes on. Bought a new car with my new money. Have been trying to get out more. With the stress of working, I have felt more of a need to party. Been going out dancing a lot with all my "single" (aka, divorced) friends. It's fun, though exhausting. My body doesn't recover as quickly from drinking and pounding my feet all night as it did in my 20s. It's worth it though, since it makes me feel alive. I love music and dancing.

Well, that about says it all. I have absolutely no expectation of hearing back from you. You certainly may if you want to. This must seem so out-of-the-blue. I can't really put a definition on what it is I seek by writing you...just interested in your life, I guess, and still feeling totally connected to you. How odd to have thoughts at times that I may never see you again...so strange a concept when meeting you has come to have been a very defining moment in my life. I sometimes fantasize over what circumstances it would take to "accidentally" meet up with you...it usually involves a funeral...how dark!

Peace! Vicki

P.S. I remembered your birthday last July, but didn't send a card. I wrote a birthday poem for you, but also did not send. I hope it was a good birthday. You have another coming up soon. Stay healthy! My 40th was fantastic...went to New Mexico and rode in a hot air balloon, as promised. Spectacular! I highly recommend it.

5/12/03

I mailed it. I don't know why. I'm entering into obsessive behavior again, and that frightens me a little. I think maybe I have a pattern and I'm not so good at letting go. I don't want to keep intruding on his life, but I don't seem able to stop, either. I talked a little about it to my cousin tonight. I felt embarrassed to say how pathetic I am. None of the reasons I usually give myself sounded remotely logical aloud to another human. I need to get over it and move on, but I am unable to pull myself out of the spiral that sends me down the same self-destructive paths time and time again.

I still think I love Michael, but I also think I'm an obsessive raving lunatic who wouldn't know love if it bit me in the ass.

Inertia

Every tide that has turned

Every chapter that has ended

Reminds me that these strong feelings have yet to be rescinded

Every strong wind of change

Gusting through, blowing through me

Doesn't sweep clean the writing in the sand that clings to me

Every rain drop that falls

Every tear drop to follow

Doesn't wash away the lumps in my throat as I swallow

Every dream that recedes

Every wish that's forgotten

Doesn't plummet to the darkness of the well's endless bottom

Every minute, every hour

Every day, every year

Doesn't heal all the wounds that my heart's learned to fear

With the passage of time

And the changing of the guard

Why this time and this place standing still, frozen hard?

Every path leads me back
Every journey takes me here
Sluggish snail steps of progress go toward nothing crystal clear
Like an Eastern tale from Buddha
Slippery knowledge not yet heeded
I am stuck inside this cycle, the lesson ceaselessly repeated
5-14-03

5/15/03
I feel a little embarrassed having gone back on my promise not to contact him. I made that promise to me as much as to him. It kept me from going off the deep end, and now I'm back in it, thankfully without the intensity of what it once was, yet still enough to bring me the entire range of feelings, from joy to anger to pain to grief to total rapture to depleting misery. Of course I indulged in the ultimate sin—I read all the emails and poems again, and listened to the tape. Why do I do that? It's like eating an entire cake. You know it's too much, you'll feel sick, but you keep stuffing it down your gullet. Sick, really, to do it on purpose like that. It's intentional wallowing, that's what it is. It almost feels good to re-live it all. Perverse, eh? I'd say I disgust myself, but I know full well that I enjoyed it in some masochistic way, and will most likely indulge in it again. Why else keep that damned box so handy?

5/17/03
Spent a long time this a.m. thinking of Michael. I don't guess I'll hear from him. Maybe he burned my letter, or threw it out unread. Maybe he laughed and showed it to his friends as evidence of me being a total psycho. Maybe it never reached him. Or maybe he's been thinking it over. Maybe he wants to tell me off, or beg me to leave him the hell alone, or tell me to seek professional help or to get a life; maybe he feels the same as me, but he's too scared to deal with it, or maybe he'll come to the conclusion that it is best left alone. Or maybe he'll come rushing down here and sweep me off my feet and ask me to never leave his side, and maybe I'll say okay. Kiss and fade out to credits...

Victoria got up off the couch, feeling irritable and grumpy. Another weekend on her own, and she didn't have any exciting plans. She'd been trying internet dating on for size, and it wasn't panning out in any real way. She'd email with different men, only to find them sorely lacking in one department or another. She'd met a few of them for coffee or lunch or dinner, but it never got past the first date. She didn't have her heart in it, and she didn't care that much when the men didn't call back or email again. She had reached a lull in the dating frenzy she'd been pushing herself into. After the initial ego boost of many responses to her online ad, the emails had tapered down to a few semi-interested suitors, none of whom she had the energy or motivation to engage in conversation. None of them came close to Michael, and he, unfortunately, was the bar that had been raised.

The battle continued within Victoria, month after month, reneging on promises to put aside her fantasies, to leave him alone and let him be. But like a persistent fly buzzing in her ear in the night, she couldn't swat away the curiosity of what he was doing and with whom, and wishing for the eight-hundredth time why it couldn't be her in the picture. Perhaps it was the loneliness getting to her again. Sometimes she felt resigned to it; other times, it infuriated her. To have had such a beautiful package presented to her, a gift she couldn't have imagined, and then to have had it snatched away before she'd even finished opening it. It still rankled her. It still depressed her. It still got under her skin. And at times, she imagined that he was the one who had taken away her chance at happiness, while at other times it seemed like some cruel joke being enjoyed by the gods or the Universe.

🎧 *"Blurry," ©2001, by Wesley Scantlin, Doug Ardito, & Jimmy Allen*

7/10/03
He's so ever-present in my mind. I wonder why some times, more than others, my thoughts are consumed by memories of him and fantasies of what might have been? Is it every time I start to feel so lonely? I don't know. I sure wish we were at least on speaking terms. I want to know what he's doing and how he's doing. I know that would be torture. I still wish I could just hear his voice. But wouldn't that be torture too? He might sound panicked and nervous as if talking to me were somehow threatening. What a lovely view of myself. And from someone who, at one time, gave me the most attractive view of myself I'd ever had.

7/12/03
I've been on a few dates now with a guy I met online. His name is Pete, and our first date was on the 4th of July. And there were fireworks that night, all right. What can I say? I was starving for it! I've been filling Sandy in on the whole thing, and she asked me how Pete compared with Michael. I really struggled to sort it out, but awoke early this morning with a clearer picture of it all.

Michael...he was like a natural disaster, well, not a disaster, but he had the intensity and electricity and power of a violent storm, snapping limbs off trees, causing flash flooding, knocking down power lines which then jerked around dangerously on wet pavement, sparking and sizzling. He was like an earthquake, shifting tectonic plates, causing rifts in the solid ground, mercilessly shaking the earth. He was like torrential downpours rapidly overflowing streams, traveling in powerful waves across the horizon. He was thunder-loud and lightning electric-hot bright. He stormed in with powerful raw beauty, a force to be in awe of, an unstoppable force against which there was no retaliation or protection. He just was. He came on fast, without warning, wreaked his natural pure havoc, then was gone, leaving behind ravaged landscapes and singed nerve endings.

Pete is like a slow steady rain. He takes his time, soaking into the soil, nourishing the flowers, slowly easing the parched earth. The hypnotic steadiness of his rainfall, leading to calm, safe places. He keeps raining until it is enough and doesn't tire or fade. And because of him, from the earth, beautiful things will grow. And he leaves behind a rainbow, glorious to behold, sparkling drops on blades of grass and sunshine peeking through the clouds.

Victoria and Pete continued dating throughout the month of July. She liked that he wasn't a totally intense experience. It felt like a soft quiet rain after Michael's torrential downpour.

And yet. Michael was still there, in the back of her mind, at all times. She was constantly comparing Pete to him. Yes, Pete was smart. Good. No, Pete didn't always get her sense of humor. But Pete liked kids! He had one of his own! And he wasn't looking for someone younger, and he lived in the same state, for crying out loud. And he wasn't bad looking. Okay, it wasn't an instant attraction. Her heart didn't explode each time she saw him, but who wanted to be exploding all the time? She felt relieved that he was smoother, calmer, less of a wildfire.

And yet...

Things with Pete didn't work out. It wasn't a happy ending, either. Things went sour. Expectations weren't met; misunderstandings turned into major issues. It turned out he did have some intensity, completely unexpected, and completely unacceptable to Victoria.

It shouldn't have come as a great surprise to Victoria that things didn't work out. After all, she still had this ghost in the back of her mind that never really left her thoughts, never really left her heart free. Sometimes it was a comfort knowing he was still there; but most of the time, she cursed his existence. It seemed he kept her from moving forward, going on with her life.

Granted, Pete had had some pretty big issues, and they had moved too quickly into a relationship, perhaps, just maybe, to help fill the void she'd been feeling, to try and drown out the echo of his voice. In a white hot flash, it was over, and she retreated to the security of her self-imposed, womb-like isolation.

She slept in a ball, curled around herself, protecting what was left of her heart, of her spirit. She whispered to Puzzle, the cat, "You won't leave me girl, will you? You will always be my constant companion," and she'd pet the cat, scratch her under the chin and behind the ears and lavish on her all the love she wished someone would finally lavish on her, and she cried silently into her pillow at night, not wanting to upset the kids, not allowing herself to actually voice her pain, which should have retreated so long ago, should not still be part of her daily existence. And she returned to the box in the closet, choosing the familiar darkness of the past over the infinite void of the future.

8/7/03
Each time I reopen The Box, its contents completely transport me back to that time and those feelings. I can't help but be excited seeing those first emails, I can't help but cry when he tells me no, and get so angry all over again at how he let me go; the audio tape makes me feel every feeling along the way and I laugh and cry and sigh; the video...the video. I see how happy and excited I was and I can almost feel it again—almost, but not quite. I can't quite reach that level again. I feel hollow inside—to have been so filled with joy and hope and expectation not knowing it would all be pulled out from under me in such a short time. His reaction to the video—so impressed and flattered and still so interested. What went wrong? I torture myself again and again, wondering how it could have been so close within my grasp, and then gone, as though it had never existed.

And then later, the emails as we tried to establish a friendship. Even then, he seemed somewhat invested.

I'm crazy, I tell you. I still even now want to see him, to touch him, as if he'd allow it! I want to drive to his house and fall into his arms and not say a word, or say everything. I want to believe that somewhere deep inside him is a part that still feels something for me, that there's still some kind of connection.

And I know I am asking for nothing less than a miracle, and I know I would be intentionally ASKING for my own heart to please be broken completely. Why would I feel driven to do that? Am I hoping for some Hollywood ending? I know I'm out of my mind. Everyone thinks so, where this subject is concerned. Why don't I want to hear that? I just don't want to lose the one brightest spot in my past that ever made any sense whatsoever. Any at all.

Victoria remained in her retreated state for some time, licking her wounds and gathering just enough strength to live out the basics of her life. She held onto the memory of Michael like a security blanket, recalling that he had been a positive and nurturing force, no matter how flashflood he had raced through her life.

Sometimes, when she recalled the times it had all seemed like a possibility, she would imagine how he felt about her, not just how she felt about him. And it soothed her to imagine he was as deeply moved and cared as intensely about her. That it had been as meaningful an event in his life as it had been in hers, and that, despite his reluctance to accept it, he somewhere, deep inside himself, recognized that they had been meant to be.

🎧 *"Again,"* ©2000, by Lenny Kravitz

At other times, she felt tortured with the memory of Michael, as if he were always going to be there, hanging over her like a dark cloud. And she wondered if it would always be this way, painful and taking her breath away, like a punch in the stomach. Would he stay there, haunting her, following her through the years, attached by that invisible chain she'd placed around her ankle, and had since lost or thrown away the key?

She beat her head with the flats of her palms, symbolically trying to beat the thoughts out of her mind. The pain had gone on too long, and she couldn't control when it set in or for how long. She unkindly chided herself about her once-fantasy to run into him years later, to reignite the spark. It now seemed it would only re-intensify the torture.

Crystal shards
In too deep
I've dug at them with nails and needles
Under the skin now
Sharp pain when I least expect it
Stepping lightly
Waiting for absorption into my system
8/11/03

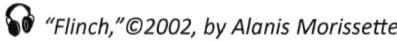 *"Flinch,"©2002, by Alanis Morissette*

8/16/03
Had a lovely dream in the early hours. I was with Michael. All I could think of was his beautiful hairy chest. I was sitting on his lap and we were embracing, and he said, "The problem is, I want more than just your legs," which, in my dream, I knew meant he wanted more than just sex. I was trying to articulate to him that I felt the same way. I can't remember much more than that, but I woke in one of my dream humps where I was sure I was having sex with him. I wish it so badly sometimes.

Victoria rubbed at her inner thighs gently, trying to recreate the feeling she'd had just before she'd awakened, but it was too late, it was gone. Her hands felt cold and unfamiliar, and he wasn't really there, after all, was he?

She stretched and moved one leg at a time slowly off the edge of the bed. She knew she needed to get up and get moving. She and the kids were heading to Baltimore today to visit her friend Liv, husband Bill and their boys. They would spend the majority of the time at the pool, then head back to Liv's and spend the night. The kids missed each other so much since Liv's family had moved to Maryland. They could only get together once every other month or so, despite the fact that it was only an hour and a half drive between the two places.

Victoria was looking forward to seeing her old friends. They were probably the only two people who knew her well enough to realize that she was finally returning to herself, the self that had existed before she'd been married. Liv had started seeing Bill while Victoria and Liv had been post-college roommates. Max had entered the picture not long afterwards. They'd been to each other's weddings, experienced the births of each other's children, and now they had supported her through her separation.

The one thing they had not been so solid on, however, had been attempting to understand and sympathize with her on the situation with Michael. And really, what was it she expected them to understand? What they knew of Michael was what she'd told them, and what she'd told them had been predicated so much on her own interpretations of events. They'd never met him, they weren't around when it had happened, had only heard snippets of the story during brief visits or short phone conversations.

Victoria realized she was having mixed feelings about the visit. It would be a comfort to be with friends who knew her so well, but it would also be a lonely existence, the third-wheel scenario, the lack of understanding of where she was in her single womanhood. They kept teasing her about finding a good one-night stand, and even had a young co-worker of Bill's in mind.

But Victoria wasn't interested. How could they possibly fathom how a one-night-stand repulsed her. How she knew that the planets could never be aligned quite the way they had that one night, so long ago, when that brief encounter had transpired, and some raw energy had been transmitted to Victoria that nothing could compare to.

And besides, they grew weary of her loyalty to this blip on the radar screen. They sent knowing glances to one another when she'd even dare to mention his name or that night. No one really believed that it had been that meaningful, and no one understood how it still so fully affected her. It was a solitary path she walked when it came to Michael. Her friends didn't really want to hear it anymore. Just like he didn't want to hear it anymore.

🎧 *"White Flag," ©2003, by Dido Armstrong, Rick Nowels,
and Rollo Armstrong*

Distance, time
Memories shift
Only the good parts remain
Smiling, sighing
The heaviness will lift
My ray of sun through the rain
Half-remembered dreams
Half-serious ideas
Half a mind to call you
Drive up to see you
Face to face
Eye to eye
Mouth to mouth
Would you run?
Would you laugh?
Would you be there?
Would you take me in your arms?
Take me?
Is there any more left?
Have you forgotten?
I could never say no to you
Day or night
Any time
I am yours
Always
Forever
Yours.
8/03

MISFIT

December 31, 2003

Victoria looked at herself in the bathroom mirror. It was speckled with dried water spots and flecks of gunk that had been flossed and flung out of her teeth. There was some smudged black (mascara?) on the middle pane of glass as well. She looked tired. She was. Her eyes were heavy and a little red. She had some circles beginning to form underneath them. No surprise, really. She and the kids had just flown back from Tucson, where they'd been visiting her sister for the past week during the winter break from school.

They'd flown out Christmas morning, an exceptionally good day for flying. There'd been no one at the airports, no lines, no waiting. It had been a great visit. Chloe and Connor had had no trouble jumping right into the middle of their five cousins and blending in. All in all, it had been a nice break from routine, and a happy reunion with family Victoria rarely got to see.

Now it was New Year's Eve. Victoria had chosen this day to fly back, hoping for as empty an airport as on Christmas and leaving herself enough time to switch back to East-coast time and to catch up on laundry before returning to work. She hadn't intended on doing anything more than getting the kids to bed and collapsing onto the sofa with some hot tea, but now they were home, it was still relatively early, and they were still awake, albeit travel-weary. The kids were begging to be taken to the annual New Year's Eve party at the Myers'.

Friends from church, the Myers held a party every year for all ages. Kids took over the basement and got to stay up to watch the ball drop; adults ate, drank, and conversed and then watched the ball drop; at about 11:30, everyone went outside to have a bonfire and beat on percussion instruments. It was fun and a safe drive back home.

Now Victoria was trying to come up with a good reason not to go, but couldn't. She thought they'd at least stay for a short time, and if they started showing signs of disintegration, they could come home and either watch Times Square from bed, or just go to sleep. So the question now was what to wear? All her clothes were dirty. She didn't feel like showering and primping at this point, but didn't want to show up in her stretch pants and a sweatshirt, either.

Victoria walked over to the suitcases that were haphazardly lying on her bedroom floor. She unzipped each one and began tossing clothes into laundry piles. After all the clothes were sorted into heaps, she pulled out a pair of jeans that didn't have any salsa stains and seemed relatively unwrinkled. These she put on, and then moved into the closet. What could she possibly pull off that was festive, cute, and clean? She finally decided on a black spaghetti-strapped satin top that was part of a mini-skirt and vest combo she'd bought for her 20th high school reunion. She pulled it over her head and went back into the bathroom. Immediately, she realized she'd need to shave her armpits. She pulled the top back off and leaned over the sink with her razor, carefully shaving, attempting not to drip any soapy, hairy water onto the waistband of her jeans. She patted her pits dry and reapplied deodorant, then donned the top again. She looked pale and dull.

Next stop: the kids' bathroom. Victoria remembered that Chloe had gotten some body glitter as a birthday present at her 10th birthday just a couple of weeks ago. Victoria pulled out a roll of toilet paper, some hair bands, and a bottle of hydrogen peroxide before she found the two tubes of glitter, one pink and one gold. She opted for the gold. She spread the sparkling lotion over her entire chest, neck, and shoulders, and even dabbed some on her cheekbones and eyelids.

That, with some extra mascara and eyeliner, and a careful application of fresh lipstick, seemed to do the trick. She tousled her hair and sprayed it liberally. As a last-minute, spontaneous thought, she dabbed some gold sparkling nail polish on each nail. It was mostly sparkle and no actual color, so it was easy to do it quickly, and still get away with an undetectable percentage of error. She was now passable as a party-goer.

Finally, Victoria put on a fresh pair of black socks and her black boots, rounded up the kids, and they headed off to the party.

❧

The party was in full swing when Victoria and the kids arrived. Chloe and Connor immediately disappeared into the basement, and Victoria was left to her own devices. Despite the popular belief that she was an outgoing extrovert, it was quite the opposite. Walking into a room full of people, even people she knew, was a daunting effort that drained her. Spending an evening talking, laughing, and looking perky was also hard work that Victoria usually needed lots of down time to recover from. That, mixed with a little jet lag and disorientation from being out of circulation for the last ten days, left her feeling shy and uneasy.

Victoria smiled and said hello to several people as she entered the crowded kitchen. She grabbed a bottled water and leaned against the counter, near the food table. This always seemed to be safe territory. No one could sneak up behind you or be watching you from the back, and as long as you were eating, you were busy with something. She took a long swig of water, realizing she was quite dehydrated from the flight.

As the night wore on, Victoria eased into conversations with friends and tried to perk up enough to enjoy herself. There was plenty of food and drink, though she stuck with water. She found herself in a ridiculous conversation with her friend Pat, as well as Bill and Kim Costello, fairly recent members to the church who had jumped right in to active participation. They were both very outgoing people, and had made many friends quickly. Bill was telling Pat and Vicki a story about a guy he worked with who had been dating an apparently psychotic woman, and there were some details about lingerie and catalogs, and the possibility of a vibrator that could be inserted into undergarments and switched on at will. The three of them were laughing and talking too loud, but generally having fun. As Bill continued to talk about his work mate, it became apparent that the guy was a divorced man in an age range compatible with either Pat or Victoria.

"Hold on!" Victoria shouted, her arm outstretched before her, her hand in a gesture as if to say, "STOP!"

"Are you telling me this guy is single? And my age? Hellooooooo....???!!!"

She and Pat laughed some more, and Bill laughed too, but then stopped.

"I hadn't really thought about that," he said, "but that's not a bad idea."

"What's not a bad idea?" Victoria asked, starting to see a red flag.

"Well, John's a really nice guy. He's available. He's financially stable, he's in great shape. You might be a good match for him."

"Whoah...wait up. I was just kidding," Victoria said. And she had been, though frankly, it had been quite a while since she'd been out on a date, and she'd become entirely fed up with Match.com and other dating websites. Here was a potential date that could actually be backed up with a personal reference from someone she trusted and knew.

Bill continued. "You'd like John. He's got two kids too, and he lives nearby."

"Really?" Victoria was not sure she wanted to go down this path, but she also hadn't had a hope of a date in quite some time, and this was just falling into her lap.

"I tell you what," Bill said, "I'll talk to John, and then, if you want, I'll give him your email or I'll give you his and let you two decide."

Victoria felt suddenly embarrassed and put on the spot. But she shyly said, "Well, okay, just check and see, then let me know, I guess."

At about 11:45, Pat and Victoria both decided that midnight on New Year's Eve was an event neither of them could stomach, even amongst friends, what with all the couples and no one to kiss. Victoria rounded up the kids and they drove home just in time to catch the ball dropping on TV. She sent Chloe and Connor off to bed exhausted, without even putting on their pajamas or brushing their teeth, and then she herself followed not far behind. As she drifted off to sleep, Victoria smiled. Maybe, just maybe this time...

≈

As the alarm clock went off, Victoria stumbled out of bed, and as had been her routine of late, started up the computer before she even peed. She then went to use the bathroom, came back and used the dial-up modem to check for any incoming email while she went and took a shower. She was back into a habit she'd hoped to have left behind some time ago: checking her emails constantly. Once upon a time, it had been Michael whose name she was looking for religiously. Now, though without quite the fervor, she was constantly checking to see if Bill had gotten back to her.

Ever since New Year's Eve, Victoria's curiosity had been piqued about this John character. Bill had said he was about 45, good looking, etc. But after not hearing back from Bill for a couple of weeks, she had thought maybe he'd forgotten to bring her up. She'd started out with a casual email to Bill asking if he'd had a chance to mention her to John. They'd emailed back and forth a few times, with Bill saying at first, no, not yet, and then yes, but John is out of town on business, or that Bill himself would be out of town for the next week. It seemed to be a very slow process, and Victoria was beginning to doubt she'd ever hear any more about the guy.

As she stepped out of the shower and toweled off, Victoria thought about the prospect of dating again. She didn't seem to have much luck with men. Her timing was off, or she picked men that had serious issues with commitment or drinking or immaturity. And she'd come to realize of late that SHE was the common factor, and that maybe she just shouldn't be in a relationship at all if she was so bad at choosing men and so poorly equipped to handle being in the relationship.

She wrapped the towel around her hair in a turban and put lotion on her body. As the steam from the hot water slowly evaporated off the mirror, Victoria caught her profiled reflection. She still had a half-decent figure. She worked out at the gym, and she didn't look bad for someone over 40, she thought. And she often lamented that it seemed a terrible waste to be someone still so vital and excited about life and passionate about sex, and not be with someone. All this beauty gone to waste, she'd say to her reflection, laughing and noting the wrinkles around her smiling eyes.

Victoria walked out of the humid bathroom towards the dresser. As was her habit, she glanced over at the computer monitor to see if any emails had been delivered. There appeared to be several. Without her contacts in, she could only see that there was a list, but not how many or from whom. She grabbed a pair of underwear out of the top dresser drawer and slipped them on, then walked over toward the computer. She had five new messages. One was from Bill. Victoria plopped herself down in the chair in just her underpants and towel turban and quickly double-clicked on Bill's email.

From: William Costello [Costello@upqst.org]
Sent: Wednesday, January 28, 2004 5:37 AM
To: vickwool@aol.com
Subject: RE: saying hey

Vicki,

I'm sorry it's been so long since I've been able to email. Work has kept me busy, and with an upcoming new assignment for me and my team, I've been putting in overtime. Kim isn't too happy about it, but she's been great.

Anyway, I finally got to talk to John. He seems very interested in meeting you. I told him what a great person you are, and how attractive you are. I did misrepresent him a little. I had said he was 45, but it seems he is 48. He just looks really young, and is in great shape from running. I gave him your email and phone number, which I believe you said was okay to do. Hopefully, you will hear from him soon.

Again, sorry about the lag time. Hope you and the kids are doing well.

Bill

Victoria blinked a few times. She was having a dual reaction. First, she was glad that Bill had finally followed through on this. While she still wasn't 100% sure she wanted to meet this guy, she had been wondering if she'd ever have a date again. Second, she was taken slightly aback by the age. While 48 wasn't much older than 45, she had been finding herself more and more attracted to men younger than herself, and certainly not much older. She was currently 41.

Then she reminded herself that Michael had been seven years younger, and she'd made it to be absolutely not a factor in whether or not two people could find each other and fall in love. So why should a seven-year difference in the other direction make a difference to her? There was one more thing that she felt a little uncomfortable about: she didn't remember saying Bill could give this guy her phone number. She really wasn't at all sure she wanted to talk to him without the safety of a prescreening through email.

It was a slightly crazier-than-usual Thursday. In addition to the usual hustle and bustle of getting ready for work, Victoria had scheduled a maintenance visit regarding the heat pump, but she wasn't going to be home, so had asked a friend to come let the guy in and hang out till he left.

The extra phone calls and logistics had left her feeling harried and frazzled. She knew replacing the heat pump would cost a ton, but it had been on the fritz and she couldn't afford NOT to fix it. She had been up since 5:00 a.m., as Thursdays were her free mornings. The kids spent the night with Max on Wednesdays and he got them to school the next morning. Vicki took this opportunity to hit the gym, though it made for a long day. After school, she'd pick the kids up and race Chloe to her gymnastics class, then race home for homework, dinner, bath and bed. Then Victoria would force herself to stay up to watch ER at 10:00. It really felt like a grind sometimes.

That night, as she tucked Connor into bed and shut his door, the phone rang. Victoria walked back into her bedroom and picked up the phone.

"Hello?" she asked, somewhat tiredly.

"Hi, is this Vicki?" a male voice asked. He had a slightly southern sounding drawl.

"Who's calling?" Victoria asked, as her heart rate increased.

"This is John Finn...Bill Costello gave me your number. Am I calling at a bad time?"

"No, no. That's fine. I was just getting my kids to bed," Victoria said as she sat down cross-legged on her bed.

"I can call back later, if you need some more time," John said.

"Nope. This is a good time to talk," Victoria said again, slightly annoyed this time.

"Great. Uh, well, I guess it seems a little strange to talk to me since we've never met," John said.

"A little," Victoria replied. "But I knew you might be calling, so that's cool."

"Good. Gee, well, where should we start? How old are your kids?" he asked.

Victoria felt a prickle of annoyance. This guy was asking about her children and she was very protective of them. She had no intention of telling a virtual stranger all about them before they'd even met. But she took a deep breath. After all, it had been her experience that most guys didn't even want to know your kids existed. Well, Michael had...but shoo that thought away. And wasn't she tired today? She swallowed back her annoyance and answered his question.

The conversation went on for about a half hour, during which time she found out that John was from Texas, had two sons, one that was 21 and going into the military, and one that was 13 and lived with his mom most of the time. It had been a rocky divorce, and John was still fresh from the wounds.

Victoria shared her children's ages, that she was a kindergarten teacher, and that Max was still a big part of their lives. Her overall impression was that John seemed nervous, understandable since he was still so raw. This was a bit of a cautionary flag for Victoria. She didn't want to deal with someone on the rebound or who was still so hurt that he was afraid to be hurt again. But then again, she had been hurt herself many times, and she had to try and give the guy a little slack. At least he was trying. And he seemed polite and kind.

They finally decided to email a couple times and then see if they wanted to meet. In the next week or so, John and Victoria emailed back and forth, exchanging the minutiae of their lives and deciding whether or not they were a good fit. John emailed a picture of himself. It looked like he had a receding hairline and a moustache, but he looked okay. Victoria had been trying to match his voice up with what he looked like.

Victoria emailed a picture of herself that she'd posted on Match.com. He gave her many compliments about how attractive she was. They finally agreed to meet for lunch on February 14, Valentine's Day. It seemed a little too symbolic for a first meeting, but it happened to fall on a Saturday when she didn't have the kids, and Victoria was partial to lunch over dinner for a first meeting.

Valentine's Day. This was not Victoria's favorite holiday, to be sure. For the past few years, she had spent it alone. One of those years, she had gotten a bouquet of roses, but they were from a car dealer who was going to give them to his girlfriend, but their plans had been cancelled, so he'd handed them to Victoria when she was shopping for a new car. It was still nice to get flowers, though.

The Valentine's Day that really stuck out, though, had been Valentine's Day of 1994, a whole decade ago. A sore reminder of the downward slide of Victoria's marriage, she recalled that awful February morning. She had given birth to Chloe almost two months earlier, and it had been a foggy haze of late- and all-nighters with a baby that didn't appear to sleep and wouldn't nurse. Victoria had begun hallucinating from the lack of sleep, and had fallen into what would later be determined to be postpartum depression.

Another night of little shut-eye had resulted in an early morning stuck in the rocking chair in the nursery, holding Chloe who would only remain asleep as long as she was in Victoria's arms, rocking. The second Victoria tried to stand or move in any way other than the sitting, rocking motion, Chloe would reawaken and start to scream.

It was a morning like so many others where Victoria had sat blearily rocking, burying her resentment that Max had slept peacefully the entire night, without interruption, and would soon be abandoning her to go to work, where he could actually have peace and quiet or speak in complete, entire sentences to other adults, having conversations that did not revolve around feedings and diaper changes.

As Victoria heard the sounds of Max starting to rumble across the hall, she thought how nice it would be to just lie down for a minute, or maybe take a long hot shower. She heard the toilet flush and remembered she hadn't peed since early in the evening the night before. Suddenly her bladder ached.

The sounds of the shower water coming on and the shower curtain being swept open and shut again, of soap dropping and skittering across the wet tub floor, all stuck in her side like thorns, reminders that she might not get a shower today at all, and if she did, it would be hastily taken, without any follow-up hair styling or primping.

Victoria kept rocking. The sun was coming up and the light in the room was slowly changing to a dim glow. She heard the water shut off and the sound of Max's heavy footfalls as he stepped out of the shower. She could hear the medicine cabinet door opening and shutting, probably him putting on deodorant. She heard the sink faucet come on, and the sound of brushing as he played out his morning routine in preparation for work.

Victoria ran her tongue over her own teeth, feeling the slime of a long night's accumulation of phlegm and saliva. Her breath was probably awful. Had she brushed her teeth last night? She was also very thirsty. Why hadn't she thought to bring a glass of water in with her? The bathroom door opened and she could even hear the sound of the light switch being turned off. She could hear Max shuffling around in the bedroom, opening and shutting bureau drawers, moving things around on the top of the dresser...perhaps keys, a watch, his pager. The TV had been turned on low volume so he could hear the morning news.

Victoria continued rocking. It had been maybe 15 or 20 minutes since Max had first stumbled lazily out of bed. Victoria figured she'd been in that chair for at least two hours. Finally the television was shut off, and Max came out of the bedroom. She saw the nursery door crack open and Max poke his head in. Victoria quickly mimed a shush, glancing meaningfully down at Chloe's restless infant head.

Max, however, tiptoed in with a Cheshire grin on his face, clearly hiding something behind his back. He took a couple of steps toward the rocker, then pulled out a large bag of pink, red, and white M&Ms which he held out to Victoria as he whispered, "Happy Valentine's Day!"

Victoria had completely lost track of time, and had no idea that it was February 14th, or that February 14th had any significance other than another day to cross off the months of tedium she foresaw with this infant. She clamped her jaw shut and smiled feebly.

"Thanks," she whispered back. Max looked expectantly at her. She realized he was waiting for his gift. Her eyes opened a little wider and she clumsily muttered, "Sorry, I don't have anything for you..."

Max's eyes lost the sparkle he'd entered the room with. He half-graciously said, "Oh, okay..." and exited the room. He left for work soon after that.

Months later, many months later, when the two of them found themselves in marriage counseling and discovered Victoria had been battling with postpartum depression for almost a year, Max admitted that it had really hurt his feelings when she hadn't even remembered Valentine's Day. He seemed genuinely incensed that she had not taken the time and effort to purchase him a card and gift and deliver them.

In her anger, she'd spat out something to the effect of, "Oh, and I suppose you would have liked them all delivered by me in a bright red teddy!" which had led to another ill-fated discussion of their greatly decreased sexual activity.

Fast-forward, though, ten years later. It wasn't 1994 anymore, and Victoria wasn't married to Max. She wasn't sleep-deprived or dealing with an ornery baby. She was in good physical shape and probably looked damned good in a bright red teddy. The question was, would anyone be seeing her in one any time soon? Today was the day. She was scheduled to have lunch with John at Bonefish, a seafood restaurant in nearby Centreville. They would meet there, getaway car at the ready if necessary.

Victoria looked through her closet trying to decide what impression she wanted to give. It was Sunday, so not too dressy, but it was Valentine's Day and a first date, so not too shabby either. She finally settled on a nice-fitting pair of jeans with boots, and a maroon paisley top that showed off her pectorals and shoulders quite nicely. She did her hair and makeup and put on a pair of heart-shaped earrings and a heart-shaped locket. She got in the car and drove, somewhat nervously, to meet yet another potential boyfriend.

As she drove, she played her music loudly, trying to scare off the nerves. She didn't feel as invested as she had in some of her earlier dating experiments, but John's up-front qualification of being a nice guy who was known by someone she knew might prove to be a better start than some of the blinder mismatches she'd blundered into via the internet.

She pulled into the empty parking lot of the restaurant. Okay, where were the other cars? Just as she was realizing that the restaurant wasn't open on Sundays, at least not for lunch, another car pulled in behind her. She looked in her rearview mirror and knew it was him. She unbuckled her seatbelt and popped a cinnamon Altoid in her mouth, then opened the car door and climbed out.

As she closed the car door, he got out of his own car, a bouquet of flowers in his hands. He was shorter and skinnier than his picture had made him appear, and he had a much-balding head, a large hook nose, slightly buck teeth, and was wearing the most atrocious cotton jacket over his white shirt. He had no ass whatsoever, and was smiling the goofiest, most nervous grin she'd ever seen.

"Hi," she said, extending her hand to shake his.

"Hello! Wow, your photograph didn't do you justice."

"Thanks," she said, feeling uncomfortable with the way he would stare, then look down shyly, then get up his nerve, swallow and look up again.

"No, really. You are gorgeous! Here," he said, handing her the flowers.

"Uh, thanks. Let me just put them in the car." She opened the car door and awkwardly stooped down from the curb so she could reach inside the car and put them on the passenger seat.

"Well," she said as she straightened back up, already feeling entirely too tall, "it doesn't appear that the restaurant is open...so, what do you want to do?"

"Whatever you want to do is fine. Do you want to go somewhere else?" He looked as if he'd almost lost, like the fact that the restaurant wasn't open meant the date might be off.

"Well, Sweetwater's is right across the parking lot there," she said, pointing some 100 yards or so away. "We could just eat there, if that's okay with you."

"Whatever you want. Sure, we can do that." He stood there smiling awkwardly.

"Um, shall we walk over? It's so close," she said, trying to get him to move and to stop gaping.

"Sure, sure," he said, and indicated that she should lead the way.

They walked down an access road, then crossed another road and entered the parking lot of Sweetwater's. He held the door open as they entered the hostess area. They were seated immediately, but at the bar, as no tables were available. They sat side by side, he to her right. All she kept thinking was, he looks like a bird and he is more nervous than I've EVER been on a date.

Somehow, they fumbled through lunch with surface details and divorce stories. Her overall reaction was that she was anxious to go home. He was perfectly gentlemanly, polite, and of course prepared to pay. But the shock of his not looking like she'd thought he would based on his picture and Bill's description had put her off; also, it turned out he was 52, not 48 as Bill had previously amended.

That was more than ten years older, and as she'd talked to him, she had learned that his own marriage and divorce had little in common with her own. There was much hostility and open pain and anger that still existed with his ex-wife. He also appeared to have some other family issues that she wasn't sure she wanted to get involved in.

Victoria excused herself to use the restroom, feeling his eyes on her the entire way there. She had to cross the bar, then go up some stairs and down an aisle between booths to get to it. It felt like running the gauntlet.

Normally, she would have been hoping her ass looked okay, but she was sure he was drooling at the bar and sweating profusely, which somehow turned her off. In the bathroom stall, she peed and held her head in her hands, saying, "Oh shit! Oh shit!" and wondering whether she wanted this to continue.

Thankfully, the bill arrived soon after she returned, and they walked back to their cars, parting amicably with a quick hug and agreeing to keep in touch. Driving home, she felt a rush of relief that the ordeal had ended, and almost felt she was escaping as she drove home above the speed limit. Back at home, she took off her tight jeans, removed her jewelry, wiped off her lipstick with a Kleenex, and plopped down on the sofa in her yoga pants and a big sweatshirt to let loose and release the tension.

All in all, it hadn't been awful. He hadn't insulted the bartender (as an earlier date had done to a waiter), hadn't smoked or drank heavily, hadn't told any off-color jokes, didn't try to kiss her goodbye, and he had assumed he was paying. Those were all good things when she checked her mental checklist.

No, he wasn't Prince Charming in the looks department, but he didn't have bad breath or a nervous tic or a crappy haircut. His clothes weren't exactly in fashion, but they weren't polyester either. He'd been intelligent, had traveled extensively, had experience in the parenting department, and was letting her call the shots. That was good, right?

※

Over the next three months, Victoria and John dated periodically. Initially, she'd only see him on her free weekends, but then started inviting him over after the kids were in bed. They had come to a quasi-comfortable place in the making out department. He was an okay kisser, and was definitely turned on by Victoria, though kept telling her they should wait and keep things above the waist. This was a bit of a disappointment in some ways to Victoria, whose body ached to be made love to; on the other hand, it was a refreshing characteristic in a man, and she had decided it meant he respected her.

However, things started getting patchy when he started bringing her gifts every time he saw her, for both her and her children; he emailed several times a day with his thoughts on her body and her mouth; he admitted that if she hadn't already said she wasn't interested in marrying that he'd propose to her today.

And then, when sex did finally come into the arena, it was with a lot of build up but no punch. He was unable to have an erection. He also had some serious issues with being afraid he couldn't please her. He started taking Viagra and changed his diet just so he could get it on with her. While she saw his inability to have sex as a problem, somehow his attempts to rectify the situation got on her nerves even more.

He was too eager to please her, afraid to speak his own thoughts and opinions, and she even noticed that he sometimes copied her. She'd say something, and then he'd repeat it. She'd remove her sunglasses, and he'd remove his. At first she thought it was coincidence, but upon running a test and discovering he would copy almost any subtle thing she did, she decided he had no actual personality of his own.

After two occasions where he mentioned introducing violence into their sex, she realized he had a little bit of a kinky side. He wanted to tie her up, and had even suggested pretending to be a bad guy with a gun forcing her to let him have his way with her. To this she had firmly and adamantly said, "NO."

When Victoria finally broke it off in May, he could not be diverted. He continued to send her gifts, call her, and email her. He even joined her church in an effort to keep seeing her. She had to tell him to stop emailing, and she returned all his gifts, much to his dismay.

In his final emails to her, he repeatedly sent song clips that made him think of her and espoused his undying love for her. He even rambled incessantly about the reasons he acted the way he did, the whys and hows of his love for her, to the point where it was making her sick just to see his email address come up in her inbox.

In the end, Victoria changed her email address, and when she changed jobs in September, she had a new work email as well, neither of which he knew.

Many months later, Victoria sat reflecting one night, thinking of Michael for the millionth time as she sat alone, dateless, loveless, aware that it could go on that way indefinitely, when it occurred to her that maybe Michael had felt about her the way she had come to feel about John.

Not that there were many similarities in the types of issues that had come up, and not that sex with John had been anything CLOSE to what it had been with Michael, but something about the obsessive way John had pursued her, even after she'd asked him to stop, first politely, and then more firmly, began to remind her of herself.

Michael had never come right out and asked her to stop emailing or writing, but she'd sensed his discomfort with her continuous attempts at communication, and he'd certainly stopped responding long ago.

It was not an attractive picture of herself to realize that maybe she'd become an email address he dreaded seeing in his own inbox. All the songs she'd picked out and recorded about him…thank God she'd never sent that tape! And the emails with all those emotions right on top, explaining her fragile relationship with sex. It must have seemed so over-the-top and sent him running for the door.

She hated to think that he could have felt that way about her after what had seemed like such a tight-knit beginning, but it certainly seemed to have ended on much the same note. She'd desperately tried to stay in touch, still did once in a while get the urge to call or write, and sadly, sometimes followed through with the impulse.

Strangely, this realization made Victoria simultaneously feel sympathy for John—if, in fact, he had one half the broken heart over her that she had over Michael--and repulsed her, to think that anyone she didn't want in her life would spend anywhere near the time fantasizing and dreaming of her that she had spent on Michael.

One thing was sure: she would never give John even one crumb of hope that there was any chance for any kind of future with her. It seemed cruel, but she thought it even crueler to let him believe there was a chance when there simply wasn't.

In fact, in many ways she wished that Michael would firmly, even assertively, tell her to bug the fuck off. It would hurt. But it might, just maybe, finalize for her that she should give up on that dream and really, truly, not just on the surface, let him go.

The other realization Victoria had was that she had not had her heart in it with John from the get-go. It didn't seem to matter what the man looked like, whether he had money or not, was single, divorced, or widowed; whether he had children, grown or still young, or was still free of that experience. No one measured up, and Victoria really never gave anyone a good chance.

It wasn't that she didn't try. She did. She wanted to move past this singular occurrence that seemed to have taken over her heart for the last two and a half years, but she wasn't able to move forward. She was losing her interest in finding someone at all. It was always doomed from the start, and that seemed like a waste of time.

She would lie in bed at night--alone, it seemed, forever--and wonder if she would ever get past this. Maybe Pat had been right when she'd said long ago it just needed time. Maybe someday, without even trying, Victoria would meet Michael again, and the time would be right. Or maybe, with time, it would eventually dissipate, recede to the far corners of her mind as a pleasant, once-upon-a-time memory. Or maybe not.

> If I saw you today...
> I hope I would say hello and how are you

I hope I would smile and look happy to see you
I hope pain wouldn't resurface and shine through my eyes
I hope desperation wouldn't control my shaking hands
I hope you would be happy to see me
I hope I wouldn't see wariness in your eyes, or avoidance
I hope I would ask how you are doing and where you are working
And all the mundane minutiae that people say after so many years
I hope if you wore a ring
And a beautiful wife at your side
That I would shake her hand and introduce myself, unjealously
I hope I would congratulate you and truly be happy for you
I hope that you would see my sincerity and not my bitterness
I hope that you would feel I'd changed and that I was safe
I hope you would be glad you ran into me
I hope I would wish you well and that you would do the same
And when I was finally alone again, and the old tears fell
I hope I would wash myself clean of all the old hurts
I hope I would let go of all the old fetters of unrealized dreams
I hope I would end the chapter gracefully and without verbosity
I hope I would then put to rest my cherished moment in time
And let it sleep and be at peace.
3/12/04

It seemed odd that another year had passed by that she'd been carrying around this lonely hope, this tiny shred of something. She kept it in that box, The Box. She didn't visit The Box as frequently as she once had. It was painful, and it took up a lot of time, which she was relatively short on these days. She was working full-time teaching, and trying to stay on top of parenting. She felt tired and overstretched. She felt lonely, but not energetic enough to pursue a remedy for the loneliness.

But The Box still beckoned to her once in a while, on weekends when the kids were gone and she didn't have any plans. There it would sit in the closet, waiting for her. She felt drawn to it like a magnet. She approached it now, not with excitement or anticipation, but with recognition. It had become part of her life. It was with her, and she didn't even try to deny it any more. She'd pull it out and look over the relics, the souvenirs, the scrapbook memories that she could share only with herself. She alone drank this draught down, knowing the consequences.

Stupor

Torturous teasing
Deep, dark waters
Diving back in
Reliving every word and deed
Fingertips tenderly brushing against your image
Breathing in the essence of your written word
Me, the happiest I ever was
Dancing and singing my soaring heart's joy
Me, the saddest I ever was
Penning the pain
Authoring awful poignant gems
Me, the most creative I have ever been
Inspired by unrivaled intensity
Desperately seeking answers
Unable to bend fate to my will
Sweet, glorious misery
Wallowing in it once more
Drinking in its potency
Gorging on the exquisiteness of its total finality

Unable to stop, unwilling to cease
Hung over after the feast
Heavy and stretched, not moving
Disgusted with my excesses
Knowing I will do it again
6/6/04

From: Victoria Woolfrey [vickwool@aol.com]
Sent: Saturday, June 12, 2004 10:42 PM
To: Sabrina Cashell & Mark Kirby
Subject: another year ended...

Dear Bri and Mark,

Phew! Another school year over! Hope yours went well! I was just looking at the picture from Deena and Todd's wedding and thinking back over the whole thing. Now they've got the baby and the new apartment. Have you been to visit much?

My year has been crazy. Still teaching kindergarten, but just turned in my resignation letter. Looking for greener pastures, and think I may have found them, though it is looking like I'll be teaching a higher grade (maybe 3rd or 4th). Seems like an awful lot of work and money these last two years gathering kindergarten stuff, but it's all packed away now and maybe someday I'll get back to it.

How is your dad doing? and your uncle, Michael's dad? It has been a long time since I have spoken/emailed with any Cashells or other miscellaneous family. Hope everyone is well. Everyone here is fine. Nothing to report. Dad is staying busy with water aerobics and politics; my kids are doing great in school and looking forward to summer. We leave for Nags Head, NC, next Saturday for a week. Can't wait. We'll be back up to Star Island in NH in July. Other than that, just hanging out for the summer. What about you?

Please email when you get a chance and let me know how you and the family are doing.

Vick

Releasing the Dove

From: BriMark Kirby [BriMark@alumni.rice.edu]
Sent: Sunday, June 13, 2004 2:44 AM
To: vickwool@aol.com
Subject: RE: another year ended...

Hey Vic,

It's nice to hear from you. Yes, thank goodness the year is over! Mine went very well, all in all.

Everyone in the family seems well, from a distance anyway. Deena and Todd bought a super fine apartment and their little boy is a huge, giggly bruiser. J.R. and Bonnie are still in Maine. Their son is pushing two, and Bonnie is expecting someone else in November. Jenna and Jerry provided David with a baby brother, Josh, at the end of May! Lindy took her Foreign Service exam and is now awaiting her results. My parents are doing ok. Dad's health hasn't really improved that much - they are currently living with Lindy while they wait for a new house to be built for them in Virginia. They should be moved in in July sometime. Maybe we'll get to see more of you guys now that the 'rents are back in Va!

I haven't heard from Michael since Deena's wedding, which hurts my feelings and makes me wonder what I could possibly have done to offend him so. He and I have always been in touch ... maybe he finally realized that we're freakier than he is. His mom died unexpectedly around the start of the year. I know that must be very very hard for him because they were really close.

Thanks for writing - have a great summer and we'll be in touch when we make it to Virginia.

Much love to all,

Sabrina

    Upon reading the news, Victoria felt her eyes tear up. His mom? Not his dad? What an awful shock. She emailed Sabrina back immediately, saying how sorry she was and that she would certainly be sending condolences. She looked through the box of cards she kept for miscellaneous birthdays, weddings, thank yous, and deaths. She found one that seemed to work, and wrote a message inside. It was an attempt to be a comforting friend, to lend support and advice, but not too pushy, not too delving. What words can you say?

It had been almost three years since they'd met. Two years since she'd lost her own mom, and been underwhelmed by his slow and immature response. Over and over, she had tried to retreat from the pull that she felt towards him. Over and over, she had reneged on her promises to herself to let it drop, to leave it alone, to let it be. Time and time again, she had fought the urge to write, call, show up on his doorstep. And time and time again, she had broken down, written anyway, knowing no response would come, but still hoping that one might.

Now, it seemed, he was alone. Although she kicked herself for doing it, she had checked online directories periodically to see if he was still at the same address. None of the cards or letters ever came back, so she assumed he was. Her fear and anxiety had kept her from calling the old number. She felt the old familiar tug, the heartstrings masquerading as love's call. She heard it, wanted to run to him. He had lost his mom. Maybe he was still unemployed; maybe he'd lost his dreams. Maybe she could help.

It was a game she had played with herself so many times before. And now, an upcoming trip to New Jersey--a trip to be used as an artist's retreat while Sandy painted and she wrote. She had her book all laid out. The story of what happens when a singular event impacts you completely and changes the course of your life. It was set against the backdrop of 9/11, and she had been researching the minute details...the timeline of events that day, the weather.

Whenever she did research, using all the old emails and poems and letters and clips from songs, the story would boil forth. Now she would exorcise the demons within one final time. And the climax? Would it end with her finally living out the one fantasy she had been too afraid to face? Would she use those Mapquest directions that led to his apartment and show up on his doorstep unannounced, birthday gifts in hand, ones she'd purchased in case she ever had the nerve to send them or even deliver them in person, attempting a casual air she didn't feel, trying to cover the pounding of her heart as her sweaty fist reached toward the door to knock?

Would she really shave and apply her makeup and fix her hair so as to appear as attractive to him as possible? Would he be a drunken slob, lost in his misery from unemployment and the death of his mother and the retreat of his dreams? Or would he be there with his live-in girlfriend, "the one"? Would he even be home? Or still live there? Would she dare to find out?

Or would this torture continue for another year or three, or five, or ten? This ebbing and flowing of her feelings towards him in a ceaseless tide of love, hate, pain, rejection, hope, anxiety, disappointment, and fear? Would this end the chapter, or better yet, the book? Could she hope to close out this part of her life and lay it to rest, therapeutically shaping it into a fictional novel in which the meaning of it all finally became clear? Or would she hold onto it forever, a bittersweet keepsake of the one time she felt as loved and as perfect as one could ever hope to feel?

DENOUEMENT

7/5/04
So much in a weekend. So much to review and process. Hanging with Sandy: the best. So much time to talk and be silly and cook and eat and do our own things. Book writing: I typed in a lot of the emails and song lyrics...very mechanical, not much creativity involved. Somehow my mind kept running into a wall. And Michael: I got the nerve up this morning to finally call. His phone was disconnected. I even tried calling some other listings for Bellamy, thinking they were family. He's gone, I think. I obsessed a while about driving to his apartment anyway, just in case (?), and even drove partway there before realizing I had no money for tolls. I had to go back to Sandy's and borrow cash and then just went home, feeling rather deflated. I'd brought and wrapped his bday gift and gone over a million versions of conversations I might start. All for nothing. I wonder now if he's received any of the cards or letters? They didn't come back, but were they forwarded? My next step is to call his Aunt Amelia, though I hesitate to...may just pass on to Sabrina that he appears to have moved. Now I have no idea where he is.

Called Aunt Amelia. As I guessed, she had all the dirt. Michael has relocated for new job at a cable station. He's had a tough year dealing with death of his mom and changes. My heart aches for him, but mostly, I was relieved to hear he was okay and employed. She will supposedly email me his new address, etc. I hope soon. I would like to touch base with him, even if he doesn't respond. I feel better at least knowing where he is and what he's doing. I of course wish, what? That I could have seen him? I don't know. It's probably best kept as a fantasy. My fantasies now seem to involve us being good friends rather than lovers or soul mates. I just want him in my life, and want to be in his life—somehow. I'm glad I called and my day seemed relaxed and happy after that.

From: Vicki Woolfrey [vickwool@aol.com]
Sent: Wednesday, July 7, 2004 1:26 PM
To: Cbellamy@wayout.com
Subject: Happy Birthday!

Michael,

No idea if this is an actual email address, but found out you were working here from good old Aunt Amelia...so glad you are doing okay...don't know if my card was forwarded to you, but of course I heard about your mom and am so terribly sorry.

It's terrific that you got a job and moved on...getting further north bit by bit, I see. Good for you! Happiest of bdays to you. Would very much like to hear how you're doing.

All the best, 35-year-old!

Victoria

From: Michael Bellamy [Cbellamy@wayout.com]
Sent: Wednesday, July 7, 2004 2:04 PM
To: Vicki Woolfrey
Subject: RE: Happy Birthday!

Hi Victoria -

Thanks for the birthday wishes...and your card, which I received last week. Very nice note and thoughtful.

Been an up and down road the past several months certainly, but things are steadily rebounding. New place, new job - both of which are working out well. The move especially was overdue - needed a change drastically. Have roommates for the first time in a while and the everyday interaction is much healthier than basically being a hermit. They're good guys and being able to go out for a few beers with them, just hanging out, or whatever is a needed change of pace.

I'm close to work too, finally and that gives me back about 10 hours a week. Got back into skiing and biking this year after 20 years away...probably as a result of where I'm working - at a company that covers it. One of the highlights was skiing in the French Alps while on assignment there back in January. Then the more local terrain of CT, Vermont and Maine. Biking is the new sport - appropriate of course, with the Tour on for basically all of July.

And you not only remembered the birthday - but the age too. And I'll get used to thirty-freakin-five soon enough...just happy to be here.

At last check, you were in a new home (same town?) and you had a new job?? Been a good summer with your guys?

Thanks again for the note and I hope all is well with you and your family.

—Michael

She read the email, still trying to catch her breath that he had responded. Initially, her hope soared again...could this be the beginning of a friendship? Did this mean the connection was still there? She had gone to the trouble of finding his email address based on the sketchy information Amelia had provided. She'd found the website of a cable company based in Connecticut, and she'd found a contact email address, then simply replaced the name of the contact person with his, and pushed SEND. At first it bounced back, but then she changed it to just an initial and last name, and sent it again, and voila! It had gone through.

What had he thought when he'd received that email? Had he been surprised? Scared? Disgusted? Or just resolved to the fact that she would always find him somehow. Had he called his Aunt Amelia and said to please not give out any more information about him? But he'd had the choice of not emailing back. He could have ignored it, deleted it, moved on. He hadn't. He'd answered, even asked questions of her, sustaining that connection, continuing that thread.

She read his email again. She tapped out a reply, explaining about her job situation, her kids, and asking more details about his job. For two weeks, they emailed to one another, giving movie reviews, discussing vacations. Then, the emails stopped. It was as if they had come to a logical conclusion, as if the fuel had finally run out. When she didn't hear back from him, she didn't panic. She didn't cry. She didn't even feel angry. And she didn't try to reach him again. Something had come full circle for her. Something had finally sunk in.

Victoria pulled out the birthday gift she'd wrapped, with every intention of hand-delivering an Adam Sandler CD of comic routines. She remembered that he liked Adam Sandler, and she thought it was an innocuous enough gift, one that wouldn't appear too sentimental or have any special meaning.

Attached to the outside of the gift was a small cardboard box, about one inch by two inches, in which were some pieces of gum. She'd found the gum at a novelty store. It was called Mofo fruit gum, and it recalled an email he'd sent to her once after which she'd razzed him for the use of that terminology. On the outside of the small orange and green packet of gum was a lengthy description in tiny print of the type of person who should chew the gum, someone who liked to chill with "bee-yatches," someone with "dawg" breath, someone who was a "bad-ass." When she'd seen it, she had immediately thought of him, and purchased it without a second thought.

Now it lay taped to the CD. She had the sudden intuition that she would never be giving it to him. She placed it in The Box, the same box she'd come to love and hate, the one she couldn't bring herself to part with. This was her memory of him, reduced to a shabby cardboard box. She closed the box up and replaced it in the closet, a constant reminder that it wasn't all a dream, that it really had happened.

But now there was nothing left to say. She'd exhausted all her yearning prose and supply of self-pitying tears; she'd survived through three years of wanting, and now she saw that what she wanted was to have a real connection right here and right now, and that he had never, not once, been right here or right now.

He was, and always had been, since that night, an electronic, tapped-out message, emerging in her mind as something more, someone real and tangible, and her own contributions to that lengthy ethernet conversation had been just as conjured. She had created a world for them both, all within the confines of words, either spoken through a telephone line, or more frequently, written with a keyboard or a pen.

It was dawning on her that, in fact, she no longer lived for his emails. And that was all he was anymore, that and a distant wavering spirit of adventure that she could sometimes almost touch, but never hold.

She sat at the computer. She went to the temporary file where she stored his emails and her responses to them. This had served for so long as some sort of permanent record that he existed somewhere outside of her fantasies. She had held onto these emails as if they were precious, the only remnants of him she could still touch.

But they were just so many ones and zeroes. There was no breath of life or fiery spirit contained in those files. She clicked on the first one, held down the shift key and clicked on the last one in the list. Then, she pressed Delete. She clicked on the Deleted Items folder and selected "Empty Deleted Items," then, when asked for confirmation, clicked on yes.

It was over. It was time to release him, let him go. But more importantly, it was time to release herself from this self-imposed prison. It was time to free her own spirit.

Dove

Seeking answers
Exorcising the old demons
Wanting closure
Unaware of how to achieve it
Dealing with ancient issues
Priding myself on creative balance
Unable to finish the story
Unsure of how it ends
Or if it ends
Projecting the different outcomes
No further from the fantasy than before
No closer to the goal
Lost, as always, within the maze
Changing lanes in futile hope
Heading back into the fray
Listening to the wrong voice
Choosing the path of pain
Determined, but never enough
To be free of the chains that bind
Unwilling to cut the final cord
Unable to release the dove
7/1/04

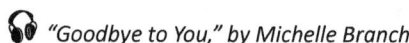 *"Goodbye to You," by Michelle Branch*

EPILOGUE

She sat on the rocks, black and smoothed from endless tides rushing over their surfaces, wearing them down over time. The waves crashed and foamed, sliding in and out of the shoreline, creeping ever closer. A brilliant blue sky and piercing sunlight faced her, a stark contrast to the leaden clouds full of thunder and ominous promises that had been there only thirty minutes before.

The Oregon coastline was raw in its beauty, rounded humps of rock periodically pushing through the water near the shore, steep hillsides butting right against the insistent tide, fir trees standing their ground, though pushed over time into a sweeping bend away from the ocean winds, gracefully arching, their branches streaming behind them like a woman's long and tangled hair blowing in strong and steady gusts.

The drive from Eugene to Yachats had taken just under two hours, with the schizophrenic Oregon weather showing off from beginning to end. What had started as a grey and rainy morning had turned into a crisp, sunny fall day, driving through falling leaves and winding roads that finally exploded onto the coastline in Florence, stunning views threatening to take her eyes off the road.

She'd stopped at her favorite beach, Hobbit Beach, pulling over to the tiny parking area just past the Haceta Lighthouse entrance. As she'd stepped out of the truck, she thought she heard thunder booming in the distance. She ran down the Hobbit Trail, careful not to slip on wet pine needles or leaves, hoping to beat the storm and see the ocean on this hidden stretch of shore. She could hear the pounding ocean, and even as she ran, the skies became darker. She wished she hadn't worn her sunglasses.

She reached the beach and saw a sky divided dramatically between bright blue to the south and dark grayish black to the north. A group of four observers stood against the rocks and hillside, watching the storm make its way closer. She was glad she'd worn her rain jacket.

Lightning struck out against the angry sky, and she marveled, having not seen any lightning since moving to Oregon six months earlier. In Virginia, lightning and thunder and showers were a frequent guest. Here, despite the ever-present rains of fall into spring, she had yet to have seen lightning.

A woman in black Lycra pants, a yellow hooded rain slicker, and loaded belt of water bottles stood a few feet away, also admiring the dramatic show Mother Nature was performing. A particularly spectacular lightning branch lit up the dark skies and the four people against the rocks cheered and turned towards the two women, as if to convey, "Did you SEE that??"

She wasn't sure how long it was actually safe to stand there watching, though it was fascinating to view the storm's advancement. Not wanting to get soaked, and hoping to reach the truck before the rain started, she turned to go, exchanging the pleasantries strangers do, "Nice meeting you," "Stay dry!"

The uphill trek through the trees winded her as she tried to walk-run her way back. The sky grew ever darker, and she had to remove her sunglasses. While that permitted more light, it became blurry and unfocused and she prayed she wouldn't trip on a tree root.

Epilogue

Thunder continued to boom, and an occasional cracking sound, as though the sky itself were literally about to open. Then another sound: the rushing of trucks and cars. She was close to the road. She ran the last hundred yards to the opening of the trail, looked both ways, and ran across to her truck as the first rain drops hit.

Inside the truck, she turned her phone on and attempted to reset the GPS. No signal. She knew approximately where the beach house was, having been to it once before, so she waited until she saw no approaching headlights, then turned back onto the road, heading directly into the storm.

The rain was heavy at times, and it even appeared that small hail was falling. She drove slowly along the winding coastal road, fixing her gaze in front of her. White patches on the sides of the road looked suspiciously like snow, but she couldn't imagine that was possible. It was in the 50s and had been sunny only moments before.

She drove the fourteen miles to the town of Yachats and found the turn off to the beach house. As she pulled into the driveway, the rain stopped and the sun shone brightly. The timing was impeccable. She pulled out her cooler, overnight bag, laptop case, and two other bags full of miscellaneous items from books and journals to rain boots and sweaters.

Once everything was inside, she ate a quick snack and thought she'd better spend some time by the ocean before the weather decided to turn again. She headed down the short road. About ten houses lined this small stretch, and the road literally ended at the sea. She turned left onto the pathway that stretched along the coast, making her way past puddles and under dripping branches. Others were out walking dogs, or sitting on benches and watching the sea.

She made her way to a stretch of beach covered in rocks that didn't look too wet or jagged and found a smooth seat on which to settle. The sun felt magnificent on her shoulders and face, and the breeze was crisp and bracing.

She was here for less than 48 hours, and she knew that there was much she intended to accomplish. This little getaway was a late birthday gift to herself. She needed the ocean to renew her spirit, and the lack of distractions at home to do some work. She was working on a book about her mother's childhood in Europe during World War II, and was stuck on how to end it.

Endings. She always had struggled with those. It wasn't so much that things could keep going forever, but more that she didn't have the words or the vision of what that looked like, how to close it gracefully, with a satisfying finality.

She'd been working on the book for almost three years now, and was very close to finishing it. She had joined a writer's group when she'd gotten to Eugene, finding kinship and good feedback through it. Sandy, who was working on her MFA, had promised to do the design work for the cover and layout for free as part of her portfolio.

Sandy had designed the cover for Victoria's book of poetry, self-published almost two years earlier. They were a collection of post 9/11 poems, all of which had the same theme--a broken heart and a doomed encounter with a man who'd become the obsession of her life.

The book had enjoyed a brief surge of popularity amongst family and friends, and she'd even earned $39 last year in sales! Never a goal, of course, but it had been fun to know her work was out there being read by someone. And it had been a brave act of total vulnerability to put those heart-wrenching words on paper that people would actually see.

This latest labor of love, though, was a family history. Her deadline had more to do with making sure her aunt and uncle, the last remaining members of that generation in her family, would see it, than any burning desire for fame or fortune. She thought it would make a great story. Her mother had lived in truly extraordinary times, and Victoria had learned so much about her grandparents, the war, and her aunt and uncle and mother, that the process had been worth it on a personal level.

Epilogue

This coast getaway had a two-fold purpose. Relax with some tea, and finish the darn book, at least enough to be able to pass it on to a couple other readers for feedback as well as her writer's group leader who would professionally edit it for a fee.

That morning, before she'd left for the coast, Victoria had gone to the gym. Her workouts these days didn't quite match the intensity of what they had been a decade before, but she was still fairly conscious of staying strong and flexible, so light workouts and yoga twice a week were part of her routine. At 55, she still felt relatively healthy, though old injuries were rearing their heads—a torn ligament from a skiing accident in college, and the torn rotator cuff she'd suffered two summers ago on a fall from her bicycle.

As she'd worked out on the lower back/abs machine, iPod tunes playing in her head, she heard a song that she'd heard before. But for some reason, that day, she listened to the lyrics and heard something different.

As the song played, time literally slowed. Her body moved as if through honey, and her swirling thoughts moved at a snail's pace. She heard her heart and she heard an echo, and she realized there was something else she needed to finish.

Now, these waves, approaching and receding, over and over, felt for a moment like the relentless returning to her past, always taking two steps forward, two steps back, making ever-so-slow progress, only to pull back again in the end.

But with age had come acceptance, at least partially. Progress was continuous...there wasn't an end point. At least, not in life and its lessons. Books...that was another story altogether.

As she walked back to the beach house, she let her mind review her situation. Did she still think about Michael? Of course. He would be with her forever, like a sweet memory, like a favorite dress that had fit in her youth, like a hairstyle that would appear dated now. She could reflect and smile now, not feel heavy emotion that weighed her down. She was comfortable in her skin, finally. A couple of boyfriends had come and gone, but she felt secure in her singleness now, not like it was a crime or a detriment or a sentence. She still felt lonely at times, but she also loved her independence and wouldn't trade it for anything. She had made a life for herself, and was continuously changing it up. This recent move across the country, alone and without any belongings, only the most recent change she'd made. She felt brave and strong and free.

Sitting with her laptop, focusing as she had on her family history book, she knew, without any hesitation or doubt, that she must first finish the other book. She realized she'd been keeping it from ending on purpose. It wasn't just that it was difficult to figure out an ending; she still had held some hope of it continuing. And that hope was outmoded.

There would be no perfect ending. But there would be an ending. With love, resolve, and peace, she would, both literally and figuratively, put down the pen.

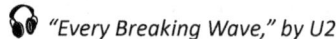 *"Every Breaking Wave," by U2*

ABOUT THE AUTHOR

R. N. Miller resides in Bend, Oregon with her cat Bo where she explores the scenic Pacific Northwest and devours books, podcasts and music. This is her second novel. Her first, *Dearsie,* was published in 2018. She has also published a collection of poetry, *Eleven.*

www.ingramcontent.com/pod-product-compliance
Lightning Source LLC
Chambersburg PA
CBHW050314120526
44592CB00014B/1900